Chicken Soup
for the Soul.

The
Forgiveness
Fix

Chicken Soup for the Soul: The Forgiveness Fix
101 Stories about Putting the Past in the Past & Moving Forward
Amy Newmark

Published by Chicken Soup for the Soul, LLC www.chickensoup.com
Copyright ©2019 by Chicken Soup for the Soul, LLC. All Rights Reserved.

Front cover artwork courtesy of iStockphoto.com/ImagineGolf (©ImagineGolf)
Back cover and Interior photo of road courtesy of iStockphoto.com/linephoto (©linephoto), photo of woman courtesy of iStockphoto.com/Evgeniy Skripnichenko (©Evgeniy Skripnichenko), photo of luggage courtesy of iStockphoto.com/karayuschij (©karayuschij)
Photo of Amy Newmark courtesy of Susan Morrow at SwickPix

Cover and Interior by Daniel Zaccari

Distributed to the booktrade by Simon & Schuster. SAN: 200-2442

Publisher's Cataloging-In-Publication Data
(Prepared by The Donohue Group, Inc.)

Names: Newmark, Amy, compiler.
Title: Chicken soup for the soul : the forgiveness fix : 101 stories about
    putting the past in the past & moving forward / [compiled by] Amy
    Newmark.
Other Titles: Forgiveness fix : 101 stories about putting the past in the
    past & moving forward
Description: [Cos Cob, Connecticut] : Chicken Soup for the Soul, LLC,
    [2019]
Identifiers: ISBN 9781611599947 | ISBN 9781611592948 (ebook)
Subjects: LCSH: Forgiveness--Literary collections. | Forgiveness--
    Anecdotes. | Conduct of life--Literary collections. | Conduct of life--Anecdotes. |
    LCGFT: Anecdotes.
Classification: LCC BF637.F67 C45 2019 (print) | LCC BF637.F67 (ebook) |
    DDC 155.9/2/02--dc23

Library of Congress Control Number: 2019940301

PRINTED IN THE UNITED STATES OF AMERICA
on acid∞free paper

25 24 23 22 21 20 19   01 02 03 04 05 06 07 08 09 10 11

The Forgiveness Fix

101 Stories about Putting the Past in the Past & Moving Forward

Amy Newmark

Chicken Soup for the Soul, LLC
Cos Cob, CT

Chicken Soup for the Soul

Changing the world one story at a time®
www.chickensoup.com

Table of Contents

❸

~When Parents Disappoint~

❹

~Apologizing and Moving Forward~

❺

~Keeping a Marriage Healthy~

❻

~How to Find Forgiveness~

❼

~Forgiving Yourself~

8

~Getting All the Facts~

9

~Ex-Spouses Ex-Enemies~

10

~Resetting Expectations~

⓫
~When You're the Victim~

Introduction

Whenever we condemn, we cloak the world in pain.
~Hugh Prather

I've read tens of thousands of personal, revealing stories from our writers during the twelve years I've been doing this job, and I've come to understand that forgiveness is an essential key to happiness. Why is forgiveness so important? It's because of the emotional weight we carry when we *don't* forgive.

I always think of those resentments and disappointments that we carry in our hearts as if they were sewn onto a heavy cloak. Imagine that cloak is covered with your collection of bad experiences, and you feel it pressing down on your shoulders as you try to move through life.

Now imagine that you've shrugged it off and that cloak has fallen behind you. It's lying on the ground, with all those bad things attached to it, but you're light and free and you're walking away from that heavy garment, moving forward toward the rest of your life. You've left the past *in the past* — where it belongs — and now you have a bright, warm, welcoming road ahead of you.

Lynn Sunday describes that process in her story, "You Take Him with You." She was so angry with her ex-husband that she felt her blood pressure shoot up every time she thought about him. She thought about him too often and talked about him all the time. Finally, her best friend said, "You might as well still be married to the man. You take him with you wherever you go."

That's when Lynn realized that the only person she was hurting was herself. There she was, living in a prison of her own making through her anger, and yet the man she resented was happily living his new life. That happens all the time; we realize that we hurt only ourselves through holding on to resentment and anger, while the other party — the person we think is in the wrong — is blissfully unaware of the whole situation!

Lynn decided to forgive the father of her sons. She says, "I felt light and buoyant, as though an emotional weight had been lifted off me... Nothing really changed except me, but that seems to have made a world of difference in my life."

Lynn finally moved forward, without her ex constantly invading her thoughts. But we have plenty of stories in which forgiveness brought people back together, too. I bet you'll say "What took you so long?" when you read them.

In "There for Each Other" Lauren Magliaro describes how her father and his younger brother were estranged for many years, not even talking to each other when they attended family functions. But when Lauren's father was hospitalized with a life-threatening brain aneurysm, his brother showed up to help, and whatever had transpired between them was put in the past. Lauren's father recovered, and the two brothers enjoyed twenty more years together, which was not only life-changing for them but for their families.

One of the best ways to find forgiveness is to put yourself in the other person's shoes and try to understand his or her motivation and circumstances. In the story "No Fault," Christy Heitger-Ewing tells us that her mother tried to commit suicide by taking pills. She was saved, and the family rallied around her to help her. When she did it again six weeks later, and succeeded, Christy felt abandoned. How could her mother deliberately leave her?

Christy says, "For several months, I remained steadfast in my righteous indignation... Then one night I saw a news segment on suicide that caused me to re-evaluate Mom's actions. Up until this point, I'd been drowning so deep in my own grief that all I could see was how Mom's death affected me. I hadn't stopped to consider what she must have been feeling."

She began attending a support group and came to realize that her mother was in agonizing emotional pain and that it wasn't her fault that she died. As Christy sees it, "She didn't choose to become afflicted by a chemical imbalance that messed up her brain any more than a cancer patient signs on to have cancer cells ravage her body." Christy was able to stop feeling hurt and instead feel gratitude for the forty-six years that she had with her mother.

We have lots of stories about parents in this book—parents who disappointed their children in some way. It's not easy being a parent and we're not perfect, so there are bound to be misunderstandings. Paul Lyons wrote his story, "Pop," about how he misinterpreted his father's guidance and support as criticism many times. It was only when Paul grew up that he realized his father was actually trying to compliment and encourage him. Paul was one of seven sons, and his father did his best. Sometimes his backhanded compliments came across as insults, especially to a sensitive teenager. And sometimes his attempts to guide his seven sons — a difficult job — were heavy-handed. Paul eventually understood that his father always had the best of intentions.

And that's when Paul decided that as much as he wanted his father to apologize, so too did Paul need to apologize to his father, for being so angry with him for all those years. Paul says, "I began seeing past the slights I kept collecting to realize that this man — a stranger to me for so many years — was my biggest ally. Dad was never against me; the world was not against me. My world was dark because I kept turning out the light."

Paul apologized to his father and then needed to forgive himself as well. There is a Chinese proverb that says, "Gold cannot be pure, and people cannot be perfect." Many of us are quick to forgive other people, but we are hard on ourselves. And that's another topic in our book: self-forgiveness. I've always thought there was something rather illogical about excusing other people's transgressions but holding *yourself* to a higher standard and deeming *yourself* unworthy of forgiveness. You'll read more about this in our book — the importance of giving yourself the same benefit of the doubt that you would give to someone else.

Giving each other the benefit of the doubt is a key theme in the book. So many disputes can be avoided when we don't expect each other to be perfect, and when we don't hold onto the past. As you read the stories in this collection, you'll go deep inside the lives of people who came back from everyday disputes, disappointing family relationships, and terrible transgressions — abuse, deliberate malfeasance, and even murder. They describe how they were able to put even the worst experiences behind them so they could climb out of their dark holes, shed those heavy cloaks of anger and resentment, and stride forward unencumbered on the road to a bright future.

Basically, if you stay angry you create more anger, and you carry it with you. Imagine walking around with that little bit of anger inside you at all times. Isn't it obvious that bit of anger would color all your experiences and somehow throw a shadow over all your interactions with people? No one likes hanging out with someone who is negative. It's not fun, and it feels bad.

We aim to help you find that open road and that joy in living again. I know that all of us are better people as a result of working on this book, and I hope you'll find it as life-changing as we did. So dive in and shed that heavy cloak as you meet all the wonderful role models in these pages.

—Amy Newmark—
Editor-in-Chief and Publisher
Chicken Soup for the Soul

August 13, 2019

Putting the Past Where It Belongs

There for Each Other

There's no other love like the love for a brother. There's
no other love like the love from a brother.
~Astrid Alauda

My father is funny, smart, hardworking and loving. He taught me to drive, throw a baseball, and fish. One other thing my dad's good at is holding a bit of a grudge. For most of my teen years, he didn't speak to his younger brother, although they were at many family functions together.

I was never sure why my dad was so angry with my uncle in the first place. But they spent many Christmases, Thanksgivings and Easter Sundays seated at opposite ends of the table. It was simply something that we all accepted at the time.

When I was nineteen, I got a call in my college dorm that my dad was having serious medical problems. My mom and grandmother picked me up in the middle of the night so I could be there the next day when he was scheduled to transfer to a better hospital. I didn't sleep that night, not a wink. I tossed, turned and was almost delirious when we arrived at the hospital early the next morning before the transfer.

That morning, as my mom and I walked down the hallway of the hospital, we could see straight into my dad's room. A tall man wearing a stylish suit stood over my father's bed with his back to us. Casually, my mom remarked how nice it was for the doctor to come by to see my dad so early in the morning. But through my sleepless fog, something about the scene struck me as odd. The man with his back to us was standing very quietly and still, looking down, but he was holding both of my dad's hands in his own. Not typical doctor behavior.

I stopped cold in my tracks and whispered softly to my mom, "That's not a doctor." I knew right away it was my uncle. But, little did I know, I would continue to reflect on that quiet moment for decades. And it would be the beginning of something truly wonderful.

The hours and days that followed were some of the most trying of my young years. My dad had had a brain aneurysm and ended up in the hospital for quite a while. My uncle stayed with my mom and me the entire time. He forced me to eat, bringing me healthy snacks and making sure I actually ate them even though I had no appetite. He gave me his mobile phone, a novelty at the time, to check in with my best friend. He supported my mom as she tried to stay strong for me. Honestly, I don't recall him leaving our side once through the entire ordeal. When I think back on those uncertain days, I remember two things: being scared, and my uncle by our side.

Thankfully, my dad pulled through beautifully. He didn't even need surgery. Somehow, the brain aneurysm healed itself. I don't have much medical knowledge, but it always seemed like a miracle. The other miracle was my father's new relationship with his brother. He couldn't hold a grudge anymore. Not only had my uncle helped him but he had helped my mom and me get through the hardest days of our life. It was the true definition of a clean slate.

After that, my dad and his brother became as close as can be. It was incredible to watch them get to know each other again, and become the best of friends. We got to know him, his wife, and his three amazing sons. Eventually, my dad even went to work for my uncle.

Years later, when I was pregnant with my son, my uncle offered me a job where I could work from home so that I wouldn't have to leave my son in daycare. Being a stay-at-home mom was my dream come true, and he made it possible. It is still one of the greatest gifts anyone has ever given me.

Four years ago, my uncle died tragically at the age of fifty-eight. I can't even put into words the great loss our family has experienced through his passing. Though devastated at the loss of his brother, my dad was there for my uncle's wife and three grown sons, the same way my uncle had been there for me and my mom two decades earlier.

I miss my uncle every day, especially seeing him and my father together. They always reminded me of the importance of forgiveness, and that all things are possible with love. I'm thankful they had twenty good years together, and I'm so very grateful that I have this story to tell.

—Lauren Magliaro—

Forgiving My Bully

Forget what hurt you, but never forget
what it taught you.
~Shannon L. Alder

I could never forget fifth grade, the most miserable time in my school career. That was when Barb started bullying me, the shyest, quietest girl in the class.

"Bully Barb" began with small, annoying acts such as hiding my pencil case. Soon, she escalated into name-calling and other daily insults and torments. She managed to convince most of the class to tease me, too. Until then, I'd liked school and had been a good student. My teacher's only complaint was that I didn't participate in class, being too shy to raise my hand even when I knew the answer.

Now I dreaded going to school. I developed suspicious stomachaches and other fictitious ailments. When my parents asked me what was going on, I admitted that Barb was bullying me.

They spoke to the teacher, who lectured the class about getting along with each other. For a while afterward, Barb bided her time. Then she sneakily started her bullying tactics again, and my misery returned.

In the last week of school before summer vacation, she did the worst thing ever. During morning recess, she crept up behind me and threw a handful of itching powder down my back. Feeling a sharp, burning pain, I couldn't help screaming.

I marched back to the classroom, grabbed my schoolbag and took the bus home all by myself.

"What on earth happened?" my mother asked, shocked to see me coming home mid-morning.

"It's that horrible girl, Barb! I'm never going back to that school again!" I sobbed furiously.

Wisely, my mother let me stay home for the last few days of school. After the summer vacation, she insisted that I be placed in a different sixth-grade classroom than Barb.

The next year, my father got a new job, and we moved to a different city.

Eventually, I grew up and became a teacher. I couldn't forget Barb, and I watched for any signs of bullying in my classroom, especially when it came to the shy, quiet students.

As the years passed, a good friend who was a therapist suggested that I try to contact Barb and let her know what she'd done to me.

"Maybe she'll ask you for forgiveness, maybe not. But then you might be able to move on," she pointed out.

Thanks to our school's alumni association, it was surprisingly easy to find my old nemesis. Barb was now living in an upscale town only ninety minutes away. I sent her an e-mail and asked if she remembered me. Her reply, which came quickly, astounded me.

Barb wrote in a very friendly tone. Of course, she remembered me, she said. She recalled that I was good at story writing and that my father, who came to pick me up from school, had a moustache.

It seemed unbelievable that, after all those years that I remembered Barb's nastiness, she didn't recall a single negative incident. In fact, she sounded as if she'd been my best friend!

Then she went on to tell me about her life. She and her mother had moved away when she was sixteen. There was no mention of her father at all. Was that why she remembered my father so clearly? Could it be that she'd been jealous of me? Was that the reason for her bullying? The idea seemed incredible. Barb had married, given birth to a daughter, and then divorced. For many years, she lived with her elderly mother, who passed away recently at the age of ninety. Barb was now growing accustomed to living alone.

Before contacting her, I wondered if Barb would admit to any of the terrible things she'd done to me. Would she ask for my forgiveness? Since she had no recollection of any of it, there could be no apology. Suddenly, my hostile feelings toward her disappeared. No longer did I feel the need to dredge up her malice in fifth grade.

All those years of resentment melted away like snow in the sunshine. Though Barb was totally unaware of it, I found myself forgiving her, feeling almost sorry for her. I realized then that my friend had given me the best advice. Finally, I felt free.

— Monica Anne Levin —

Act 3

We cannot destroy kindred: Our chains stretch a little
sometimes, but they never break.
~Marie de Rabutin-Chantal, Marquise de Sévigné

Most of my childhood memories of my father include watching him as he sat at his desk, typing away on his typewriter for hours almost every night. He dreamed of publishing a novel. He worked tirelessly on it for years. It was a serious, unsentimental novel, much like my father, who was a serious, unsentimental man. Or so I thought.

Despite being fearful of my father, I could not help but be fascinated by his never-ending typing. Dad used his index fingers to type, and he typed very loudly. *Peck, peck, peck* emanated constantly from his corner of the family room.

Although I was a generally obedient child, I morphed into a teenage hellion. While I was busy rebelling against my overly protective parents, my father continued working on his novel. Between heated arguments, he and I ignored each other. Looking back, I believe this was how it had to be for us. During this time, I fell in love with the written word, but never shared this new passion with Dad. His *peck, peck, peck* was just background noise to me during those teenage years.

When I was twenty-two years old, my father and I had a monumental argument that led to my dramatic departure from his house. I refused to return for another four years. And during those four long years, I did not utter a single word to him.

While I was on this self-imposed sabbatical from my father, my career progressed nicely. My life appeared to be pleasant and stable. And yet, I often dreamed about my father, feeling melancholy and empty when I awoke. Eventually, my mother shared with me that he frequently cried in his sleep, fretting about my absence. Given that he was an outwardly unemotional man, I did not know how to react except with disbelief. I wanted to return to him, but he and I were worlds apart, at least in my mind. It seemed like we could not coexist peacefully.

Still, I was completely torn. Throughout my twenties, I did some extensive soul-searching. Finally, I had a stunning breakthrough: My father and I were actually the same! Both of us were strong-willed and proud and, most importantly, we missed each other dearly. I realized it wasn't his job to be the person I wanted him to be. It was my job to love and accept the person he was. These epiphanies led to a miraculous and long-awaited reconciliation with Dad that shocked everyone. Our silent war was finally over after four emotionally excruciating years.

He never asked me why I drastically changed my attitude toward him. He just took me back into his open arms without asking for even a semblance of an explanation — just what one would expect a loving and forgiving father to do. To be honest, at the time, I didn't know if he had forgiven me or I had forgiven him. But looking back, I realize that we had forgiven each other.

During the golden years of his life, we had a wonderful time together. Eventually, he started to talk to me about his novel. *Peck, peck, peck* became a newly comforting sound to my ears. But I still never talked to him about my love for writing. Mostly, I felt I had to "forget" about writing to pursue a more practical career. Or perhaps I feared I would never be as talented a writer as he was. After all, the last thing I wanted to do was to disappoint my father.

As I grew closer to Dad, I thought I knew everything there was to know about him. Little did I know about the surprise he would leave me.

When I was thirty-two, he passed away right before Father's Day. After the funeral, I was organizing his belongings when I found a very old manuscript that I did not recognize. As I began to read it, I realized that it was an extremely romantic account about my mother, a love letter so to speak, written by my father! I was in shock as I read his beautiful words. Was the hopeless, sentimental romantic who wrote this letter actually my frequently stern, serious father? I could not believe it, and neither did anyone else.

My mother had little recollection of this letter, which led me to suspect that I was the first person to read it. It was as if my father had let me in on his life's secret so that we could continue our relationship even after he had left. I missed him even more.

One of the biggest ironies of my life is that I understood my father better in death than I did when he was alive. The way I see it now, this love story between Dad and me happened exactly the way it was meant to. For most of my life, I didn't really understand him, and when I was ready to truly know and appreciate him, he was gone. But in his absence, Dad left me a hidden treasure in the form of a romantic account, a love letter, about my mother so that I could discover the man that he was underneath.

Perhaps I was meant to find his letter later in life so that he could inspire me to write again. Dad passed away before realizing his dream of completing his novel. However, I know in my heart that he is sitting right next to me, finishing his novel as I type these very words. I can hear the *peck, peck, peck* — the sound of my father, the secret hopeless romantic.

As an aspiring screenwriter, I have been taught to tell my stories in the classic three-act structure of most films. When I look back at my relationship with my father, I realize that our relationship played out just like a classic tale of forgiveness. In Act 1, I misunderstood him. In Act 2, I fought him. But in Act 3, I loved him.

— Kristen Mai Pham —

Once More with Feeling

Find the love you seek, by first finding the love
within yourself. Learn to rest in that place
within you that is your true home.
~Sri Sri Ravi Shankar

On the day the movers arrived to dismantle our home, the piano was left behind. "Get rid of it," my wife said. There was no space for the piano in our new lives.

It was a dark brown spinet with a sticky, middle C. I couldn't even tell you the brand because, at some point, the manufacturer's metal label became dislodged and was lost. The piano had been with us for the entirety of our marriage. We lugged it across twenty-two years, four states, and the birth of two children.

One spring afternoon in our home outside of Boston, we asked our daughters to join us in the living room. Olivia, sixteen, and Claire, fourteen, sat on the piano bench with the wobbly leg and my wife Katherine and I on the sofa across from them. Claire absent-mindedly examined a few strands of her long, brown hair for split ends, and Olivia placed her fingers on the piano keys.

"Daddy, Play 'Malagueña,'" Olivia said. It was her favorite piece.

"Perhaps," I said while clearing my throat, "after our family meeting."

When I was a child, I begged my mother to allow me to take piano lessons and she demurred. Many of our neighbors had pianos in their living rooms, shiny, black baby-grand situations with gold and silver framed photographs artfully arranged on top. Here was a photo of a family on the outer banks of North Carolina, everyone in khaki shorts and white button-down shirts. There was a photograph of the mother resting her chin on a hand, looking wistfully into the middle distance. Someday, I hoped, my own family would be in those frames, and I at the piano, with strains of Brahms and Beethoven channeled through the deft touch of my fingers.

Mom and I struck a deal. I would pay for the lessons with the earnings from my newspaper route, and I could commence only after I played football for one season. I sensed the reticence in the words she left unsaid: boys play sports, not the piano.

"I want you to know that I love you," I told my daughters at the start of our family meeting, "and your mother too." My wife furtively glanced at me and then at the girls, nodding her head that yes, this was the truth. My daughters both looked up then, the serious tone shifting their emotions from indifference to concern.

"Is someone dying?" Claire asked.

The spinet was a castoff, unused by a family friend. We had it moved into our home on Latham Road in Greensboro, North Carolina. As a youth, I spent hours at the piano, my fingers striking and memorizing the black and white keys while Mom tended the rose garden in the back yard. When the final measure drifted through the air, I'd wipe my brow and glance through the screen door. Mom would be looking off into the distance as if she heard something in the music that I could not.

I became a piano performance major in college and fell in love while listening to Liszt's Sonata in B minor. The piano notes cascaded through the open windows of the music building and tumbled through the long green corridor of oak trees shading the front campus. The music called to me, and so I stood outside of the practice room, waiting for the person who produced such beauty to emerge.

"Nobody's dying," I replied to Claire. "But here's the thing."

Katherine moved to sit next to the girls and placed her arms around each of their shoulders. I studied their faces. Claire had her mother's strong chin, and Olivia had in her eyes the look of vulnerability I saw in mine. I took a mental photograph, and tucked it away, as if someday

I might rummage through the attic in my mind and pull it out again, to see them as they were before.

"I'm the same person today that I was yesterday," I said, "but now I want you to know something—I'm gay."

The girls fidgeted and then looked at their mother.

"I don't understand," Claire said.

"Your father is gay, sweetie," Katherine said, squeezing Claire's shoulder as if repeating the phrase might make it more understandable.

Katherine and the girls left long before the movers ever arrived. They were unable or unwilling to watch our lives divided and packed-up. My pile consisted of just a few artifacts — Katherine's unwanted items steeped in too many painful memories. They returned to Virginia and moved into a small three-bedroom house and I into an apartment in Waltham, Massachusetts. Katherine needed her support system back home, she told me, and I was too racked with shame to argue. There was no room in my tiny basement apartment for the piano, and it took up too much emotional space for the girls' new home.

After the movers left, I wandered the house, lingering by the doors of my daughters' empty bedrooms, and then stood by the piano. Whenever Claire had a tummy ache, we had this ritual. I would pour her a glass of soda and rub her feet. She would then sit next to me on the bench and rest her head on my shoulder. I opened a window to let in a cool autumn breeze, sat down at the piano and played Debussy's "Girl with the Flaxen Hair." It was Claire's favorite, and in that vacant house where the wind danced with the curtains, it echoed.

I knew his music, that boy from college who played Liszt before I knew his face. He was tall with dark brown eyes and wavy, auburn hair. Before he opened the door of the practice room, I'd already fallen for him. We became friends. We played Mozart's "Fantasia in F minor for Two Pianos," my refrain answering his, a statement through music that I could not produce in words.

I fell in love with him, but our relationship was doomed. My fear of eternal damnation prevented me from returning his affections. However, something inside of me had changed. I came out to my mother, but she pushed me back into the closet. This time the words were spoken out loud: "Boys like girls, not other boys." The world would never alter, and so I had to. I left college and my dream of becoming a concert pianist behind, but the piano remained.

When Katherine asked me to get rid of the piano, I placed an advertisement to sell it on Craigslist. I received only a few replies: a man who would wire a great deal of money into my checking account if I provided him with my account number, someone who could take the piano off my hands if *I* paid *him*, and a woman who was seeking companionship.

After I moved into the basement apartment, it was the music of life that I missed the most, the trill of the girls' laughter and tears, the percussive opening, closing and sometimes, slamming of doors, and the chords from the old, brown spinet with the sticky middle C. I created an online dating profile to fill the void, and after a few tragic encounters with other men, I met a father named Paul.

On our first date, when the waiter led us to our table, Paul placed his hand on the small of my back to guide me. He was tall, kind and good-looking, the soccer dad, next-door type who did not recognize how handsome he was. He pulled out three crisp photographs of his children from his wallet and laid them down on the table with a snap. I pulled out my tattered school pictures of Olivia and Claire and placed them next to his.

A couple of months into our relationship, I was watching him stir green beans and butter in a red plastic bowl when it struck me that I could watch the way Paul's fingers gripped that spoon for the rest of my life. He led me into his living room, pulled out his piano bench and said, "Play for me." Our children's photos found a home together on the top of his piano.

When all efforts to sell the old, brown, spinet piano fell through, I asked a co-worker, Greg, if he would like it, offering to give it to him.

"My son wants to take piano lessons," he said, "maybe now's the time."

On the day after the movers dismantled my old life, Greg showed up with a white pickup truck and pulled up to the front porch. We rolled the piano through the house and hoisted it onto the truck. We sat there on the front steps, wiping our brows and drinking a couple of beers. Overnight, a storm had swept through, and that morning, the autumn sunlight dappled the maple leaves yellow. I told Greg why my marriage had ended.

"I think my son might be gay," Greg confided in me. "It's okay. I just don't want life to be hard for him, y'know?"

Greg smiled, but his brow was furrowed, and he tilted his head as if to say, *sorry, no offense.* "No offense taken," I assured him. He was a stoic New England guy, solid as White Mountains granite.

"You can't change who your son is," I replied, "and life would be harder for him if you tried."

It was one of the most difficult lessons to learn. But, years after my world changed, I watched Mom dance with Paul at our wedding to a song without words, sweetened by a resolution of forgiveness and acceptance.

I watched Greg pull off. The piano weighed the truck down, and the tires dug trenches into the softened earth. Just as I was about to run down the steps to help push, he kicked it into gear and waved his hand through the open window. The piano shuddered a final chord, and then it was gone.

— William Dameron —

A Purifying Rain

Sometimes a thing needed opening
before closure was found.
~Hugh Howey

Water from our raincoats pooled at our feet as we situated ourselves in a small conference room at the public library. Gazing out its glass wall, I wondered why my father had selected this location for our proposed reconciliation. The fishbowl effect of the room seemed to scream, "No privacy here!" Perplexed, I eyeballed him across the table.

"I meet here with my Alcoholics Anonymous sponsors. It's free, it's quiet, and we aren't likely to bump into nosy neighbors here. Best I could do," he said.

I rolled my eyes and shifted in my rigid chair.

"Shall we dive right in to discussing the letter then?"

In response, I held up my hand and closed my eyes. I had requested this meeting, but now that it had come, I felt myself panicking.

"Is everything alright? Do you not want to do this?" my dad asked.

"I'm okay. I just need a minute."

"Well, I got your letter and your list," he said. "And when I got it, I was pretty hurt."

The list to which my father referred was more of a catalogue of all my unhappy memories. Given that I was the nineteen-year-old daughter of a recovering alcoholic, it was long. Each entry documented the pain, neglect, and letdowns I had endured.

"I didn't mail it to hurt you, Dad."

And that was the truth of the matter. I had written the letter three months earlier during a retreat near the Shenandoah National Park in Virginia. While on retreat, I thoughtfully completed the introspective exercises and sought serenity in the forest. But when stress continued to smother me, I sought out the priest leading the retreat for advice. I spent hours with him, unburdening my soul. When I found I could cry no more, he challenged me to take control of my life.

"You need to stop feeling sorry for yourself," the priest told me, "and move forward in life. Take time to tell your father about your pain. Then, whether your father feels the need to make amends or not, you need to work to forgive him. You do this, not to excuse his behavior, but to guarantee it no longer holds power over you."

Appreciating the wisdom of the priest, I resolved to confront my father. But my father was terrifying; I simply could not do it face-to-face. Instead, I sent him a letter. In it, I listed every unhappy memory I could recall. I explained that these were the open wounds keeping me from joy. He could help me heal, I told him, by helping me find a happy memory to cancel out each unpleasant recollection.

Back in our windowed library room, my father set the list of grievances on the table between us.

"I've always loved you, Nini. I hope you know that."

I grabbed the list off the table and felt instant disappointment. He was supposed to write something in response to each of my items, but more than half of the entries remained blank. Exasperated, I turned to my father for an explanation.

"I did the best I could, Nini."

"Well, this hardly seems like an A+ effort, Dad," I retorted.

"I meant in life. In parenting…"

I was gobsmacked.

"Seriously, Dad? How could my childhood possibly have been the result of you trying your best?"

"Look, Nini, I know it is hard for you to believe, and maybe when you are older you'll understand better, but I honestly thought, given the circumstances, I was doing the best I could."

"Given the 'circumstances'? Really, Dad?"

"Nini, please just stop. I messed up. Big time. Multiple times. I'll own up to that. And, as evidenced by your letter, I clearly didn't cope with my issues as well as I thought I did. I've talked to you about this before. I have talked to you about how I became an alcoholic. I've tried to help you understand that when I was going through everything, I just kept sinking deeper and deeper into my whirlwind of self-loathing. And clearly, I became overly focused on my own unhappiness. I was so focused on my own problems that I didn't even know half of this stuff on your list happened. You hate me for stuff I have no memory of doing!"

At this, he began crying.

The word "pathetic" came to mind as I sat watching him cry. This man, who, throughout my life, had been intimidating, aggressive and controlling, suddenly seemed fragile and vulnerable. He was broken. I'd lived through his battles with his inner demons, but had never realized how deep his wounds were.

"I wish I could go back and change things, Nini. But I can't. Life doesn't work like that. And that's the hell I have to live with every day — knowing that I screwed up, and that you, your mother, and your brothers all had to pay the price for it. I can't change any of it. All I can do is own it, apologize for it, and promise to do better. I hope you'll give me the opportunity to try."

At that, we fell into silence, each looking down at the table between us.

It seemed abnormal to let go of nineteen years of pain in a single moment, and yet I knew that, before I left the library, I would. I had always feared my father, but having revealed his own fragility and self-hatred, my father ceased to be my tormentor and adversary. As a vulnerable, lonely individual seeking love, I could relate to the flawed, broken, and profoundly sad man who met me in the library that day. We could each be stronger, I decided, if we could support one another.

"Dad?"

He met my gaze.

"I can't say it's okay because it isn't. None of it. But I want you in my life. I'd like us to get along. So, I'll promise to work with you to create enough happy memories to wipe out this list if you promise to work really hard to do that with me."

"You're serious?"

"Yes."

At that, he came bounding around the table.

"Yes. Yes, I promise! Can I hug you?"

I let myself become enveloped awkwardly in his arms.

After some time, we dropped the embrace and agreed that we should probably get going. We slipped into our raincoats and made our way out of the library. As we stepped out into the night, I reconsidered the rain. The same cold and dreary weather now filled me with hope. The rain, it seemed, was a symbolic cleanser, wiping our slates clean.

— C. Goodheart —

Rebound

*Grudges are for those who insist that they are owed
something; forgiveness, however, is for those
who are substantial enough to move on.*
~Criss Jami

The woman speaking to me at the basketball game looked vaguely familiar. She said, "Joe? Is that you?"

"Marci?"

"It *is* you!" she exclaimed, smiling broadly. "Gosh, it's good to see you again!"

It was good to see Marci, too. Off and on during the past few decades, I'd wondered about her. I almost tried to track her down a few years ago after talking to a mutual friend who had indicated that the 1980s had been pretty rocky for Marci. So bumping into her at the basketball game was, at the very least, fortuitous.

We spent a few minutes catching up on the business of our lives: kids and careers, spouses and houses, education and recreation. (It's always a little disconcerting to see how few words are required to summarize twenty years of living.) We played a little "Have you seen…?" and "Did you know…?" And we reminisced about the good old, bad old days.

Then Marci grew quiet for a moment, looking out over the crowd milling about the concession area. "You know, Joe," she said, "I've always wanted to tell you… how… you know… how sorry I am for the way I treated you."

I squirmed. One does not like to remember when one has been unceremoniously dumped.

"It's okay," I said. "No big deal." *At least,* I thought to myself, *not anymore.*

"But I was such a jerk," she continued.

Yes, you were, I thought. "We were both pretty young," I said.

"I know," she said. "But that's no excuse for..." She hesitated, and then continued. "It's just always bothered me, remembering how mean I was to you. And I've wanted to tell you that I'm sorry. So... I'm sorry."

The smile on her face was warm and sincere. And there was something in her eyes—it looked a lot like relief—that melted any vestiges of icy resentment that may have built up within me during the years since she had slam-dunked my heart.

"Okay," I said. "Apology accepted!" Overcome by the sweetness of the moment, I reached an arm around her shoulder and gave her a quick hug. Just then, the crowd erupted with a huge cheer, and Marci and I both returned our attention to the game. By the time I looked over to where she had been, she was gone. But the warm, wonderful feeling of our brief exchange was still there and continues to this day whenever I think about it.

We all bear wounds—some slight, some not so slight—that have been inflicted upon us by others. The healing balm of forgiveness can soothe a troubled conscience and bring peace to an injured soul—even years after the fact.

Even at a basketball game.

—Joseph Walker—

Free to Remember

*Hanging on to resentment is letting someone
you despise live rent-free in your head.*
~Ann Landers

One afternoon, I was flipping through the movie channels on my TV, and I spotted Reese Witherspoon. She's one of my favorite actresses, so I decided to watch for a minute. Reese's character was having coffee with friends, and one of them told her she needed to move on and let things go.

"I love my grudges," she said. "I tend to them. Like little pets."

I burst out laughing. The line painted such a great mental picture of someone literally feeding her grudges and past hurts so she could keep them alive forever. It was hilarious.

That night, I was talking to my friend Sarah who works as a special-education teacher. I'd resigned from teaching a decade before, but I had also worked with children with special needs. I'd taught preschool-aged children with special needs for eight years. We were commiserating about how often special-education teachers are made to feel like their work matters less than teachers who work with typical kids. Much of this attitude revolves around standardized test scores. Because my students had special needs and were too young to take the state test, I was especially targeted by this attitude.

"The principal of my school made me feel like I was just a baby-sitter," I said. "One time, when the paychecks were being handed out, the principal's and mine got mixed up. When I handed it back, I joked that I'd love to get paid what she does. In front of several other teachers, she said, 'If the school district paid you my salary for the job you do, I'd laugh my head off. They may as well give the cafeteria workers a six-figure salary.' I just stood there, unable to believe she'd insulted me in front of everyone. I couldn't think of anything to say in response, so I just ran to my classroom and cried."

"I'm so sorry that happened to you," Sarah said. "She was completely out of line."

"I know," I said. "As I cried in my classroom, my hurt and embarrassment turned to anger. I began to think of all the things I should have said to her, if only I could get that moment back."

She nodded. "I think everyone does that. We replay that moment in time in our head, but we have the perfect comeback in our mind to put that mean person in her place."

"It feels good to do that, even if it doesn't really teach that person a lesson."

She was quiet for a minute. "How many years ago did that principal say that to you?"

"Like, thirteen years ago. No, fourteen."

"Diane, I know that lady really hurt you. She made you feel unimportant, like the vital job you were doing was insignificant. I know that hurts because it's happened to me, too." She looked right at me. "But that experience happened fourteen years ago, and you're still talking about it, still replaying it in your mind."

"No, I'm not."

"Diane, I've heard that story more than a dozen times. Every time we talk about my job, you tell me what that terrible principal said to you. Is it possible that you've never gotten over that? That you've never forgiven her?"

I sighed. "She never asked me to forgive her. Besides, it's not as though it's impacting my life. I don't still see her. I don't even live in the same city anymore."

"Did you like being a special-education teacher?"

"I loved it."

"But when you reflect on your teaching days, what's the first memory that comes to your mind? Do you remember the look on a student's face when he finally got a concept you'd worked on for so long? Do you think of your students' parents, who adored you and appreciated everything you did for their children? Or do you remember that awful Friday morning in the office when that awful principal said that awful thing to you?"

My shoulders slumped. "That awful thing. That's what I remember."

"You've allowed that woman to tarnish your memories. You were a great teacher. You made a difference. But when you look back on those years, you feel shame and regret that you didn't stand up for yourself."

"You're right," I said, wiping tears from my eyes. "I loved teaching, but I recall that moment in the office more clearly than any in my classroom."

"That's got to change. You can't let one mean comment color your view of those years."

I remembered the TV show that morning. Was I like Reese Witherspoon's character, tending to my grudges instead of letting them go?

I had to admit that I was. But until that moment, I never realized that it was harming me. I'd thought that since I was no longer in contact with that principal, I didn't need to forgive her. I'd thought I could just replay her awful comment in my mind, but that my perfect imaginary comeback made everything all right.

But the truth was, that day had made me feel differently about being a teacher. I'd always been proud of what I did, but her comment took that away from me. I felt devalued, and worse still, she'd devalued my students.

And after all these years, even after I'd left the classroom to be a stay-at-home mom, her words made me feel insignificant, like my work had no value.

I'd given her words power over me by re-living them so many times through the years. But no more.

I made a list, writing down the name of every student I could remember. Then next to his or her name, I wrote something I'd taught that child.

Jamie had spoken his first word in my classroom. We'd been

doing a puzzle, and I'd asked him what sound a cow makes. I'd cried when he said, "Moo."

I taught Shelby how to put on her shoes. It might not sound like a big deal now, but to her worn-out mom, it was huge.

The list spanned multiple pages. With each entry, I remembered that my time in the classroom had mattered. It had made a difference.

I forgave that principal—not because she asked for it, but because I wanted to be free to remember my days in the classroom, not that one awful moment in the office.

—Diane Stark—

Growing Up and Letting Go

*Incredible change happens in your life when you decide
to take control of what you do have power over instead
of craving control over what you don't.*
~Steve Maraboli

P eople tell us that growing up poor can be a character builder for later years. That may be true, but it's a lesson not realized until time and circumstances have turned for the better. However, until that lesson is realized the transition can be a bitter pill to swallow.

As the oldest of three children, I never had any hand-me-downs to wear like other poor kids. Instead, Mom acquired my wardrobe from generous neighborhood mothers. Imagine the fun other kids had when they saw me wearing their discarded clothing. It definitely wasn't a self-esteem builder.

Perhaps my biggest challenge came from Charlie. He came from an upper middle-class family I considered wealthy at the time. I had very little, so it was easy to be envious of someone with anything.

As far as I was concerned, Charlie's primary mission as a youth was to taunt me for my lack of social status. It was a task he would enjoy throughout our childhood. During those years of Charlie's persecution, I slowly learned to hate. I hated Charlie for making my life miserable, but I also hated myself for not being able to change my situation.

But situations do change, and America is indeed a land of opportunity. That opportunity came after high school when I enlisted into the U.S. Navy during the Vietnam War. The Navy made me a social equal for the first time in my life, and the GI Bill gave me a college education.

Hard work and a few lucky career choices eventually elevated me into middle-class America. Couple that with a wonderful bride and child, and I found myself living the American Dream.

One beautiful summer afternoon, my buddy Gallagher and I celebrated Friday with a delicious ribeye from Jackson's Steak House. That is when I realized that my life had changed forever. For the first time in almost twenty years, I saw Charlie. Not only did I see him, but he spoke to me. I could tell he didn't recognize me, but I surely recognized my childhood tormentor. His words were brief, but I'll never forget them. He said, "Sir, what kind of dressing would you like with your salad?"

The tables had turned. Charlie was calling me "Sir." While hundreds of inappropriate responses raced through my mind, I could only give a two-word reply: "Blue cheese."

Gallagher could tell from the expression on my face that something was up. After filling him in on all the circumstances, Gallagher insisted I use this occasion as payback for all the misery inflicted by Charlie so many years ago. As much as I wanted to taste the sweet flavor of revenge, I refused to do it. I wouldn't put another person through what I had gone through as a child. It was time to put childish things behind me and embrace the new opportunity that life had given me.

Without realizing it, sometime during the past twenty years I had forgiven Charlie for those years of childhood pain. I left him a good tip and I didn't say one word about recognizing him.

— Raymond C. Nolan —

The Staircase

Don't ever underestimate the power of forgiveness.
I've seen it free people. I've seen it lift burdens that had
weighed them down and kept them from moving on.
~Buffy Andrews

The image of that staircase never left my mind. It had been forty years since I graduated high school, but the staircase haunted my memories. The concrete steps led up to the Smiley Building. I climbed those steps several times each school day to get to math class or visit my locker.

Boys would sit on both sides of the staircase, rating the girls as we walked by. They'd call out a number between 1 and 10. If they thought a girl was really ugly, they barked.

Every time I walked up or down those stairs, the barks, woofs, and laughter rang in my ears.

"Just ignore them," my mother advised. And I did. On the surface. But inside the painful message that I was ugly burrowed deep into my soul.

Eventually, I graduated, got accepted to college on the West Coast, and left small-town Colorado behind me. I earned a degree in Communications, launched a rewarding career as a writer and teacher, got married, and raised two amazing boys. But when I looked in the mirror, the doubts returned.

Then I got an invitation to my fortieth high school reunion. "Why would you want to go back there?" my brother asked. "I thought you didn't like high school."

I didn't, but I wanted to go back and tell those boys off. I wanted to tell them how hurtful and unkind they were. And I wanted to show them they were wrong. I had a husband, a family and all the things they'd made me feel I wasn't worthy of.

I practiced my speech in my mind as I ran errands, cooked dinner, and exercised at senior aerobics.

In September, my husband and I flew into Denver, met my sister, and drove down to the town where we'd spent our high school years.

I put on my favorite blouse, touched up my make-up, and steeled myself for the Friday night opening reception.

Maybe it's true that memory is the first thing to go. People greeted me politely, drinks in hand, flattering me with "You haven't changed at all." I'd look at the face and study the nametag with the graduation photo, but it didn't ring a bell most of the time.

Had I blotted out that whole period of my life from my memory? Was I at the wrong reunion? No, some women remembered my mother being their Girl Scout leader. Others had kind things to say about my father, a local college professor. A woman I couldn't place at all thanked me for including her in our circle of friends when no one else would.

My planned speech wilted on my lips. Instead, I chatted breezily about my two grown sons, living in Seattle, and writing résumés for Boeing workers. People were nice enough, but aside from a couple of friends, I felt like I was talking to strangers.

The next day, my sister and I walked around the old campus. The school had moved to a new location, but the old buildings were still standing. I recognized the Smiley Building right away. The staircase was empty and still. I knew what I needed to do.

"Let's go inside," I said.

I took a deep breath and walked up the stairs for the first time in forty years. The echoes of barking seemed to fade in the bright sunshine.

Inside, I found that the building had been transformed. We passed the Smiley Café, a yoga studio, and a piano school. I walked up and down the hallways, marveling at the change. The building was now a community arts center, with rooms rented out to painters, photographers, sculptors, teachers, graphic designers, and massage therapists. What had once been a place of pain for me was now a celebration of creativity and healing.

It was pointless to hold a grudge against people I couldn't even recognize. I was only hurting myself by replaying those memories in my mind. I knew I needed to forgive.

That night, the reunion organizer read a letter from an anonymous classmate who had not been able to attend the gathering. "Looking back," the man wrote, "I realize that in an effort to make people laugh, I said things that were hurtful and acted like a jerk. If you remember me that way, please forgive me."

I let him stand in for all the boys I couldn't remember, and in the silence of my heart, I said, "I forgive you. I forgive you all."

A dark sorrow lifted from my soul. I felt happier, more self-confident and attractive.

Back home, our senior fitness instructor noticed that I was wearing a new T-shirt. "You are really rockin' that shirt," she said.

I smiled. She'd said that before, but this time I believed it.

— Christine Dubois —

I Forgive You, Mom

*Forgiveness is a sign that the person who has
wronged you means more to you than
the wrong they have dealt.*
~Ben Greenhalgh

As Mom and I stood waiting for my husband to pay for movie tickets for *Cinderella*, I hoped I wouldn't regret this outing. Mom seemed pleased when I invited her to come with us. But ever since she'd moved from California to our rural Midwestern town a year earlier, I'd wondered if we'd made a huge mistake in encouraging her to relocate.

Mom still mourned the loss of her apartment and possessions due to a fire. She'd had to stay in a motel for a week, find a new home for her beloved cat, Perky, and say goodbye to friends and familiar places she'd known for three decades. Not easy adjustments for an eighty-seven-year-old.

Because my brother had died several years earlier, I was Mom's only remaining child. Although I wanted her near us, my feelings were frequently hurt by the many ways she invalidated me, opening wounds from my childhood that I thought had healed.

When she interrupted me repeatedly at work to chat on the phone — even though I'd explained many times that I couldn't talk while on duty — it reminded me that she'd rarely honored my requests when I still lived at home. She would often ask what I wanted to do, but then forge ahead with her own plans.

Now, every time she gloated when I repeated a story I'd already told her, I remembered her ridicule throughout my childhood and the hundreds of times she drew attention to my faults and failures.

If we treated her to a meal in a superb restaurant, she'd complain that the meat wasn't tender enough or the air conditioning was too cold.

Things weren't any better at her assisted-living facility, where she complained that broccoli was served too often and the maid didn't make the bed the way she liked it. She also grumbled at her church, where people didn't speak up during prayer time. But her number-one complaint? People who complained all the time!

"Oh, Lord," I'd moan, "I want to honor my mother and not let her get under my skin. But unless you help me in a big way, and somehow change my heart, I don't know how much longer I can last!"

I had attempted to set boundaries with her. Sometimes, they worked; sometimes, not. If I tried to explain gently how something she said or did upset me, she would apologize for offending me and say, "I didn't mean to hurt you." I was convinced of her sincerity. Of course, she wasn't purposely bringing up old wounds to ruin my day. She simply didn't think about how her words or actions might affect me.

And I was sincere every time I responded to her apology by saying, "I forgive you, Mom." But there was always a next time, accompanied by fresh pain. I found myself afraid to joke or be my usual transparent, cheerful self around her for fear she'd ridicule me or use my faults to draw attention away from her failing memory and skills. I became uncharacteristically subdued in her presence.

I fought my anger at her for reopening my childhood wounds. I also struggled with anger at myself for allowing her to upset me nearly every time we were together. Shouldn't I be more mature than this?

Then *Cinderella* happened.

Mom said nothing throughout the entire film. A couple of times, I looked over to see if she'd gone to sleep. But she was awake, taking in every word. Except three.

Near the end of the familiar story, Prince Charming found Cinderella locked in the attic by her evil stepmother, realized the glass slipper fit her, and took the young woman by the hand to lead her to safety. As the couple descended the stairs, Cinderella turned suddenly to face the woman who'd tortured her for years and said, "I forgive you."

At that exact moment, Mom leaned toward me and asked, "What did she say?"

I sat riveted in my plush theater seat, my heart pounding with shock, my eyes wet. This was an opportunity to extend forgiveness to Mom without her asking for it. I could say, "I'll tell you later." Or I could whisper the words in her ear in the darkness of the theater, knowing she'd have no inkling that I was speaking for myself, but believing I was only telling her the line of the movie she missed.

I spoke the words. And when I did, something burst inside my heart. Some of the pain and hurt, like mud caked on old boots, began to crack and fall away. I was telling Mom that I chose to forgive her for a lifetime of misunderstandings and disrespect. She didn't need to say, "I'm sorry; I didn't mean to hurt you." I was offering her forgiveness of my own free will because I wanted to walk with my head held high and my shoulders back, stooped no longer by anger or resentment.

On the ride to Mom's apartment, I asked her if she liked the movie. "Yes," she said, "it was good. But I thought it was too loud."

I smiled to myself. The one line she missed, the one that wasn't too loud, was the one she needed to hear—and I needed to say.

Now, every time I see a new version of *Cinderella* or read the story to my grandkids, I'll remember the power of those three words: "I forgive you."

— Pam Kennedy —

Understanding
Someone's Actions

No Fault

Your pain is the breaking of the shell
that encloses your understanding.
~Khalil Gibran

I crumpled into a ball of hysteria on the floor of the sporting-goods store. "No! No! No! No!" I kept repeating. My hand grasped my cell phone so tightly that my knuckles turned white.

How could this be happening again? Only six weeks earlier, my sixty-eight-year-old mom had called me and blurted out, "I just took a bunch of sleeping pills."

I had sprung to my feet, trying to sound calm but inwardly freaking out.

"A bunch? Like how many?" I asked.

Within minutes, she was mumbling incoherently.

I was able to get the paramedics to her, and she survived, for which I was grateful. But I was also confused and angry.

When I visited Mom in the hospital, I wanted to scream, "What were you thinking? How could you do something so stupid?"

But she looked like a frightened child, and her whole body shook like a panicked dog during a nasty thunderstorm.

"I'm sorry," Mom whispered, her mouth dry and lips chapped from the tubes that had been shoved down her throat to pump her stomach.

I was desperate to say the right thing and paranoid I'd say the wrong thing. Mostly, I said nothing. I just sat beside her on her tiny hospital bed and gently squeezed her trembling hand, trying to make sense of the senseless.

"I love you, Mom," I said slowly, almost methodically. I wanted to be sure the message got through and that she never did this again.

The next several weeks were spent talking to my dad and various doctors about how best to help Mom. We locked up all her medications. We rid the house of guns and knives. Dad promised not to leave her side. After a while she seemed to be doing better so Dad went back to work.

Now I was at the store with my boys, shopping for new bike helmets when the phone rang. And Dad had just said, "She did it again. Only it's way worse this time."

"I'll come right now," I said. "I can be there by midnight."

"I don't think you'll make it in time," Dad said.

I collapsed, knowing that, for all intents and purposes, my mom was gone.

The next several hours were spent waiting for the dreaded phone call. In those hours, I worked myself into a lather of anger.

"How could she betray me like this?" I cried, my face hot with rage. "How could she choose to leave me?"

I spent the evening replaying all of the times in my life when Mom had rescued me. When I was twelve and had dropped to seventy-three pounds, she hospitalized me so I wouldn't succumb to anorexia. When I was thirty-three and going through a painful divorce, she invited me and my son to live with her and Dad until I got back on my feet. When I was thirty-nine and had to have carpal-tunnel surgery on both hands, Mom cared for my toddler. Time after time, she saved me. And now, when it was my turn to save her, I had failed miserably. Guilt and gut-wrenching pain ate away at me.

I had just drifted off to sleep when the shrill ring of my phone led me to my worst nightmare.

"She's gone," Dad said. With those two words, my world turned to gray.

The next week was spent planning Mom's funeral — picking out her clothes, coffin, flowers, and songs. I was furious at her for putting me in this position. For anyone who died of cancer, a car accident or a heart attack, their death was outside of their control. But Mom chose this! She thought about it, she did it, and she lived. Then apparently she thought about it some more, did it again, and died. How could she intentionally put her family through such torture?

From the inside out, every part of me hurt — my heart, my head, my whole being. One night I sat alone on my bed, seething. Through clenched teeth, I screeched at the top of my lungs, "Why did you do this to me? Why didn't you love me enough to stay? Why did you leave me? Why?"

My heart pounded hard and fast as I continued reeling, going through the house like a rabid animal, frantically ripping down every photo of my mom so I didn't have to see her selfish face staring back at me.

For several months, I remained steadfast in my righteous indignation as I constantly teetered on the precipice of a meltdown. Regularly, I broke down in the aisles of the grocery store, at the park while my son was swinging, and — my personal favorite — while balancing on a rubber exercise ball at the gym, sobbing like a madwoman between ab crunches.

Then one night I saw a news segment on suicide that caused me to re-evaluate Mom's actions. Up until this point, I'd been drowning so deep in my own grief that all I could see was how Mom's death affected me. I hadn't stopped to consider what she must have been feeling.

About this time, I began attending a support group where I was surrounded by others who had also lost loved ones to suicide. I gained some valuable insight there, too. After a while, it became clear to me that prior to her death, my mom was in agonizing emotional pain that never subsided. I wanted her to hold onto life, and I think she did for as long as she could… until she lost all strength.

Something clicked inside me, and suddenly I had a newfound perspective, and with it, a newfound mercy for Mom. Clinical depression was her cancer. It was her car accident. It was her heart attack. She didn't choose to become afflicted by a chemical imbalance that messed up her brain any more than a cancer patient signs on to have cancer cells ravage her body. So while my mom died by suicide, it was depression that killed her. It wasn't her fault. The power to forgive provided me with both strength and clarity that enabled me to move through the hurt so I could heal.

"I'll always be sorry I couldn't save you, Mom," I said one night as I lay in bed. "But I'm not mad at you anymore. You fought hard, and you stayed with us as long as you could. You needed rest, and now you have it."

Tears ran down my cheeks as I continued, "I'm more aware and educated now. I no longer blame you, Mom, because I know you didn't do this to me. I hope you'll forgive me for my anger because I certainly have forgiven you."

Forgiveness enabled me to release the "whys" and embrace the "wows." As in, "Wow, I was lucky to have such a wonderful mom for forty-six glorious years."

— Christy Heitger-Ewing —

The Angry Child

If someone is facing a difficult time, one of the kindest
things you can do for him or her is to say,
"I'm going to love you through this."
~Molly Friedenfeld

The raven curls framing her eight-year-old face were soft and sweet — a dark contrast to the two coal-black eyes filled with fire and rage. Her small frame was stiff and unyielding as she sat in the chair facing me. An iron rod of anger, she raged and snarled at me for daring to accuse her.

I knew she had stolen the money from my bedroom. I knew because she had access to it, and also because of her history. It wasn't the first time she had stolen. She stole from the kids at school. She stole from her parents. And the night she had a friend stay over, she stole her video game. She was an accomplished thief, and she was the only one who could have taken the money. Yet her determined indignation and denials weakened my resolve.

She was not an easy child, and stealing wasn't her only vice. She tortured her brother, hitting, pinching and tripping him incessantly. She had no friends at school because she fought and bullied the other children. Temper tantrums were the norm, accompanied by kicking, screaming, throwing and breaking things. She had perfected the art of cheating, and lying was second nature to her.

Looking across the table at the small, angry child, I pondered what to do. She was braced and ready for a fight. Her muscles were tense, like a panther ready to lash out. She wore her anger like a spiked collar, daring me to try and best her.

I hadn't known her as a baby. My son adopted her shortly after he married her mother. But I knew there was more to her than the furious little girl covered with a thick, hard armor of rage. Occasionally, she lowered her guard and I saw flashes and glimpses of an intelligent, curious, loving girl.

She glared at me, prepared for the battle she knew was coming. Usually, she won by wearing out her opponent. She never admitted guilt and she never backed down.

"Aly, I know you took the money."

"I didn't take the money, Grandma. If you loved me, you'd believe me."

Her anger came from a deep place. She wanted to hurt the world because she was hurting. Punishing her would only fuel the anger further. It would feed the beast that was consuming her. So I tried a different tactic.

"I love you, Aly. I don't understand why you took my money, but I want you to know you don't have to steal from me. When you love someone, you share what you have. You can keep the money you took, and I will also give you anything else you want. What else do you need? What can I give you?"

She scowled at me. "I didn't take your money! I don't want your stuff!"

I went to the kitchen and picked up my favorite mug. "I love this mug." I set it on the table in front of her. "You can have it." Her dark eyes softened slightly, and she looked confused.

Then I started gathering other items and placing them before her. "Take these earrings. Take this change. Take this…"

She protested. "No, Grandma, no. Stop it!" The heavy armor of anger was weighing on her shoulders, pushing them down.

I ignored her shouts and continued putting pictures, jewelry, and knickknacks on the table before her. As the pile grew, the fire left her eyes, her head dropped, and then something broke. Her thin shoulders began to shake and heave with sobs. Only then did I stop and wrap my arms around her. "I love you, Aly. Just ask me, and I will give you anything you want. You don't have to steal from me."

She didn't admit guilt, but the stolen money reappeared. Aly didn't change overnight, but she did change. She is still moody at times and often tries my patience, as most teenagers do, but the screaming, out-of-control, raging beast has gone. Aly is a high school senior, a lettered softball player, a cheerleader, a princess in the Homecoming court and an almost straight A student. I am so proud of the beautiful young woman she has become.

She has learned to be empathetic and care about people's feelings. She is witty and hilariously funny sometimes. I feel lucky to call her my beloved granddaughter.

As an added bonus, I can leave any amount of money lying around. I know with certainty that she will not take it. She has not stolen from me since that first time. Sometimes, love is the best punishment you can give a child.

— Vickie J. Litten —

By the Grace of God

*Throughout life, people will make you mad,
disrespect you and treat you bad. Let God deal
with the things they do 'cause hate in your heart
will consume you, too.*
~Will Smith

Several months ago, I stared blankly at the television, huddled in the corner of my sofa with a blanket. Resting between my fingers was a cigarette, curling a thin, gray cloud of smoke toward the ceiling. The police were buzzing around my home like bees in a hive, but I barely heard a word they said. I had been through all of this before... so many times. I should have been used to it, but I wasn't.

After everything I had taught her and tried to instill in her, after every excuse I made for her, every time I stood up for her, and every lecture I had given her... she had not changed. Not one bit! All I could think about were the incidents leading up to this night: a fight at school; disrespecting a police officer; suspension from school; a court hearing; community service; a behavioral-adjustment seminar; a $375 fine; a failing school year; five stolen or snuck-in cell phones; multiple inappropriate photos, videos, and chats; a make-out session in a public park; hair bleaching; an attempt to pierce her own lip; an attempt at breaking and entering; countless lies and manipulations... and no help in sight.

The police asked me questions that had become second nature to me, as I had already answered them a million times in past incidents with hospitals, counselors, psychiatrists, psychologists, behavioral therapists, teachers, parents, friends, and family. I was falling deeper and deeper into a pit of despair. All I wanted to do was go upstairs, crawl into bed, cry what little tears I could after having shed so many over her before, say my prayers, go to sleep, and never wake up again.

One might think this is a pretty dramatic and elaborate reaction, but it is mild compared to what some parents with a sociopathic child go through.

Yes, my daughter is a sociopath.

I remember telling my sister over the phone that I was afraid of my daughter and that she was evil. My daughter followed me everywhere, even into the bathroom, but she always stayed behind me and to the side, just out of my peripheral vision. She was always so angry, and I was just waiting for her to plunge a knife into my back or kill me in my sleep. My husband and I had even put a lock on our bedroom door because I had nearly fallen down the stairs twice due to her actions.

I'd spent countless hours researching all of my daughter's symptoms, and I'd considered every diagnosis. If it weren't for my husband reading up on sociopathic tendencies for his job, I doubt we would have ever figured it out. My daughter had completely drained us of anything good. We were mentally, physically and emotionally exhausted.

One night, out of the blue, I saw a short video on Facebook. It was from the *Dr. Phil* show, so I looked up the episodes online. After watching a few of them, I realized we were not alone! There were numerous clips of parents with extreme children who had done some pretty unspeakable things. That was the first time I heard of "Oppositional Defiance Disorder." Apparently it's the diagnosis for sociopathic children. I thought it was rather humorous! Eighteen and older, you're a sociopath; seventeen and younger, you are ODD.

Things were very bleak. Everything seemed to be working against us. We felt doomed to spend what seemed like an eternity with someone we were growing to hate. I do not use the word "hate" lightly. I love easily, forgive quickly, and the world is generally good and agreeable in my eyes. So, when I say that I was beginning to hate someone, it would take insurmountable forces to push me to it. That's just the way God built me.

Then it hit me... God! Now, I'm not a religious person, and I've always considered myself more spiritual than ritual, but God was truly the answer! Did I start going to church? No. Did I start reading and memorizing the Bible? No. Did I start behaving like a perfect angel? No. Did I start pushing my revelation off on others? No. All I did was take a deep breath and let go. I let go of my anger, resentment, sense of betrayal, righteousness, and pride.

I am unable to carry such a heavy burden on my own, but my husband, in-laws, sister, friends, animals, job — and God — have gotten me through and kept me going. God hasn't "cured" my daughter of her sociopathic tendencies, but he has filled me with an internal calm, patience, and knowledge that everything will turn out all right in the end. Things haven't changed miraculously overnight, but they have gotten much better!

Now I can speak with my daughter on a personal level, and she actually listens and interacts. She has come to me with her own issues, and we work through them together. We can laugh and be silly with one another again. I can hug her with my whole body, heart, and soul, and when I tell her I forgive her, I mean it!

My daughter is a sociopath. She is angry and defensive. She lies and manipulates. She is going to betray my trust and confidence in her. She is going to make mistakes and live with the consequences of her actions. She is nothing like me, but she is my daughter, and I love her by the grace of God. That is all that matters.

—Lea Welch—

The Kaleidoscope Effect

Life is like an ever-shifting kaleidoscope —
a slight change, and all patterns alter.
~Sharon Salzberg

I stood at the altar next to my husband-to-be and said, "I do," not fully comprehending that I was also saying "I do" to two ex-wives and three stepchildren, the youngest of whom was five years old. Although I was thirty-one, I knew little about being a wife and even less about being a stepmother. But I loved Bill and accepted the circumstances willingly, confident I'd figure it out along the way.

Days after our honeymoon, my husband's second wife called, insisting Brené, the youngest, spend part of her summer with us. "We can do that," Bill said without hesitation.

Just like that, the honeymoon was over. My wedding-day confidence nose-dived, and my stomach shifted uneasily as I suddenly faced the reality of an ex-wife's demands on our lives.

"You okay with this, sweetheart?" Bill asked after the fact.

"Sure," I said cheerfully, keeping the anger and disappointment from my voice. "I want you to have a relationship with your daughter." I readied our spare bedroom for Brené, shoving aside my feelings of resentment toward Bill's ex-wife while contemplating how to establish my own relationship with a little girl.

The next day, Bill and I picked up Brené. She was an energetic, petite girl complete with blond pigtails. My heart melted as she placed her tiny hand in mine, allowing me to escort her to our car. During her visit, Brené and I spent lots of time together, feeding ducks at the park, making cupcakes for her daddy, and giggling while watching kiddie movies. She was the daughter I couldn't conceive, and my heart was full of love for her. But I reminded myself that Brené wasn't my daughter and I could only hope that she'd accept me as a mother figure in her life.

During subsequent visits, Brené acted lovingly and was comfortable in my company. By Christmas, her attitude and behavior toward me shifted. "You can't tell me what to do!" she shrieked.

I froze. "Brené," I said softly, regaining my composure, "don't you want to go to the Christmas party?"

"No!" she replied, shaking her head fiercely. "You can't make me. Mommy says so." She stormed into the bathroom, slamming the door.

"Let me talk with her," Bill said. "She's probably just tired."

He disappeared into the bathroom, emerging moments later cradling a teary-eyed Brené. "We're not going to the Christmas party," he said curtly. "It seems that Shannon has filled Brené's head with the notion that you're like the evil stepmother in *Cinderella*. Now she's afraid of you."

"What? Why would Shannon do such a thing?"

"Honestly, I don't know, but I'll talk with her," Bill answered, his eyes blazing with anger.

The following day, Bill confronted Shannon. "Why did you tell Brené that Lillie's like the evil stepmother in *Cinderella*? What an awful thing to say!"

"That's what Lillie gets for stealing my daughter from me!"

"Lillie doesn't want to steal Brené from you."

"Yes, she does!" Shannon shouted, her face reddening. "You just don't see her for the wicked person she is."

"What?" His eyebrows drew together in a scowl. "Why would you think such a dreadful thing?"

"Well, all I know is that every time Brené visits you, all she talks about is 'Lillie and I did this. Lillie and I did that.' Lillie can't have her own children, so she wants mine. No one can be Brené's mother but me."

"You're crazy," Bill snapped back, putting Shannon on the defensive.

Hoping to diffuse the situation, I turned toward Shannon. "You make a valid point. Perhaps I was overzealous, but I certainly had good intentions. I wanted Brené to feel welcome in our home. I never intended to infringe on your relationship with Brené. I apologize."

"I don't believe you, not for a second. You're evil!" Shannon's lips twisted with scorn. "No one gets to be Brené's mother but me. No one. I'll see to that! Now both of you get out of my house!"

As we scurried toward the front door, Brené stopped us. "Daddy, when will I see you and Lillie again?"

Bill collected himself and knelt down, looking directly into Brené's eyes. "That's up to your mother. She'll call us when you're ready to visit."

"I'll be ready very soon!" Delight rang in her voice.

I choked back the tears, feeling as if I was somehow responsible for Shannon's outrage. "You've done nothing wrong," Bill assured me. "Try not to fret about it. We'll work with the situation as best we can."

Shannon called eventually, and Brené visited with us regularly throughout her childhood and teen years. Not wanting to be further misconstrued, I spent little time alone with Brené. But the evil step-mother label was firmly planted in Brené's mind, and any hopes I had of having a relationship with her had been vanquished. "You've always been and always will be the evil stepmother," Brené said frequently. Even now, some thirty-five years later, those same hurtful words fly from her mouth when I don't meet her expectations or demands.

For years, I blamed Shannon for the shattered relationship between Brené and me, harboring disdain and contempt toward her for villainizing and diminishing me. I saw Shannon as the enemy, and I was her helpless victim. The dark side of me wanted to lash out at her and exact some form of revenge. But I just couldn't be that ruthless. Being vengeful would've hurt Bill's relationship with his daughter and only worsened the situation.

I decided to step back and look at the situation in a different light. Shannon was playing an illogical story inside her head, one that she truly believed. With that false narrative, I was the villain she feared would destroy her mother-daughter relationship, and she had no option other than to diminish me in order to protect that relationship. She used her fear creatively to place a wedge between Brené and me while at the same time striking out at her ex-husband. Oddly, that same fear became the heart of their mother-daughter dynamic. By adulthood, Brené had too much vested interest in the story she'd been fed; she couldn't let go of the evil stepmother label for fear of losing her relationship with her mother.

Although I couldn't change or influence the situation, I understood it better. With that understanding, my perspective shifted in much the same way the patterns shift in a kaleidoscope when it's held to the light and the cylinder's turned. Something new was created in me — a feeling of compassion and forgiveness for Shannon and Brené. The shift from feeling like an angry victim to being a compassionate and forgiving person was profound. Shannon and Brené were no longer my enemies, only frightened, fragile, and flawed women. More importantly, I realized that we're all a kaleidoscope of complexity — thousands of different facets of light and dark yearning to be understood.

— Lillie Houchin —

Before I Crash

Forgiving is rediscovering the shining path of peace
that at first you thought others took away
when they betrayed you.
~Dodinsky

T he words glowed on my cell-phone screen. "May I visit between 1:15 and 1:30?" I tensed up and could barely breathe. My heart pounded.

It was a simple message, but nothing with her was simple. This was the woman who could never show me love. This was the woman who taught me to fold in the face of adversity, suggesting I was worth nothing. This was the woman who taught me it would be better to drown in whisky than it would be to stand and face the world. This was the woman who preferred the bottle to her own daughter.

So, yes, it was a simple message, but nothing about this was truly simple.

I closed my eyes and breathed deeply. What could I do to keep her away? I could tell her I was sick. I could tell her I had to work. I could even tell her I was leaving town. None of it was true, and my heart sank when I thought of telling these lies.

I could smell the pot of fresh coffee that had finished brewing moments before. That brought me back to the present. I noticed the morning light streaming in through the tilted blinds of my patio door, casting a beautiful, striped pattern across the room. The air was cool and crisp through the open window. I basked in it all, every small pleasure of the senses, and overcame my momentary panic.

I texted her back: "Yes." She confirmed the appointment soon after. Politely cold was her usual style of communication with me, although she could definitely yell up a storm. I thought of how she would yell, her slurring voice, the bouts of outraged intoxication. As her children, my brother and I learned the dos and don'ts of Mommie Drunkest. He was better at submitting to her than I was. I grew up feeling fundamentally rejected, struggling to know my own worth. It was as though my thoughts were an old, failing computer program crashing from corrupted lines of code.

My father had told me a secret about my mother at one point. He made me swear not to tell her I knew. She had been raised in the 1950s in a small Midwestern town, the youngest of five siblings and the only girl. When she asked her mother how they chose her name, she'd said it came from the obituaries. When she told her mother that her father came into her room at night and touched her, she wasn't believed. Her father had died when she was sixteen, and she felt tremendously guilty about the relief she felt. Both her parents drank heavily, and that, I imagine, was how she learned to deal with anything that hurt, carrying on the continuum of pain that ran in her family. She was raised to never speak out, so she smothered her voice with alcohol.

At 1:23 in the afternoon, she arrived at my apartment. We sat awkwardly across from one another in the living room. She held a printed paper, folded in half, her legs and arms pinched rigidly inward as if to minimize her presence.

"In AA," she began, referring to the Alcoholics Anonymous group she'd joined after nearly dying of alcoholism, "we are supposed to make amends for the wrongs we have committed against others in our lives." Then she unfolded her paper and read some pre-crafted words aloud. "I know that I have never apologized to you, even after many years of sobriety. I did not know how to apologize. Today, I want to tell you I am sorry. Sorry for not knowing how to love you, sorry for not being the mother you needed, sorry for the cruel things I have said and done to you. I can't change the past. I know I can only change myself in the present." She finished a few more sentences of her script, and though she could hardly stand to look me in the eyes, I could sense the incredible effort it took for her to speak these words. In her own broken way, she was being courageous.

"I forgive you," I told her. It was effortless to say. Then, she did look at me, her eyes surprised and relieved for a moment before they flooded with tears.

Nothing in the past could be changed, not even with a thousand apologies. What could change, I realized then as clarity came rushing to me, was I could end that old program. I could be the one to stop the legacy of suffering that had plagued our family through generations. I could be the healer of my own wounds. The way to end it was to forgive.

I forgave her, yes, but I knew I must also forgive her parents, and the parents before them, realizing that the wounds within compel us to wound those around us. I didn't want to perpetuate this ancient pain, letting it rot my being, and so I made a promise to myself: I will end that old program before I crash.

—L.N. Felder—

My Mantra

Empathy is about standing in someone else's shoes,
feeling with his or her heart,
seeing with his or her eyes.
~Daniel H. Pink

When my children were teenagers, I purchased a magnet with what was said to be a First Nations or Native American prayer. I placed it on the door of our refrigerator in full view. I found the words to be thought provoking and hoped they would teach my children to have more patience and be more forgiving of others.

Oh, Great Spirit, grant that I may not criticize my neighbor
until I have walked a mile in his moccasins.

Although my children are adults now, with homes of their own, I've kept the magnet on our fridge door for the past twenty-five years. During that time, I've often found that the message has helped me see situations from a different perspective.

For example, a number of years ago, I was on my way to a farewell function with several colleagues. A popular department manager was retiring. As we were leaving the office, we bumped into our colleague, Wendy, who had previously planned to attend the event with us. I asked Wendy if she wanted us to wait for her, and she responded in a fairly rude manner, declining our invitation. One of my other colleagues was quite annoyed and clearly resented Wendy's behavior.

"I don't know why you even bothered to invite her," she said.

Reflecting on how frazzled Wendy appeared as she rushed away from us, I commented that perhaps we should just give Wendy a break and forgive her for declining at the last minute. She was obviously having a bad day, and it wasn't worth holding a grudge against her if we weren't aware of what provoked her unusual behavior.

A week later, I learned that when we bumped into Wendy, she was returning to the office from a medical appointment where she was told she had pancreatic cancer. She died a year later. Wendy wasn't being rude to us; she had just received a very traumatizing diagnosis. On reflection, I'm amazed she was able to respond at all.

Whether it's a family member who let me down, a friend who betrayed a confidence, or a difficult colleague, the quote on my fridge guides me. Although it's not always easy to forgive, I've been able to shed a lot of resentment over the years by focusing on my mantra.

— Kathy Dickie —

Once Upon a Time

Forgiveness does not change the past,
but it does enlarge the future.
~Paul Boese

Having spent a large part of my life putting as much distance as possible between myself and my abuser, the last thing I imagined was that I would be at his bedside when he died. Nevertheless, there I was on a chilly Midwest fall evening almost 1,000 miles from the comfort and safety of my home, sitting in a hospital room as the man who had filled my childhood with terror was facing death.

I'd received a call the night before from a relative telling me that my father was dying. Truth be told, my first reaction was "Oh, well." The next morning, however, I found myself packing a suitcase and traveling from Colorado to St. Louis with no idea why.

When I arrived at the nursing facility, I was greeted by a woman who was both warm and curious since the staff was not aware that "Bill" had a daughter. After listening compassionately to a very brief sketch of my tragic family history, she assured me that even though I had traveled a long distance, I was in no way obligated to put myself through any further discomfort. In fact, she offered to put me up for the night and provide transportation back to the airport in the morning… guilt-free.

I deeply appreciated her empathy and consideration, but decided to push through with whatever it seemed I was there to do. Stepping into an elevator, this same thoughtful human being kept a reassuring arm around my shoulder. When the doors opened, I almost gagged at the smells of incontinence, talcum powder and disinfectant. As I approached my father's room, I admit to reconsidering the offer of a guilt-free escape.

I was stunned when I walked in. It had been more than thirty years since I'd seen him, and the form in front of me resembled nothing of what I remembered about my father's angry and menacing frame. Tightly curled into a fetal position, he was frail and small. His mouth was slightly open, his breath barely detectable. I stood motionless just inches from this man of my nightmares. I haven't a clue why it happened, but suddenly all of my fear washed away, and I knew why I was there.

I put my hand on his shoulder and said, "Once upon a time, there was a little boy named Billy. Billy was born with the birthright of all children — to be loved, to learn, to play, to grow in confidence and to experience all the wonder of living. There was a moment, however, probably very early on, when Billy got hurt — deeply hurt — and no one helped to heal that hurt. Perhaps the pain had no words — only tears that he may have had to shed when he was all alone. The hurt remained with Billy and grew with fierce intensity until it finally broke through and hurt everyone around him. But it's okay now for Billy to stop hurting. It's time for Billy to feel safe and loved. It's okay for him to finally go home."

For the next eleven hours, I sat there singing lullabies, telling stories, and sharing candidly all of the feelings I had dealt with over the years. It dawned on me that this man had never been loved by another human being. And he had been incapable of loving anyone else. I think he knew what he had done, and I sensed that he was terrified of leaving this life without someone "hearing" his story and without the possibility of "asking" to be forgiven. Several times during those quiet and profound hours, I told him that he was forgiven. He was "free" and so was I.

I knew almost nothing of my father's story, but I had heard that he was a sullen child, withdrawn and suspicious. I have seen only two photos of him as a child, and in both he appears sad and hurt, even as other children in the picture are smiling. How does a child get to that point? I don't believe that any child is born with a fiercely held shield against the world. What really happened, I'll never know. Everyone has a story, and everyone needs for that story to be told. The generic story I told that night did not excuse what he had done. It did, perhaps, explain it.

About 8:30 the following morning, exhausted after a long flight and sleepless night, I gave into both physical and emotional fatigue and rested my head on the bed. Immediately, I felt the slightest twitch of his hand against mine. When I looked up, I saw that my father's journey had ended. And a part of mine had just begun.

It's been more than twenty years since this event took place. Have I forgotten the traumas of my childhood? No. Nor should I. Our lives are the sum of our stories. I have come to understand that when things are happening to us, beyond our control, we may be the victims in those stories. But when we forgive, we become the storyteller, empowered and boldly wrapped with the authority to share the story in hope that forgiving doesn't happen in a vacuum.

I am free from the pain of my past. I hope with all my heart that my father is, as well.

— Dale Mary Grenfell —

Swept Away

Distance not only gives nostalgia, but perspective,
and maybe objectivity.
~Robert Morgan

Troop 312 met in the Girl Scout hut behind the community center in my small hometown of Forest, Mississippi, near Dog River. The building was known affectionately as Kats Kave. It was a simple building with one large room and a small half-bath but it met all the troop's needs. We sang songs and pledged our allegiance to the American flag and to the Scouts. We marked off badge requirements and created artwork. We even prepared for summer day camp by making "hobo stoves" out of soup cans, corrugated cardboard and paraffin wax. We filled our weekly meetings with varying activities, but we always ended with "The Chore Chart."

That afternoon, that "fateful" Tuesday, it was my turn to sweep. I was sweeping diligently to make sure that every little dust bunny was gathered, and each tiny speck of glitter was captured and trashed. It was hard to get between the chairs, table legs and girls' legs. It was rigorous and tedious, but I was working hard.

Then the scout leader, who happened to be my mother, came up and jerked the broom from my hands. She said, "Give me that! You don't know how to sweep. I'll give it to Kathy Greener. She's a good sweeper!"

Crestfallen, I saw myself as a failure, destined never to succeed at cleaning. I continued to see myself this way many years into adulthood, cursing Kathy Greener every time I picked up a broom. Then one day I learned that my childhood troop-mate was going to be a missionary, and I decided to pray for her every time I swept. I don't know if the prayers helped her or my floors got any cleaner, but I found healing for myself. Feelings of failure and blessing can't coexist.

After having children of my own, I was able to look back at that scene from a mother's viewpoint. Let's just say it looked a bit different and played out something more like this: Girls were running around everywhere because we were hyper from all the fun, and a huge mess had to be cleaned up before we were done. We should have been gone fifteen minutes earlier, and some of the mothers were waiting impatiently for their daughters to come out. Everyone was complaining about the chores they had been assigned or trying to get final instructions from the scout leader, who had three other children waiting at home.

Perhaps my sweeps were more like giant pendulum swings of the broom, almost hitting passersby, stirring up the dust and making everyone cough. Or perhaps I had saddled it like a witch's broom and was flying all around. In my mother's defense, I can totally see her frustration and need to "end the insanity" by getting someone a bit more focused and responsible to sweep.

Now, when I pick up a broom, I don't have a sick feeling in my stomach. I feel satisfaction in knowing that I am doing a good job—and thankful for my scout leader, Mom. There's nothing better than time and maturity to sweep past hurts right into the dustpan.

—Dea Irby—

Chapter 3

When Parents Disappoint

The Right Number

The most important thing about being a father is being
able to forgive yourself. If you don't forgive yourself,
you're not going to forgive your kids, either.
~Evander Holyfield

I'd dialed this number repeatedly in the past and I thought I knew it by heart. He answered immediately, but his voice seemed different.

"Papa?" I asked.

"Yes!" he cried enthusiastically, although he still sounded strange. When I hesitated for a moment, he continued, "Eloisa?"

"Oh!" I stammered. "No, I'm sorry. I must have dialed the wrong number."

"You and everybody else," he snarled. "Big surprise!"

I apologized again and moved to hang up. The receiver was halfway to its cradle when something compelled me to stop. I pulled it back to my ear and spoke into the mouthpiece.

"Are you okay, sir?"

I heard him inhale deeply before replying, "No."

"Is there anything I can do? Would you like me to call an ambulance?"

"I should have known it wasn't her. I was a terrible father," he lamented as if he didn't hear me. "I thought you were my daughter when you called me 'Papa' like she used to — that by some miracle she was reaching out to me before... Well, I thought you were my daughter."

"I'm sure you were a good father," I soothed nervously as his voice trailed away. "All parents make mistakes. It's…"

"Not like me!" he interrupted.

Suddenly, it was like the proverbial dam burst. In a ragged voice, he began recounting a story eerily similar to my own.

"There was a boy… a loser. Her mother and I both forbade her from seeing him. I told her if she continued, she was dead to us. A week later, she turned eighteen, packed her things and left. She tried calling once, but I hung up before she could say anything. I was so stupid."

He paused, catching his breath, and then went on. "Six months ago, my wife, Cheryl, died."

I murmured sympathetically, but he ignored me and went on.

"I sold our home and I'm supposed to move out in three weeks. When I was going through Cheryl's things, I found Eloisa's phone number. They had kept in touch without my knowing. I've wanted to call Eloisa, but I'm afraid. It's been nine years now. She'll surely hate me even more since she never had a chance to say goodbye to her mother."

I swallowed hard, wondering if I should speak or keep listening. He made the choice for me.

"I knew I was wrong years ago, but I was too proud to admit it. I miss my little girl. I've missed her since the day she left."

This time, I responded. "Please, listen to me," I urged him gently. "I want to tell you something…."

I proceeded to relate my own story about my father, a difficult, stern, old-fashioned man. His word was law in our home, and he demanded unquestioned obedience from his children. He was especially strict with me, his only daughter, watching me like a hawk — more so during my teens. He selected my TV shows and music, and screened all my friends. I was not permitted to go to sleepovers or on dates. I couldn't wear make-up, short skirts or even clear nail polish. He practically controlled my every breath, sneeze and cough. My curfew, unlike my brothers', was 7:00 p.m. If I disobeyed, punishment was immediate and painful.

"When I turned eighteen, Papa announced he would choose my husband. He was making arrangements to bring an older man from his home country, Poland," I told the stranger on the other end of the phone. "That's when I ran away. We didn't speak again until I was twenty-five and had been married five years. He sent a message through one of my brothers inviting me to spend Christmas with the family."

"You forgave him?"

"What's your name?" I asked him softly.

"John," he replied.

"Yes, John, I forgave him. He had many flaws, but he had a lot of good in him, too. He provided for us, making sure we were all well fed and had the education that he never got because of the war. My memories of him weren't always bad ones. We were poor growing up. Life was hard. I'm sure there were times he wished he could walk away from four children who always needed something. Those needs probably destroyed any dreams he had for himself. Yet he stayed and did what he honestly believed was best for us. I often wished he was different, but he wasn't, and he's the only father I'll ever have — just like you and Eloisa. Make that call, John."

"What if she refuses to talk to me?"

"What if she doesn't?" I countered. "You'll never know unless you try, right? Nothing will change if she does. You're not in touch now, so what will change?"

"You're a very wise young lady," he told me gently after a long silence.

"Will you do it?"

I heard him inhale deeply and then expel a whoosh of air.

"Yes," he told me. I could sense the newfound strength in him.

"Can I call you and see how it went?" I asked.

"Yes, of course."

I reminded him I'd dialed a wrong number. When he gave me his number, I was stunned to hear that the last four digits weren't even close to my father's. I couldn't understand how I'd managed to make such a huge mistake.

I called John the next day. This time, his voice was animated—filled with joy and hope.

"We talked for two hours!" he told me excitedly. "She's married, and I have a little granddaughter! Her husband is the boy I disapproved of, but he's given her a good life, and she's happy."

He went on to tell me Eloisa knew her mother had died. An aunt who'd also kept in touch told her. The same aunt tricked John into leaving the funeral parlor for something to eat so Eloisa could say goodbye.

"She's forgiven me for everything!" John exclaimed jubilantly. "She wants to see me. They're coming tomorrow! I have so much to do!"

"That's wonderful." I laughed at his delight.

"It's all thanks to you, Miss, um, you never told me your name," he prodded.

"It's Marya."

"Marya, I literally owe you my life." His tone grew serious. "When you called yesterday, I was about to take all my wife's leftover pills. I wanted to die. I'd lost all hope. You gave it back to me. I can't thank you enough for listening."

I gasped in horror. "I'm so glad you didn't! There's always hope—and no thanks are necessary. Go and be happy. Make your wife proud!"

"I will," he promised.

"Good luck, John," I whispered and hung up.

We never spoke again. I called a month later, but his phone was disconnected—probably because he moved. I often wished I'd gotten his last name. Hopefully, he and Eloisa made up for the years they lost.

—Marya Morin—

A Mother, Without the Mothering

Letting go doesn't mean that you don't care about someone anymore. It's just realizing that the only person you really have control over is yourself.
~Deborah Reber

When my mother died, I felt nothing. She was sixty-two. It was a short life, lived hard, cancer taking her well before old age did.

Inside, I was a white canvas, a hollow devoid of feeling. Where there should have been a riot of grief and emotion, there was only blankness. I worried I was heartless, but I'd spent forty years learning to live with and love a mother wrecked by alcohol and drug addiction.

But something feels wrong about feeling nothing. People who knew me and knew her murmured their condolences.

"I'm not sad," I said, and I'm sure I meant it.

"No matter what, she's still your mother," they'd reply.

It's a line I got stuck on. Because she was my mother — without the mothering.

I visited her three weeks before she died. The throat cancer was a lump the size of a golf ball sticking out from the side of her neck. After a biopsy, it was covered by a bandage, which did nothing to make it less visible. I had a hard time not staring at it.

Her frame, always small, had shrunk to half its size. She was bird-like and frail, the size of a child under the hospital blanket. Her face was drawn, and the haggardness was there in deep lines, telling me what I already knew about her life.

There had always been a hardness to her face, which I had often mistaken for something bordering on meanness. When I was a little girl I saw that meanness in her eyes and was afraid of it. It took me years to realise that what I was looking at was likely only her own fears and insecurities.

She had every right to those fears and insecurities. Her own childhood was one that hurt to hear about. I garnered only snippets here and there over the years.

She was the eldest of six children living poor in a small country town. Her father drank too much, and while he worked hard as a labourer, he was also a hard man. My mother was sexually abused at a young age, did poorly in school, married the wrong man, and had two children by the age of nineteen.

She went on to have five children with three different men. My twin brother and I were the two she kept by her side as she journeyed through a life of addiction and dysfunction.

She told us we were the lucky ones not to be given away. In her darker moments, she threatened to abandon us to foster care. Sometimes we wished silently that she would — thinking there had to be something better. Then, in some twisted logic, we were terribly grateful when she chose to keep us and stay on as our mother. Better the devil you know...

She was never physically abusive, but her neglect stands out as violent as any visible scar.

She wasn't one to share. I had the briefest glimpses into her past, enough to give me understanding about why she became the person she was and the mother she wasn't.

Her cancer spread quickly, and she died within weeks. At her funeral, the celebrant talked up a good life. Really? I felt for the celebrant. She had little to work with.

How does one honour the life of a woman who gave so little of herself, with those little bits mostly vague or venomous? I couldn't help the celebrant write a better eulogy because I was stuck myself.

How can death be peaceful when peace was never made? Did I miss the miracle of a deathbed confession, some cleansing to free her spirit to move on to a better place? No, I don't think that happened. I don't know where she's gone.

At her funeral, my twin said it best when he chose not to speak about our mother at all. He spoke to the grandchildren instead. He told them to make good choices in the big things but especially in the small things.

Strangers may remember you for the glorious act or the huge achievement, he said. However, what really counts to those you love are the small, kind things you do every day.

My mother reaped the consequences of a life lived hard. It was never my job to make her into someone different. Perhaps she was capable of change, but the insidious nature of addiction to alcohol, drugs and men stole her willingness.

Ours was a relationship with fragile layers, complicated and at times overwhelming in its emotional dysfunction. Those intense troughs of my early years when my mother wasn't there or didn't care drove me to the edge of sanity.

While we never stepped over that cliff, I know how violence happens.

I grew up frustrated and sometimes desperate. My saving grace was an inexplicable core of hope and belief that things would get better.

The time I spent at her hospital bedside was strained and shallow. I'd spent our life together pretending *nothing* was wrong. I'd spent our time apart dwelling on *everything* that was wrong.

Why did I think it was going to be different at the end?

In those last minutes together, I made my peace with her by acting kind. I made ordinary conversation about the things I knew she was interested in — her plants and her dog. I avoided the topics we should have, if we could have, resolved many years earlier.

As I walked out of her hospital room, I told her I loved her. I'm not sure I meant it. Despite the chasm of things left unsaid churning inside, my shallow words would have brought her some kind of peace. I know, despite the acting, that I did well.

That empty void I felt after her death was disturbing, but also welcome.

After all, if I'm not burying things from the past, then perhaps the hollow wasn't heartlessness, but a canvas made blank by some anaesthetic salve I'm going to choose to call forgiveness and healing.

—Jennifer Watts—

Writing to My Dead Father

Forgiveness is an inner correction
that lightens the heart.
~Gerald Jampolsky

My father died when I was in college. For years after that, I locked away my feelings about him, safely buried under school, teaching, writing, and turbulent relationships with boyfriends.

He was an unhappy and distant man with great musical talent. He had studied at Juilliard and played the violin like a concert artist. I inherited his love of music, taking piano lessons from grade school through high school, and later, flute lessons, even studying, too, at Juilliard.

He denied himself the pleasure of his music, though, except for tortured Sunday mornings when his violin wept and screamed with frustrated beauty. He quit a community orchestra because "they weren't good enough," and, when I showed him an ad in the paper, he wouldn't audition for the second string section of the Philharmonic.

With a growing family, he settled for a second-rate administrative job that used a sixteenth of his intelligence. He barely tolerated the small-mindedness of his boss and co-workers.

My father had two methods of communicating with his family: the sarcastic putdown to which you couldn't retort, or a cold silence that permeated the whole household, punctuated by unpredictable eruptions of temper. We all lived in trepidation. My brother scurried to his room. My mother turned to the kitchen. Yet when she complained to me about him, or more accurately, complained under her breath in my hearing, I always defended him.

"He's tired," I'd say. "He's overworked. He's hungry."

He might not have known I defended him, because he hardly talked to me. The few times I tried to share a detail or two about my life, he grunted and turned toward the television, eventually falling asleep.

Years after his death, I took a personal-growth workshop called "Dealing with Our Past." The leader's instructions were to choose an "unresolved issue" and write about it. Instantly, my father came to mind.

The first few lines of my letter to him were stiff and awkward. But as I wrote, sitting on a metal bridge chair in an overheated room full of people, the memories threatened to overwhelm me. I could hardly write fast enough, pouring out everything I'd kept bottled up for so long.

> *Dear Daddy,*
>
> *Please, see me, Daddy. Notice me. Talk to me. You've always been so preoccupied with work. Or too angry with your world and your family — me — and I never knew why. Or too tired after work to do anything but stare in front of the television and fall asleep.*
>
> *How often did I see you smile? Maybe three times in my life. Once on vacation when two fawns pranced across a field. Once when a neighbor's kid crawled into our bushes. And once, the time I cherish most, when you smiled right at me.*
>
> *It was a Sunday, and I was about 10. We'd had a house full of relatives visiting, and after all the goodbyes, you and Mom drove our car to the highway entrance with them following. The kitchen and living room were piled with the leftovers of entertaining — dirty pots, dishes, glasses, napkins, and crumbs over every surface.*
>
> *While you were out, I gathered it all up, threw out the garbage, scrubbed every pot, and did sinkful after sinkful of dishes, as Mom had taught me. I put everything away and wiped every surface.*

As I was scrubbing the sink, you came home. You looked toward me in the kitchen and smiled — that third time — and said, "You're a good kid."

I've carried your look and those four words in a deep place inside myself. They were the only compliment you ever gave me.

Everything else was storms and crises, fuming and cursing, frowning at my clothes, looks, or not-quite-perfect grades, or worse, ignoring me.

Look at me now. I'm still a good kid. See what I've done. Could you be at least a little proud of me?

Daddy, as you kept away from me, you kept me from knowing you. I wanted to, so much. But I could never get through.

Except once. During my freshman year in college, we went to a concert together, just you and me. This was the only time I remember we ever went out alone. I felt very grown-up in my skirt and blazer, low heels, and little earrings, taking the subway straight from my last class at the city university to meet you outside Carnegie Hall.

We had hamburgers and French fries in a place across the street and almost really talked for the first time. I vaguely recall telling you about my courses and friends. Across the table, for the first time, I had your attention. You even told me a little about your music studies.

The concert was sublime, although I've forgotten the program. Mostly, I remember sitting next to you, watching you sideways. Then we took the late train home back to suburbia.

You began having pains on the train. You kept groaning, trying to stifle them, and there was nothing I could do. I hear those groans now. When we got home, you took some potion that helped momentarily.

Only weeks afterward, at midnight in your big bathroom, you crashed into the glass shower door and collapsed on the floor.

I know you were struggling for years and years. Your last illness, I'm convinced, was a stockpile you couldn't stop, everything that bothered you, stuffed down for so long it had to explode.

I understand now and know why you were so angry — the Wagnerian motif of your life, the unfulfilled promise, the wasted talent. And I forgive you.

Forgive me, too, for intruding on your life so you had to earn money at something you hated and weren't appreciated for instead of following and developing the music career you loved.

And I see now, unexpectedly and with shock, how much I've learned from you.

I've learned from your strength and grit, your intensity and passion for music. Even though I don't play now, the music you gave me continues to nourish me as I listen daily.

I've learned to apply your passion to my writing. It continues to nourish me daily.

I've learned from your insistence on doing a thorough job and seeing it through, despite your disdain for your colleagues. I emulate your push for perfection in my refusal to let my writing go out until, after many drafts, I'm satisfied, at least for today.

I've learned from your outraged disdain for slackers, and I now demand the fullest from clients and friends.

I've learned from your love of quality and genuineness, whether of violins or cars or people, and I don't settle for imitations.

I've learned from your ferocious honesty, and I now can ask probing, even embarrassing, questions of others to get to the truth.

Daddy, you were the best you could be for me. I wish I'd known you, adult to adult. I forgive you and love you.

After I wrote this letter, changing positions on that metal chair in the stuffy room, I felt lighter than ever before. The armor of resentment and unexpressed sadness dissolved, yielding to long-buried love. With tears, I felt great gratitude for all I'd learned and, finally, for writing to my dead father.

— Noelle Sterne —

22

A Precious Jewel

You can't selectively numb your anger, any more
than you can turn off all lights in a room
and still expect to see the light.
~Shannon L. Alder

My mom impressed two maxims upon me when I was growing up: don't embrace hatred and never hold a grudge. Unlike most teenagers who go through a period of rebellion as they seek their autonomy, I was obedient and determined to never hold onto anger or a grudge.

On Friday afternoons, as I watched *American Bandstand* and practiced new dance steps, my mom did fancy footwork as she paced at the window and complained about her tardy husband. The minute my stepdad walked through the door, she'd shift gears and pretend everything was fine. Was this forgiveness? If she displayed anger, would that be holding a grudge? Her messages and actions weren't always compatible, and I was often confused, upset and apprehensive about displaying honest emotions.

Mom and I never had a screaming match, even though she had been overprotective to a fault, and I had plenty of reasons to be upset with her. At seventeen years old, I had a steady boyfriend and vowed to get married when I graduated high school. I couldn't wait to escape our restrictive house rules.

One Friday, I brought home a senior-ring brochure tucked inside my English homework. My heart was set on a dainty ring with a royal blue stone.

"Mom, I know money is tight, but…"

My mother looked at the ring of my dreams circled in permanent red marker. It cost $35. She cut me off. "There is no extra money for a class ring. Period."

I offered to earn the money by ironing or doing odd jobs for neighbors.

"Don't you dare approach neighbors! You'll have a wedding ring on your finger in a few months, anyway. You don't need a class ring."

"But, Mom! I want one. I'll be the only person in my senior class without one. Please?"

My begging fell on deaf ears. She turned away and went to her bedroom; her mind was made up. Mine was filled with anger, but I wasn't allowed to display it. I wasn't supposed to hold a grudge. I flopped down on my bed to read a book, but I couldn't see the words through my tears.

The weekend before the money was due, I attempted one more time to persuade her. I waved my hand and pretended I was showing off my pretty senior ring.

"There is no extra money! I said 'no'!" she told me.

I quashed my anger and swallowed vicious thoughts. When my stepdad walked through the door, late as usual that night, he handed Mom a five-dollar bill. I was hopeful. She left the house and returned with beer for him. That's when I decided that my anger was an honest emotion and I could hold a grudge as long as I wanted — as long as they didn't know about it.

As it turned out, I wasn't the only student in class without a senior ring. And Mom was right — I flaunted a diamond wedding ring on my finger within months of graduation.

Yet, for years, whether my hands were soaking in sudsy dishwater or changing diapers, I secretly yearned for that sapphire stone.

As the years passed, Mom and I went on to have a wonderful mother-daughter relationship. She was the best grandma. She visited frequently and doted on her grandchildren.

The kids grew up. I divorced. Mom and I grew older.

We sat at my kitchen table one afternoon dunking donuts, discussing life and our belief systems. She admitted she had made many child-rearing mistakes.

"You did a good job, Mom," I said. "But I've changed my way of thinking about something you taught me. Even though anger and hate are scary and powerful emotions, we shouldn't deny our kids or ourselves those feelings."

Mom jumped at the chance to lecture me. "Holding on to bitterness will destroy you. I've always taught you…"

"I know, but holding it in is just as destructive. Mom, not holding a grudge isn't as easy as slipping a ring on or off my finger." I made the motions. For a moment, I think my mother thought I was talking about my failed marriage. Then she nodded and lowered her eyes when she realized what I meant.

"Your senior ring?" She tried to explain her position. She never fully understood mine.

"It's okay, really, Mom. I just want you to know that I believe feeling angry is all right. Staying angry isn't."

That day, as I massaged my ring finger, I symbolically slipped off decades of hurt as I released repressed emotions attached to an absent gem.

Forgiveness really is a precious jewel.

— Linda O'Connell —

23

A Last Look

Forgiving people isn't always about giving them
another chance. It's for closure so you can move on.
~Sonya Parker

I parked my car at the far end of the street called Via Segundo. I wanted time to walk through the old neighborhood and anticipate, or perhaps delay, my arrival at the house where I grew up.

I stepped from my Honda Civic into the cool, moist air and high leafy shade that made my hometown ideal for growing azaleas. The street was narrower than I remembered. Sycamores uniformly planted as street trees, slender and upright in my youth, now reached high as if to escape the front yards they had outgrown. Arching boughs touched and mingled overhead, creating a natural arbor that led me into the past.

I walked along the sidewalk, aware that I had walked these same streets in my dreams many times before. I crossed at corners and read the street names: Via Primero, Via Anacapa, Via Lucero. As a child, I had come to understand that the names were Spanish and held meanings: Via Primero and Via Segundo, First and Second. I reached our old street, tucked behind Via Segundo, and read the street sign: Via Rincon. Corner.

I walked past the first house, where as children we dared each other to walk, fearful that one of the old spinster sisters who lived there would jump from the bushes and snatch one of us to boil for their dinner. I looked in vain for the crosses etched in the sidewalk, marking property lines, but also the bad-luck squares one had to jump over to stay safe.

I had lived there for twenty years, until the day of my wedding, but now Via Rincon looked unfamiliar. I identified the house where a friend had lived, and another where they gave out the best Halloween candy, but the houses were different now, the yards redone, the rose-bushes gone. A woman passed by, holding a small child by the hand. Although I had a smile ready, she did not look at me.

I came upon my parents' house almost by surprise. It was smaller than I remembered, painted brown by its new owners and missing the lush rhododendrons that had dominated the modest front lawn. I spied the single-car attached garage my father had built and the narrow driveway where my sister and I had played Two Square.

I remembered the last time I had stood in this same place, staring at the house, working up the courage to walk up to the front door and ring the bell. For six years, my parents had refused to talk to me, angry that I was seeing a therapist and talking about them behind their backs. It did not matter to them that I had been suicidal and needed to understand how childhood abuse had damaged my psyche and kept me fearful and confused. They could not forgive my disloyalty.

That visit failed in the sense that I could not find a way to recon-nect with them. They made it clear that they no longer considered me their daughter. They had no interest in my life and could not fathom why I was sitting in their living room trying to make conversation.

Although my visit did not change their attitude toward me, it did change my attitude toward them. For the first time, I saw them not through the eyes of a frightened child, but with the clear gaze of an adult who had experienced real love, healing and forgiveness. From that day on, I felt pity for them and a growing sense of compassion. I began to pray for them — not for their punishment, but for their release from stubborn hatred. I stopped having nightmares about being hurt by my parents and started dreaming about them as they might have been under different circumstances: gentle, loving, secure enough to be kind and generous.

Now, with both my parents long deceased, I looked at the house and tried to connect with that long-ago life. I stared at the front window on the right, which looked into the room I had shared with my sister. I pictured the closet where my child-self had hidden from angry voices. I imagined the pale green walls standing silent witness to beatings, terror and sexual intrusions on my innocence.

I felt sadness layered with a comforting sense of distance. I knew the memories would always be there, in a deep corner of my heart, but through decades of living and loving, that corner had become smaller. I had outgrown the old pain. My identity had shifted from throwaway child to beloved wife and mother, cherished friend and valued daughter of God. I could afford to be generous, to be kind. Out of the great store of grace I had received, I could afford to forgive my parents.

Standing on the sidewalk on that early May morning, I grieved for my mother and father. I ached for the cruel upbringing they each had endured at the hands of their own parents, for the lies they believed that had twisted and hardened them, making them resistant to love and forgiveness. I missed the friendship we might have shared had circumstances been different.

A sweet-scented breeze whispered across my face and rustled the sycamore leaves above my head. I looked up into boughs fluttering with green, anticipating a new season of growth.

This tree was an old friend of mine. I had raked its leaves in autumn and hidden my face against it when playing hide-and-seek in summer. I noticed the sidewalk had cracked and risen in places where its roots had expanded far and deep, searching for water, the tree taking what it needed to survive.

I stepped closer and laid a gentle hand on its rough side. I studied the trunk, noticed how the old bark loosened and fell off in patches, leaving smooth living wood beneath. On impulse, I broke off a three-inch piece to take with me as a memento and token of farewell. I knew I would not be coming back. My business here was finished.

I turned and walked down the street. I did not look back but cradled in my hand the fragile evidence that life is strong and generous and works for our good when goodness is what we seek.

—Judith Ingram—

24

Patriarch

Inner peace can be reached only
when we practice forgiveness.
~Gerald Jampolsky

My father is having brain surgery. His right leg drags, and he cannot speak coherently. This man who spent our youth drilling us on perfect public speaking and demanding perfect grammar now struggles to talk. This man who ruled his castle with a leather belt in silent rage is tethered to tubes and wires, needles and gauges.

He has an IV, heart monitor, and catheter. He pulls up his gown, fumbles at the tube draining urine he cannot control, and lets my sister make pretend adjustments. It calms him, and he relaxes back onto the pillows, allowing her to cover him, seemingly unaware that he exposed himself. When the medical staff comes in, we speak for him, identifying ourselves, as he would do if he could. Birth order is important, and we instinctively step forward, oldest to youngest — first me, then my two brothers, and finally my sister — as our father beams from the bed. Patriarch still.

We talk softly, stroke his cold hands, and massage his cramping legs. He smiles as we gather around, telling him he's strong, declaring love for him, promising to be there when he wakes up. He offers no complaints, but he cannot talk. Maybe he's screaming inside. My sister talks for him and helps him eat. The older of my two brothers speaks with the surgeon, gathering and sharing information as if they were colleagues. The younger brother tells jokes, mumbling funny things at inappropriate times.

I do nothing but sit, watching the drama around me. All the others seem to know their roles, but I don't know mine. Thankfully, our familiar father is gone, replaced by this fumbling stranger. Over his bed, I look at my sister; she catches my glance and hurries to fix the pillows. "Need the bed raised, Daddy?"

They will shave his head, peel back his scalp, take a piece from his skull, and remove the mass — blood clot, tumor, whatever it is that has stolen his abilities. He requires attention and care from the doctors and nurses, but he needs much more from us — his progeny whom he spent a lifetime trying to shape into the people he thought we should be. He could be proud of those people even at the expense of our own pride.

He is frightened, and so are we. We hope for recovery — at least to walk and speak like he could a week ago. It's hard to hope for better, for reinstatement of long-lost mental function. Is that even possible? No one will ask.

I realize what I want. I want him to live — to return to me the love I am trying to give to him. And I hope for forgiveness — not *from* my father, but *toward* my father for the uncertainty and anxiety that were my legacy, the burden bestowed upon the eldest by the man of the house.

After he is released from the hospital to a rehab unit, we four take turns observing and assisting in therapy sessions. We scribble notes and share information from doctors, nurses, and other staff. In six weeks, we move his belongings to an assisted-living facility.

We divide the week into four parts, to each have time with our father. I sit by his bedside every Monday and Tuesday, all day and into the night. I push his wheelchair, take him outside, watch *The Andy Griffith Show* and *The Lawrence Welk Show* reruns with him. Sometimes, I bring my two-year-old grandson to visit. He sings for Papa, whose face is wreathed in the biggest smiles of all.

We learn how to communicate in new ways. I hold his hand and smile into his eyes, which look back with a mix of sorrow and pleading. When I chatter on too much, he squeezes my fingers as if to say, "Quiet, now." We settle into an easiness that feels strange, then suddenly right. He pats my hand, my arm. I help him eat, steadying the fork or spoon he holds, guiding it to his mouth. He's hungry, and I feel my heart swell with gratitude for that.

One afternoon, we sit outside in the sunshine. Holding my attention with a tight grip of my hand and a powerful gaze into my eyes, he whispers, "I'm sorry."

And I answer, "I know. I love you, Dad."

I forgive you.

— Sue Armstrong —

25

A Bitter Absence

Gratitude is the healthiest of all human emotions.
The more you express gratitude for what you have,
the more likely you will have even more
to express gratitude for.
~Zig Ziglar

As a child, I knew I was unwanted by my absent father. It was a fact, but not one I could easily accept. As the years went on, it got harder and harder. I had no father's shoulder to cry on, no father to dance with or call me his little princess. It was a constant ache.

Eventually, I felt like I wasn't worthy of my dad, not worthy of his attention or want. As a teenager, I'd pace in my room and sob, wondering why he didn't miss me. I'd wonder what was so un-special about me that he could live without knowing me. Not even his own mother begging him to act like a father could pull him from his drunken stupor to try.

At some point in my teens, I decided to use my anger toward him as motivation. He only *thought* he didn't want to know me, I told myself. How different he'd feel if I became famous, did something remarkable, or became someone that others wished they knew! How would he feel when I stood up for an acceptance speech, and his name was missing from those I thanked? I was determined to be great, not because I wanted to be, but because I wanted to spite him. My motivation turned from bettering myself into making him pay for not wanting me.

This continued for years. When I wanted to give up on something, even if it was something that was no longer for me, I'd bitterly push forward anyway. I'd imagine his face when I finally reached the pinnacle of success, crushed by all he had missed out on. Making him sorry for all the tears I cried would finally make me feel better. I was sure of it.

Gleefully, I'd think about how it would be my turn to make him sad. I'd turn him away once he reached out in repentance. I'd make him feel the same way I felt my whole life. Such revenge would surely heal my heart, wouldn't it? Of course, it would!

But I never became famous. I never received the on-stage accolades I dreamt up in my revenge plots. But I did achieve my ultimate dreams outside of him — I conquered cancer at nineteen. I went on to get married, have two miracle children, and start a charity to help those suffering through infertility and loss following my own multiple miscarriages and permanent infertility. I learned what I truly wanted in life and the goals that made my heart soar — not with hopeful revenge, but with pure happiness. I found appreciation for life and everything I did have instead of focusing on everything I didn't.

That's when I learned that clinging so tightly to my anger, wanting so badly to spite that missing father and make him pay, was only holding me back and hurting me more. It took decades to learn this important lesson. I had to retrain my mind. I had to learn to make goals for my own happiness, to learn what I truly loved instead of what I pursued for revenge purposes. I deserved a good father, but even more than that, I deserved to be motivated by more than just anger.

As I grew older, I realized that not everyone is meant to be a parent. I examined what I knew of him and realized how bad my life could have been had he stuck around. Was there still a part of me deep down that was sad I grew up having to feel unwanted? Of course. But maturity showed me that sometimes absence can be a gift. He didn't leave because I wasn't special enough to stick around for. He left because he was too flawed and selfish to be a good parent. I was much better off without him. Once I realized that his absence wasn't a reflection of who I was as a person, I was able to let go of the anger.

Sometimes, I still fantasize about making it big. But now, when I imagine myself on that stage, I don't think of his face full of regret. I don't think of his face at all. I think of all the people who helped me get to where I am and all the people who have made a positive impact in my life.

It's a much better fantasy now that I can let go of what didn't happen and embrace all the good that did. Allowing forgiveness to calm my anger gave me a new viewpoint on life and an appreciation for the man I chose as a father to my own children. There's no greater delight in my life than knowing I chose better for them. I learned an important lesson about who *not* to choose so my children would never have to go through what I did. My father's drunken, abusive, and irresponsible behavior, which was passed down to him through his family, ended with me.

—Jill Keller—

26

Only Human

Forgiveness, for me, means letting go of the energy
that is keeping me bound to the hurt.
~Christine Laureano

We were as close as a mother and daughter could be. Mom and I truly enjoyed each other's company. For as long as I could remember, we were pals, giggling over lunch, spending an afternoon at the mall, or sunning ourselves at the beach. Yet, with Mom there was always one caveat to keeping our plans — she had to feel well enough.

Plagued with chronic obstructive pulmonary disease (COPD), Mom was in poor health for as long as I could remember. There were spring nights when the air was so full of pollen that I could hear her wheezing through her closed bedroom door. Summer was no better when high humidity would cause her to gasp for breath. Neither was fall with its threat of mold spores or winter when the sharp sting of frozen air would keep her indoors for days on end. But, when the weather cooperated, and Mom felt well enough, there was no stopping us.

During my early twenties, it seemed that Mom got more frequent reprieves from what she called "her attacks." Thanks to some new medications and guidance from a nutritionist, she gained significant lung function and strength. Soon, she began to "feel well enough" more and more frequently. Oh, the fun we had during those times. With Mom no longer a slave to her lungs, we could schedule outings at any time. We even vacationed together.

During one of our weekend travels, I became concerned about Mom's newfound energy. I was in good shape; I'd been known to walk several miles each day. Yet when I had trouble keeping up with my mother on a walking tour, I became suspicious. "Mom, where did you get all your energy from today? You practically sprinted through that tour," I half-joked in the hotel that night.

She extracted an amber-colored plastic container from her travel bag. The small round pills inside made a rattling noise. "I just take an extra one of these," she laughed, referring to the steroid medication prescribed to keep her asthma at bay, "and then I have all the energy I need."

So that's what Mom was doing, I thought as a sinking feeling hit my stomach. "Are you sure that's a good idea? It doesn't seem wise to fool around with the dosage of your medication."

My mother waved her hand dismissively. "The doctor told me I could increase my dosage if I needed to. He said it's okay as long as I cut back once I feel better."

Well, I thought to myself, wanting to believe her, *as long as the doctor says it's okay*... But I had doubts about the wisdom of her practice — and the wisdom of her doctor to dispense such advice.

Years went by, and Mom continued what seemed to be her harmless habit of adjusting her medication according to her needs. I went on to move into my own home and marry. Although Mom and I remained close, we inevitably saw less of each other. She still seemed to be in improved health, but now sometimes complained about fatigue. Soon, I began to notice that she also reached for her inhaler more frequently. When I'd question her, she'd just smile. "I'm getting older, you know."

One day, I noticed something that sent a chill down my spine. Mom rolled up her shirtsleeves, revealing oddly shaped red and purple bruises covering both her arms. "It's a side-effect of the medication," she admitted. After years of misuse, the steroids had begun to attack her body, she explained. The medication that she depended on to keep her alive was now killing her.

I have had the unfortunate experience of seeing several friends and family members suffer under a variety of serious illnesses. In some situations, it was a long, sad journey to the finish line. My mother's case was no different. Her body broke down piece by piece, year after year. I cared for her every step of the way, taking her to doctor's appointments, sitting by her side in the hospital emergency room, wheeling her in her wheelchair, bathing and feeding her. Until the bitter end. And then, she was gone.

And I was angry.

That anger became an emotion I couldn't shake. Not that I wanted to. I was entitled, I thought. My mother had chosen her own fate when she misused her prescription medication and, in the process, took me down with her. I looked in the mirror. My face was sullen and drawn. My hair had started to gray. The strain of the situation had been so great on me that even the bags under my eyes had bags under them.

And what about all my other sacrifices? What about all the time spent away from my husband, all the social invitations I had turned down, all the friends who no longer bothered to call? I had given it all up to care for Mom. And she died anyway, thanks to her own poor choices.

The whole situation had me so furious that for months I couldn't look at a photo of my mom without wanting to tear it to shreds. I refused to cook or bake anything involving a recipe she had handed down to me. I threw her clothes in the trash and gave her jewelry to a relative. I didn't want any vestige of that woman near me.

Then one day, as I shuffled through some old files, I came across a photo of the two of us. There we were, smiling side by side on one of our vacations as the sun shone across our shoulders and waves crashed in the ocean behind us. I remembered that day so well. We had giggled together in a boutique as we both tried on revealing bathing suits we would never have had the courage to wear in public. Later, we shared a light lunch of field greens and grilled shrimp on the very same balcony where the photo was taken. It had been a glorious day, a day my mother might never have been able to enjoy without her medication. Finally, I understood.

I took that photo and wrote across the bottom, "I forgive." Aloud, I said, "I forgive you, Mom, for wanting to enjoy life and for doing the only thing you knew to accomplish that goal. You were only human, Mom, and I forgive you."

Then I forgave myself for all the months of anger and bitterness. I forgave myself for being human, too.

— Monica A. Andermann —

27

Joseph's Miracle

*The most beautiful people I've known are those who
have known trials, have known struggles, have known
loss, and have found their way out of the depths.*
~Elisabeth Kübler-Ross

I stood shivering in the vestibule of the apartment building, waiting for my student to let me in. It was unusually cold for early November. Quickly, we said our hellos, and on the way up to his apartment in the elevator, he said, "You can call me Joe, or you can call me Joseph. But don't ever call me Joey. I hate the name Joey."

"Okay," I said hesitantly. "Joseph it is."

The serious look on his face faded, giving way to a beautiful, toothy smile. "Most people just call me Joe," he said. "I like Joseph." The ice was broken, and we instantly became relaxed and comfortable with each other.

"Will a parent be home this evening?" I asked.

"I don't have any parents," he said. "I live alone." His answer caught me off guard. A parent was always present when I taught. But Joseph was a twenty-year-old college student. And I wondered why social services had requested a tutor for an adult living on his own.

His apartment was sparsely decorated, but warm and inviting. And spotlessly clean. He was polite and soft-spoken, but firm about his expectations of our tutoring sessions and me. We sat at the dining-room table, split a can of Pepsi, and got to work. "Do you want to get your homework out so we can go over it?" I asked.

"Yeah, but I want to ask you a question first. Do you know anything about digital cameras?"

"A little. Why?"

"In a couple of weeks, I'm going to the White House. I was invited to a movie premiere. Afterward, I'll be meeting Vice President Biden and the cast from the movie. I bought a camera so I can take pictures of the event. But I don't know how to set it up. Can you help me?"

"Sure," I said. "How did this all come about?"

"Well, it's a long story. And it's kind of sad. When I was eight, my mother died. My father remarried two years later. His new wife and I didn't get along. We fought a lot, and my father always took her side. He told me to keep my mouth shut and do whatever she said. I tried. But we still fought. One day, when I was twelve, my father took me for a ride. He took me to Kennedy High School on the other side of the city. Do you know where that is?"

"Yes. It's near my home."

"He pulled into the parking lot and told me to get out. He said he and his wife didn't want me living with them anymore. I begged him to take me home, but he wouldn't. When I finally got out, he drove off. It was summer. I had nothing but the clothes on my back. No money. No way to buy food — no way to buy anything I needed. I didn't know where to go or what to do. I thought maybe he was just trying to scare me, and when he calmed down, he'd come back. So, I stayed in the park across the street and slept on a bench for three nights, waiting for him. He never came back. I was terrified."

"I walk my dog in that park every day," I said, searching my memory, trying to recall if I had seen him there — not that it mattered now. The truth is, there were always kids in that park, playing hoops or just sitting in the grass, talking. Had I seen him, I would have thought he was just another kid hanging out in the park. I felt awful for him.

Then I got mad. *How could a father throw away his own son like that?* I thought. *It's unconscionable.* The more I thought about it, the angrier I got. For five years, Joseph lived on the streets — abandoned not only by his father but his entire family. He ate out of trashcans and slept wherever he could find a safe place to hide, never sleeping in the same place twice. He had to keep moving.

"Joseph, why didn't you get help?"

"I didn't know where to get help," he said. "A couple of times, the police were called. But I was so afraid of getting arrested that I ran. When we had those big snowstorms, I slept on my friend's sofa. But his parents only let me stay overnight."

"They didn't try to help you?"

"They didn't know how."

"You mean they didn't want to get involved."

"Maybe. But eventually, I got used to living on the streets. The first winter was the worst, though. I didn't have a warm coat. On really cold nights, I huddled in the entrance of an open building downtown so I wouldn't freeze to death."

"How did you survive on the streets for so long?"

"God," he said with conviction. "I prayed for help every night. And I had faith he would keep me safe until I graduated and could find a job."

Joseph became quiet, and I began thinking about his faith, comparing it to my own. While it was strong, I doubted whether it would have lasted as long as his — living without shelter, going days without food, and being consumed by fear.

"I can't believe you managed to stay in school through all of that," I said. "But I'm glad you did."

"I knew getting a good education was the only way to get off the streets. It was the key to my survival. That and forgiveness."

"Why forgiveness?"

"I hated my father. But I realized, as long as I hated him, I was no better than him. I didn't want to be anything like him. I wanted to be a better father to my kids than he was to me. That was the day I decided to forgive him. I stopped being so angry at him and started focusing on my goal. I wanted to have a good life."

I looked around the room and saw firsthand what his faith and commitment to forgive his father had done for him. "You're an extraordinary young man, Joseph. I'm not so sure, given the same set of circumstances, I could be as forgiving as you. But I can't deny the miracle that has resulted from it."

Shortly before the end of his senior year, a teacher had learned of his homelessness and contacted social services. Joseph was almost eighteen then. Too late, really, for them to do anything. But that didn't stop them. They got him off the streets and gave him a jump-start to a better life. They gave him the apartment and paid his living expenses. He was enrolled at a community college. And when he graduated, he would start his new job at Child Protective Services. Because he was doing so well, they sent him to Washington to attend the special event with the vice president.

Joseph passed his courses with flying colors. My work was done. On our last day together, beaming with pride, he said, "I'm going to my family reunion. It'll be the first time I've seen anyone on my father's side of the family since becoming homeless."

—L.M. Lush—

28

Glasses or No Glasses

You can't let your past hold your future hostage.
~LL Cool J

I walked home from school every day, past the neat straight rows of streets with their neat, straight houses getting newer and newer as I walked farther from the school. Our street was the straightest, but our house wasn't the neatest. It was beige that tended toward pink, and the paint always seemed to be peeling. The grass was often dying and it seemed like at least one tree was always struggling, too. Our cars were clean but not new, especially with my father's propensity for fixing everything rather than buying new.

I always paused a little, gearing up to walk up the straight walkway. In rain, snow or sunshine, I always needed a minute.

When I opened the door, I would call out for my mom or anyone who was home. If it was my mother, I would brace myself, waiting to see her face.

My stomach would pitch if she was wearing her glasses, because that meant she didn't have the energy to put in her contact lenses.

On no-glasses days, she'd ask, "How was your day? Do you want to go to the library?"

Books were my sanctuary. In their pages, everyone was happy, living interesting lives all over the world, in much more interesting places than my boring Montana town. In books, no one had to deal with horrible things like addiction. If they did, they overcame it, usually in a lovely seaside town.

If she was wearing her glasses, the conversations were different. Sometimes, I would go to the kitchen to make sure that the oven, microwave, stove, or toaster weren't running, as she tended to turn them all on simultaneously. Sometimes, I would feel a surge of hatred for the sadness on her face. Why wasn't she happy? Why wasn't I enough to make her happy? Sometimes, I would feel fear or shame. And, sometimes, I would feel nothing at all.

"Hi," she would say. She wouldn't ask about my day or offer to take me to the library. Sometimes, I would beg if she had promised, but to no avail. Usually, I would avoid her, grabbing a snack — anything — to make me feel better.

One time, when my father was out of town, my little sister and I were alone. My mother came home. When she walked in the door, I thought everything was okay at first — no glasses — but soon she was crying.

Sitting on the floor, she was so out of it that she couldn't speak.

"Mom, Mom, what's wrong?" My little sister was crying, too.

I tried to make coffee, having heard somewhere that coffee made people sober. I didn't know how to make coffee, so I burned myself.

Desperate, I called our neighbor, a lifelong family friend, whose two daughters were the same ages as my sister and me. The neighbor rushed over.

Later, my friend said they had listened to the call. "I don't know what to do," I said into the phone. "I tried to make coffee. I don't know what to do."

They said they imagined me hiding under the kitchen desk, scared to come out, making the call in secret. They envisioned my sister and me huddled in the dark and crying.

That's not how it happened, but that's how it felt, even though I was standing in the light, watching my mother fall to pieces. Although I never hid from her, I often felt like I was alone in the dark.

Looking back, I don't remember how old I was when my most vivid memories happened. How old was I when I discovered a bunch of liquor bottles hidden in my sister's trunk among the stuffed animals? Was I fourteen as I dug through the box, searching out every bottle so my sister would never see them?

How old was I when my mother picked me up from soccer practice in our old white minivan, so drunk that she was swerving all over the road? So drunk that my dad drove around in his big white truck, trying to find us.

How old was I when she came to my apartment to tell me that something was wrong with me after I failed a class in college? When she told me she'd never felt connected to me like she had with my siblings?

I don't remember. I don't have much of a sense of self in these moments. I'm that girl under the table, alone in the dark.

It came to a head when I was in college. Even now, I don't really understand what happened. At the time, I didn't want to know. There was an accident; my mom crashed the minivan (this one newer and greener). She finally went to rehab. It was summer, and I was working in a new town. My first love had just broken up with me — an event that seemed extra traumatizing under the circumstances — and we were supposed to meet our family at the lake. My father, sister, brother and I went while my mom was away in rehab.

"I really wish your mom was here with us," my aunt told me one day. I didn't agree.

"Your mom is going to call later. Do you want to talk to her?" my father asked, a desperate edge to his voice. I didn't want to talk to her, so I didn't.

When we got back from the lake, I started therapy.

"You are strong," my therapist told me, almost from day one. I loved her and her room felt like a sanctuary. I felt understood because her son was an alcoholic, too. He was in prison for aggravated assault, and I felt like she knew what it was like to be alone in the dark. To feel like you've failed someone. Like you aren't enough to make someone happy.

"Sit with your inner child," she would say, and I didn't scoff like I thought I would. It was hard to sit with that girl hiding under the table. Even now, years after I first tried it, it's not easy. It's much easier to avoid the girl with the hand burned from coffee, with a pit in her stomach that never quite went away.

"You have a big life ahead of you," my therapist would tell me. After many sessions, a part of me started to believe her.

Through therapy, I became interested in mental health and went on to study more about addiction. I began to understand that addiction is a mental-health crisis, not a weakness. It's not the "easy way out."

After years of study, I know a lot of things about addiction — at least my brain does. Logically, I know what depression and anxiety do to the brain. I know that no one is at fault. I know all about the specific chemicals that can cause depression and anxiety. I've been on the other side of therapy, treating children with these diagnoses.

However, it's much harder to convince my heart that it's not my fault than it is to convince my brain.

Recently, I became a mom. My journey into motherhood included some of my own mental-health struggles, primarily severe postpartum anxiety.

The day after we brought our baby home from the hospital, I followed my husband into her room, intending to discuss the organization of her clothes.

"We probably shouldn't leave the baby alone in the other room," he said, after a few minutes. "Let me go check on her."

It was like a slap in the face. For those few moments in time, I'd forgotten all about my baby.

"I'm the worst mother in the world!" I sobbed inconsolably.

Later, I talked to my mom, crying into the phone. She reassured me as no one else had.

The only bright side of my new anxiety is that my mother understood and supported me without a qualm. Sometimes, we almost feel like friends. My own experience has given me a capacity for forgiveness that I never thought possible, even after years of therapy and thinking I'd moved on. It's that whole brain-heart connection again.

Recently, I met my mom for coffee — her drug of choice these days, albeit a much more socially acceptable one. As a new mom, I never say no to a little extra caffeine.

In the coffee shop, I saw my mom waiting with a cup in her hand. She had on her glasses, but my stomach doesn't pitch as much as it used to. I wear glasses myself. They don't mean anything, just that I can't see well without them and don't feel like putting in contacts.

"Hi, sweetie." My mom smiled at me and held out her arms to snuggle my sweet baby. "How was your day?"

—Amy Mac—

Apologizing and Moving Forward

29

Kindness Is Precious

*A single act of kindness throws out roots in all
directions, and the roots spring up and make new trees.*
~Amelia Earhart

The sound of glass breaking is instantly recognizable. I'd been telling my best friend Missi a silly story and had spun around in the living room when I heard that sound and froze.

When I looked down at the rug, it was covered with tiny shards of sparkling red, pink and clear glass. Missi said, "Oh, no, not the vase."

"Why? What did I do?" My face reddened.

"Abby, that glass vase was one of the few items my relatives brought when they came to America," Missi replied nervously. "If you'd broken anything else in the apartment, I would've gladly said I did it. But you're going to have to tell my mom that it was your fault, and she's going to be really mad."

I was terrified. I'd destroyed a priceless family heirloom. Why did I have to spin around like that?

We gathered up the shattered pieces. I kept saying that maybe it could be fixed, but Missi said gently it didn't look possible. I insisted we keep the pieces. The glass was so fragile, like a colorful, swirly light bulb had exploded. Some of it broke even more as we tried to sweep it up carefully.

Missi said her mom would be home by six. My stomach was in knots. Would her mom yell at me or punish me? Would she tell me

I couldn't stay in their apartment for the weekend? I couldn't stop playing those fifteen seconds over in my mind, me spinning fast and the sound of glass crashing. The only thing I could think of to say was "I'm sorry."

A couple of minutes after six we heard a key turn in the door. Her mom was home.

Right from the start, we could see she was in a good mood. "Hello! It's hot today. I want to treat you girls to that frozen yogurt I know you like. Let's go!" her mom said. She pointed at the open door.

"B-before that, I need to tell you something," I said.

"We can talk at the yogurt place," her mom said.

"No, I need to tell you now. It's important," I insisted. I could feel my voice shaking and tried not to cry.

"What is it, dear?" her mom asked. She closed the door and walked closer to me. Our hands almost touched. I could feel her eyes study me, and she watched me quietly. My heart beat faster.

"I'm sorry," I blurted out. "I-I came into the apartment with Missi, and we were talking and laughing. I spun around and didn't look beforehand. The glass vase behind the couch fell. It broke. We saved the pieces, and if it can be fixed, I will pay to fix it. But it all looks like small pieces of glass now. I'm so sorry."

Her mom looked at me. She was expressionless and said nothing for what felt like forever. This terrified me even more. Then she erupted into a loud scream of joy that filled the entire apartment. She embraced me, kissing me on both cheeks.

"Oh, thank you! I always hated that ugly vase, but I had to keep it because it was passed down in my family. Now it's gone! You've done me a huge favor!" her mom crowed with delight. She kissed me again.

I couldn't stop the tears running down my face. I was so relieved to have apologized, but I was also in shock. This was not at all the reaction I had expected. Missi looked shocked. Her mom talked to us a bit more, sounding happy and telling us about her day. Then she went to make a phone call in her bedroom.

"I am telling you right now, if I broke that vase, she would have killed me!" Missi whispered. "I never knew she didn't like it."

"Well, I'm relieved she feels that way. I still feel awful about it," I whispered back.

We went to the frozen-yogurt shop around the corner from her apartment. Missi's mom asked us what our plans were for the weekend, and I sat quietly as Missi talked about wanting to see a movie in Greenwich Village. I remember eating swirled-chocolate-and-vanilla cones with lots of frosty air conditioning to soothe us on a hot and humid day, and thinking again about the beautiful, colorful, swirled-glass vase I had broken only an hour ago. I was expecting her mom to be furious with me, but it was as if nothing bad had happened. By the time we got to the Chinese restaurant for dinner, I was laughing at Missi's jokes and had started to unwind.

I'll admit it wasn't until I reached my adult years that I recognized what a profound gift her mother's generosity and warmth in welcoming my genuine apology was. She probably was not happy I'd broken the vase. But she realized it was an honest mistake and impossible to fix. Now, when I receive a genuine apology, I try to remember Missi's mom, to consider the people's feelings so that when they say, "I'm sorry," my response shows them their apology was fully heard and truly appreciated. Missi's mom taught me a lesson that has stuck with me and guided me many times.

— Abigail A. Beal —

More than a Facebook Friendship

Everyone makes mistakes.
Everyone deserves a second chance.
~Mo'ne Davis

For my fourteenth birthday, my mom offered to take me and several friends to the city nearest our small town to visit a mall, go shopping, eat pizza in the food court, and then catch a movie. Afterward, we would all return to my house for a slumber party. It was just the kind of celebration that a teenage girl craved.

All the friends I'd invited to join me on this birthday excursion attended school with me except one. We would pick her up on the way to the mall. Yet one of the friends whom I'd asked to join us hadn't attended school that day. When it came time to climb aboard the bus and ride together to my home out in the country, Nora didn't show up.

I felt confused. Where was Nora? Was she still going to join us for the birthday outing? How would we meet up with her?

Then I felt mad. Why didn't she tell me she couldn't make it? Why would she tell me she'd come to the party and then back out without letting me know?

So, after getting home from school, the other two friends and I took a walk around the dirt roads of my neighborhood, stewing over how Nora had let me down and abandoned the party. During that walk, we decided to call Nora and get some answers.

By the time we returned to my house and reached for the beige telephone hanging on the wall, I had worked myself into a fit of indignation.

Stretching the phone cord into the bedroom I shared with my little sister, I punched in Nora's number. When she answered, I demanded to know why she had ditched my birthday celebration and me.

"It's my birthday! And you're not coming to my party, and you didn't even let me know. What kind of friend are you? How could you do this to me?" I wanted to know.

Then Nora explained that she'd had to stay home from school because she had gotten sick. She couldn't ride the bus home with me and my other friends or join us at the shopping mall for food-court pizza and a movie because she had been too sick to come to school.

Nora began crying on the phone, hurt and surprised that I was furious at her.

"Okay, so you're sick… But how was I supposed to know if you didn't tell me?" I answered. "How am I supposed to figure out that you're skipping my birthday party if you don't tell me?"

It only grew worse from there, and Nora sobbed as we hung up the phone moments later. Immediately, her mother called back. Angrily, she told me how much I'd hurt her daughter, how much Nora had wanted to join us, and how she had been the one to change Nora's plans when she didn't allow her to go to school sick that day.

Still thinking only of myself, I ended the call with Nora's mom and still felt resentful. Later, my mom loaded up my two other friends and me, and then we swung by to pick up the last member of our party.

At the mall that night, the four of us (plus my mother) had a blast listening to Bon Jovi tunes as we browsed racks of mini-skirts. We scarfed down our slices of pepperoni pizza and watched a movie on the big screen, a treat for us small-town girls.

I barely gave Nora or her absence from our festivities another thought. At school on Monday, I found it easy to avoid her since she and I had no classes together. For the rest of the school year, we barely spoke, and I forgot about my hurtful call with Nora as time went by.

The next year I started at the high school, with twice as many students as my middle school. I made some new friends and kept some old ones. Maybe I glanced at Nora with a small smile once in a while as we passed in the halls, but our friendship had been relegated to the past. It happens sometimes, and I shrugged it off.

Years later—just over twenty, to be specific—I discovered that Facebook had suggested Nora as an online friend. We'd attended the same schools, came from the same town, and had many Facebook friends in common; it made sense.

So, I reached out and sent the friend request that Facebook had recommended. Nora accepted, and we were now able to keep up with the posts and announcements that we shared via social media.

After a year or so of polite online interactions, I began to reflect on that ugly phone conversation I'd initiated with Nora all those years before. Now, I regretted it—deeply. I recognized how selfish, self-centered, and self-absorbed I'd been. How did I even think she would have let me know at school? There were no cell phones back then. I didn't even give her a chance to tell me once I got home, and I didn't think about how disappointed she must have been, or even ask how she was feeling.

I wanted to make things right. Regardless of the fact that decades had passed since that telephone call, I didn't want to dismiss it simply as typical teenage behavior. I wanted to acknowledge my need for Nora's forgiveness.

I logged into Facebook and began composing an apology letter to Nora. I would have preferred a face-to-face conversation, but since we lived in different states, the private-message option via Facebook would have to suffice.

I labored over the words, prayed over the phrases, and then clicked Send. I wondered if Nora would even remember the incident. But only a few days later, she responded with a message of her own—one of heartfelt receptivity and forgiveness.

She told me how she'd missed me after that ill-fated birthday celebration weekend. Nora had thought I was "cool" and wanted to stay friends with me. I expressed remorse that the opportunity had been wasted—all because of that one phone call and how I'd handled it.

Apologizing and Moving Forward |

Nora and I did not begin keeping in contact apart from Facebook posts updating the world about our children, jobs or a new recipe attempted in the kitchen. But we did bring a sad moment from the past to a healthy conclusion — because I was willing to ask for forgiveness and Nora was willing to grant it.

— Allison Wilson Lee —

Toying Around

*Guilt is also a way for us to express to others that we
are a person of good conscience.*
~Tom Hodgkinson, The Freedom Manifesto

Mum had purchased the contents of a home via an estate sale, and my new husband and I were helping her go through all the rooms full of boxes, furniture, books, and memorabilia.

The home had belonged to a ninety-year-old lady. The family was eager to clean out the house and get it on the market. Mum had an antique store and was in the business of buying the contents of homes in search of that perfect treasure. Over the years, she had found a few treasures, and she loved discovering unique items for her customers. Her fondness for antiques and clever business sense gave her a discerning eye, so she gave us instructions on how to handle the contents of boxes or whatever we came across. There was a container for items that might look unusual and would qualify for the possible "treasure" category. Those would be put aside for Mum's store.

"Toss if it is unusable," she told us. "Make a pile for things you aren't sure about, and I will check those later. Then sort out any clothing, toys, books, and donations and put them in the labelled containers."

We were assigned to clean out a couple of the bedrooms while Mum worked in the living room and kitchen area. She told us she had had a quick glance around the bedrooms where we were working, and she hadn't really noticed anything that she might call a treasure, but to go ahead and check just in case.

Apologizing and Moving Forward | ☰

"Just keep aside what you think might sell," Mum said. "I trust your judgment."

Mum headed back to the living room.

My husband and I were working together for a while, sorting and piling. Then I came across an interesting box in the closet. It was tucked high on a shelf. As I opened it, I was intrigued. There were some old toys, a tin motorcycle, a few pretty little dolls, an old rubber bendable toy, along with a couple of older picture books. There was more in the bottom, but it didn't look too interesting.

"Put it in the donate box," my husband said. Obviously, he thought they weren't collectibles.

"But I really like these dolls," I said.

I collected dolls and old toys, but not for monetary reasons. For toys to be in my collection, I had to like the look of them. And I liked this little box of goodies.

"So keep them," my husband replied. "There's not much in there for your mother anyway."

I justified keeping the box of unusual toys by telling myself there really wasn't anything worthy of shelf space in Mum's store. I tossed the box in my car and went back to work. I felt a little sneaky, but I told myself that Mum had bought so much stuff already she wouldn't miss it.

Once I got home and emptied the box, along with what I had already seen I found a unique little pull toy, a Barbie from the 1950s, a metal truck, a spinning top and a game that looked very old. I contemplated giving the box back to Mum, but I was afraid to tell her what I had done. So the toys ended up in a cabinet in my house. I tucked everything a little closer to the back of the cabinet so Mum wouldn't notice anything when she came to visit. Once, though, she did admire the toy assortment in my cupboard.

"That's getting to be quite a nice little collection," Mum said one day. "I think that Barbie is worth something. It's in good condition."

My heart beat overtime. I thanked her and changed the subject quickly. Guilt had already been gnawing at me, but I shooed it away, thinking it was too late to say anything. The damage was done. It would be silly to talk about it. Besides, she didn't even know about the box of toys.

Time had passed, and I thought it was over. But it wasn't. Every time I looked at my toy collection, the joy it once brought me was replaced by a still, small voice inside reminding me what I had done.

It was not easy, but I made the decision. I told my husband, and he said to follow my conscience. I found a cardboard box and tucked the toys in there, feeling slightly relieved already. Was I ready to face the music with my mother? That part wasn't making me feel very good.

I knew I had to do it anyway. What I did was wrong. Just because Mum didn't know about the box was not a justification for me to help myself. Her words, "I trust your judgment," continued to haunt me.

It had been months since we had finished helping with the estate sale. Mum had been happy with her purchases and had most items in her inventory. She had been none the wiser about anything that might have been amiss. But I still had to tell her what I had done.

Eventually, I mustered up the courage.

"I want to show you something," I said.

"What are those?" Mum asked as I sat on her couch and peeled back the flaps on the cardboard box.

Then the tears came, and my confession and remorse. I admitted how I had helped myself. I didn't try to worm my way out by justifying my choice. I simply told her that I had taken the box of toys because I had liked the dolls on the top. I told her how I had felt since I took them. I admitted I was wrong, and I asked for her forgiveness.

"What you did was wrong, but I don't care about these things," Mum said. "What I care about is your knowing in your heart that what you did was wrong."

I continued to sniffle and apologize.

Finally, Mum told me to come to her. I did. As she wrapped her arms around me, I felt a peace wash over me. "Of course, I forgive you," she said. I was so grateful for the undeserved grace. I learned a lot that day about trust, love and mercy.

After some conversation, my tears turned into laughter. I was forgiven, and the freedom I felt was incomparable. Mum wiped away my tears, just as she had when I was a little girl.

"Now let me look at that Barbie!" Mum said, with a big smile.

—Glynis M. Belec—

Putting My Tail Between My Legs

An apology is a lovely perfume; it can transform the
clumsiest moment into a gracious gift.
~Margaret Lee Runbeck

I was having a bad day at work. A really bad day. We all have them, but this was an especially awful day because I got a call from a vendor who had done some work for me months earlier. She should have been paid already by our central finance office, and when I learned that she had not, I was mortified and embarrassed. Our finance office had a reputation for slow payments, and I went ballistic.

I called the finance office and launched into a tirade the moment someone answered the phone. Even while I was screaming at the poor woman, I knew I was out of line, but for some reason I couldn't help myself.

I had never done that in a professional setting before. I knew plenty of people who acted like that and I had always looked down on them. And here I was doing it! Before I slammed down the phone, I told the woman to make sure my vendor got paid immediately or I was going to march over to their office and really make a stink. I don't recall the woman saying one word back to me.

No sooner had I hung up the phone than remorse set in. What had gotten into me? I'm a nice person; people like being around me.

Apologizing and Moving Forward | 115

And I'd never treated anyone like that. It was as though the devil took over my soul and turned me into an instant ogre. It wasn't like this was some huge gaffe either; the non-payment was a pretty minor issue. My reaction was completely uncalled for and I knew it.

The next day, I was scheduled to work from home because I had a lot to do and needed a quiet environment to get the work done. But try as I might, all I did was stare at my computer screen. I kept thinking about that poor woman whom I tore to shreds verbally. I was sure that I had ruined her day, maybe her evening and the next day, too. I wondered if she got so upset that she took it out on her kids or spouse or the clerk at the grocery store. What domino effect had I started because of my bad humor? After hours of non-productivity, I decided I had to right my wrong. I looked up the number for the finance office and called.

"Hello, finance office," a voice said.

"Um, hello. I called yesterday about non-payment of a vendor invoice. Are you the person I spoke to?" I asked meekly.

There was a pause, and then I heard the woman suck in a breath of air, perhaps steeling herself for whatever I was going to launch at her next. "Yes, that was me. My boss wants to talk to you."

"I understand, but before I talk to your boss, I have to apologize to you."

"What?" the woman said, a note of shock in her voice.

"I am so sorry for screaming at you yesterday. I don't know what got into me. You didn't deserve that, especially over something as minor as a bill not being paid. Seriously, I am really sorry."

"Oh," the woman said, the tone in her voice taking an upturn. "That's okay. I get yelled at all the time by people whose payments are late."

I was nearly speechless. "Are you saying that my despicable behavior yesterday is a normal occurrence in your office?"

"Oh, yeah. It happens just about every day, sometimes several times a day."

I hardly knew what to say, and then I blurted out, "That's awful. You shouldn't have to put up with that. You need to find another job!"

"Naw, I'm used to it. So, are you going to scream at me again?"

"Oh, no, no, no. But I do want to speak to your boss and tell her how sorry I am."

"Okay, I'll put you through."

After a few rings, another woman answered and identified herself as the department manager. When I told her who I was, I realized quickly that an introduction was hardly necessary; she knew exactly who I was. And she was ready for my tirade, which she didn't get. Instead, I apologized profusely and admitted my wrongdoing. She went quiet.

"Are you still there?" I asked.

"Yes, I'm here," she responded, "and I have to say that I don't ever recall anyone calling in and apologizing for screaming at one of my employees. In fact, you may be the first."

"First or not, I feel terrible for what I did. It was so unlike me; it's not in my nature to treat anyone like that. I want to do something to make amends. Does your employee like flowers or chocolate? I want to send her something."

"Totally unnecessary, but a nice thought," she said. "My employees are trained to take whatever angry managers throw at them. They get nasty calls every day."

"Yes, she told me that."

I reiterated that I would still like to send her employee something to show my contrition, but she said emphatically not to, that an apology was enough. Obviously, this manager did not want me to do anything else. And really, I didn't want to make the employee's job any more difficult than it already was.

After I hung up the phone, I felt a little better and was able to get back to my project, though what I'd done wasn't lost on me. Asking for forgiveness was a humbling experience. While I was remorseful and knew in my heart that I would never, ever treat someone so terribly again, I also knew that bad days would still occur, so I had to change and anticipate how I would react to them. I decided that I was going to begin following some notions that I often talked about, but had been lax about following. Clichéd or not, they imparted wisdom that was well worth practicing.

Apologizing and Moving Forward | 117

View the cup as half full, not half empty.
Look for the positive in everything.
Assume the best of everyone, even if facts indicate otherwise.
Believe in silver linings.
Be the light in the darkness.

It wasn't long before those ways of looking at the world became habits that in turn influenced my actions. Annoyances became inconsequential. After a while, nothing bothered me. I let both minor and major irritations slide. Instead, I focused on the good. I'd learned that nothing was worth getting so upset over that I would lose control and mistreat someone. My only regret is that it took hurting someone for me to get my wake-up call.

—Jeffree Wyn Itrich—

33

Just Hit Delete

Never does the human soul appear so strong as when it
forgoes revenge and dares forgive an injury.
~E.H. Chapin

The voicemail was long-winded and particularly cruel. The voice was shrill as it uttered cold, hard words. I was close to tears and just couldn't bring myself to listen to the message in its entirety. I didn't need to. Her message was clear.

I had been working as an online elementary teacher for several years and had grown accustomed to the occasional unkind parents who hid behind their computer screens. Didn't these parents realize I was a person, too? I was a teacher who had taken a pay cut from our neighborhood elementary school to take a work-at-home job that would benefit families who chose to school from home. Every day, I used my expertise to help students who were too ill to attend traditional school or who lived in a remote location. I had compassion for these families, and I was there to help. I wanted the best for all the students in my class, just like they did.

The parent's words — "difficult teacher," "impossible" and "ridiculous" — gave me a kick in the stomach.

I prided myself on my efficiency in e-mail and phone calls. Didn't this parent know I had other families in my class? Wasn't I allowed to be on the phone with another family for a brief ten minutes when this woman needed me? I also taught live, online classes throughout the morning that required me to silence my phone. My schedule was

Apologizing and Moving Forward | 119

certainly full. Why was this woman's tech issue a life-altering event that required an immediate halting of my work tasks? Wouldn't a call into tech support have been a better option? Couldn't she wait ten minutes for my availability?

Instead, this woman left me a long, berating voicemail full of unfair accusations and insults. I had never had a problem with this woman before. In fact, I had had several supportive conversations with her. I always followed up our conversations with e-mails full of free resources that would support her son. I had gone out of my way to customize her son's education, always offering support as she engaged in the often-difficult task of schooling from home.

Suddenly, a quick e-mail shot into my inbox. Clearly, the voicemail hadn't been enough. The message was short and curt, her fingers raging across the keyboard, I imagined.

More insults. Apparently, I was still ridiculous, and I never answered my phone. She was going to follow up with another phone call to my administrator to let her know what kind of employee I was.

I was ramped up. I began composing my response to her, starting with some quick defensive moves: *I am unable to hold a discussion with two families at the same time.* Scratch that... *I understand you were trying to get a hold of me...* Scratch that. Too nice... *First, I don't appreciate your tone...* Scratch that. I sounded as if I was waggling a ruler in her direction in that response. After several false starts, I put my head down as I composed the message.

> *Dear rude parent,*
> *First off, I am a parent, just like you are. I can understand a frustrating moment as you work with your son. However, I am a human being who works hard every day to assist families who choose to school from home. I have a high number of families that I currently support. I receive in excess of 50 e-mails per day at times and receive several phone calls. I pride myself on respond-ing quickly and in a supportive manner. I was shocked to receive such an unkind message to start my morning. It would be to your benefit if we had a supportive, mutually respectful, professional*

relationship. I am a professional, and I ask that you treat me as such. Keep your anger in the confines of your own home.

As I was re-reading my e-mail, checking for errors and deleting the last sentence, I got a text message.

"I just left you a very unkind voicemail," it began. "I was frustrated with things that were not your fault. I said things that were not true and am rather embarrassed."

Suddenly, my blood calmed. I sat back in my chair, relaxed my shoulders and allowed relief to settle in a bit. Taking a breath, I hit the Delete button on my e-mail. Had I ever responded in anger when it came to an issue with one of my own children? Yes, I was humbled enough to admit.

I texted the woman back. "What voicemail? I've been on the phone all morning. Let me hit Delete. Friendship restored."

The woman responded with lightning speed: "You are the best."

A handful of words and, like that, all was forgotten. Easy.

I promised myself I would try to do that more often. Easy.

Okay, not easy, but I knew I would try.

— Michele Boom —

34

The Weight of Forgiveness

To err is human, to forgive, divine.
~Alexander Pope, An Essay on Criticism

As a woman of "mature years," I was proud that I could handle Facebook, FaceTime, Instagram, and WhatsApp almost as well as my offspring. But, as the saying goes, pride comes before a fall. And fall is just what I did.

My son Jim had finally proposed to his girlfriend. We were delighted and we'd already welcomed her with open arms. Besides being pretty, Debbie also had a great sense of family, and valued Jim's relatives as well as her own. In my book, that won her many votes.

Elated by their engagement, Debbie went off in pursuit of the wedding gown of her dreams. When Jim was safely in another room, she showed me a picture of the one she'd chosen. She made me feel special when she confided that, other than her mother and her maid of honor, I was the only other person to whom she'd shown the picture. It was indeed beautiful, and I totally approved of her choice. I looked forward to seeing her walk down the aisle in that glorious dress — and could imagine my son's reaction when his beloved made her appearance on the big day.

The date for the wedding was six months away, and Debbie knew she needed to lose twenty pounds or so for the dress to look really fabulous. She was confident that she would be able to achieve her goal in half a year. She'd always struggled with her weight, but now she had something tangible to aim for.

After a couple of weeks, I asked Jim casually how Debbie was doing on her diet.

Jim sighed. "Not well. She just can't seem to get a grip on it. Our engagement coincided with Debbie starting her new job. With the pressures of work, she's just not been able to face the rigors of a diet. I've offered to pay for her to go to a gym, but she's definitely not in the right frame of mind."

"Well, she's still got a few more months to go," I said. "Hopefully, she'll find her mojo soon."

Several more weeks had gone by when my husband, Alan, suggested we take our children and their other halves out for a meal. We agreed upon a date, and the restaurant was booked.

My daughter, Jen, had set up a family WhatsApp group so that we six could communicate easily with each other in the lead-up to the wedding. Jen and I had already been communicating regularly via our personal, non-family WhatsApp link, so this was a welcome addition.

On the morning of the family lunch, Jim phoned to say he'd managed to persuade a very reluctant Debbie to join a diet program. I was delighted to hear this. We were both fully aware that the "countdown" was in full swing.

Just then I heard a ping. It was a WhatsApp message from Jen. "Look at what I picked this morning!" Proud of having her first garden, Jen's photo was of a bowl of beautiful red strawberries.

"Clever girl!" I messaged back, and then added, "BTW, Jim has gotten Debbie to sign on with a diet program. She's got to do something now if she wants to get into that beautiful wedding dress!"

Almost as soon as I sent off that message, I heard another ping. "Mom! Are you mad? You sent that message on the family WhatsApp."

I could see on my phone that Debbie had already read it. I was distraught.

Immediately, I called her cell phone, but it went to voicemail. Obviously, Debbie didn't want to talk to me. I left a message — a profuse apology. "I'm so sorry, Debbie. I never wanted to hurt your feelings." But I had.

Jim messaged me to say that Debbie was in floods of tears. "We won't be coming to lunch," he said. "She knows there was no malice in what you said, but she can't bear the thought of everyone looking at her, that we all think she's a failure."

From my perspective, it was me who was the failure! I'd damaged Debbie's fragile ego with my carelessness.

Jen advised us to postpone the family lunch until things calmed down. But when would that be? My voicemail conveyed how bad I felt, but Debbie had not responded. According to Jim, Debbie continued to cry off and on all day.

I knew I had to do something to patch things up between us. But what?

That's when Jen came to the rescue. "There's a beauty place that Debbie sometimes goes to. They do facials, manicures, pedicures — all kinds of stuff like that. Why don't you get her a gift certificate?" I flew to the phone and did just that. Then I bought a funny card about how I always seem to put my foot in it, stuck the voucher in the envelope and mailed it to Debbie.

Then I waited. Alan kept saying, "Stop fretting. You didn't do anything wrong. It's just that Debbie is understandably very sensitive at this time, and you hit a nerve."

Jim, too, kept reassuring me. "You've always been great with Debbie. She'll come around."

But I plagued myself with thoughts of how long that might take.

Several days later, my card was delivered to Debbie. I heard a familiar ping — this time a message from Debbie via her personal WhatsApp: "Thank you for my card and beauty voucher. It meant a lot to receive it. That was very kind and thoughtful, and it certainly put a smile on my face. The last thing I want is a fall-out with you. Ever. I love you, you're my mother-in-law-to-be, and we have a great relationship. Onwards and upwards."

When I read Debbie's message, I cried tears of relief and love. As she said to me later when we finally got together for the postponed lunch, there was nothing to forgive. She knew that it was never my intention to hurt her. Forgiveness was needed, but in reality, I needed to forgive myself. And I learned a lesson: to be very careful when using WhatsApp!

But here's the happy P.S. to my story. My "booboo" has proved to be the trigger that Debbie needed. She's now lost fifteen pounds and is well on her way to reaching her goal: to be the perfect bride in her perfect gown on the perfect day.

— Marilynn Zipes Wallace —

What I Didn't Deserve

*A broken friendship that is mended through forgiveness
can be even stronger than it once was.*
~Stephen Richards

My friend Lynn and I had worked well together for over a dozen years, but as I pushed away from my desk that May morning, I dreaded telling her what I had done. Owning up to my mistakes wasn't difficult if I forgot to make a copy of the schedule or lost someone's favorite pen, but this could have ruined our friendship. For weeks, Lynn suspected her job was in jeopardy, but what she didn't realize was that my actions might have been the catalyst.

Lynn and I worked in a nonprofit office, making sure everything ran smoothly for the people we served. We relied on each other to cover phones and answer the door. We helped each other with projects. But more importantly, we were there for each other whenever we needed to talk.

However, things had changed in the last several years. Lynn's family was her priority. Always. With a husband she adored, children, grandchildren, plus a large, extended family, she was forever busy. She tried to attend every sporting event, party, bridal shower, play, and concert. All that, plus her job responsibilities kept her "on the go."

One day during a staff meeting, Lynn announced she was no longer going to work on Fridays. Our boss, an easygoing guy, said, "Sure, no problem. I understand your family is important to you." Looking back, that was the moment I began to feel like she was neglecting me.

Over the next several months, people stopped by the office looking for Lynn, and I told them she wasn't there on Fridays anymore. I tried to help them if I could. But many times they walked away disappointed or angry. It fell to me to smooth things over. Soon, other staff members started grumbling, as well.

Lynn said she was working from home, but all I could see was how her absence inconvenienced me. I decided to complain to my boss's supervisor, Tom. To my surprise, he also was concerned. "I've noticed what's been happening, and I'll talk to her about this," he said. Relieved, I left things in his hands.

Things improved over the next few months. Lynn switched to working half-days on Fridays, and the mood in the office lightened. As time went on, though, the situation reversed. Lynn's absences annoyed me until I could think of little else. Lynn started planning all her family parties. She scheduled even more vacations. And I grew more irritated. Lynn left me to handle everything in our busy office, and I wasn't able to keep my hurt to myself.

As the year progressed, Tom increased his demands on Lynn's time and repeatedly expressed his disappointment in the way she did her job. What was worse, though, was that Tom began accusing Lynn of things she didn't do. More than once, she sought shelter in my office and cried.

I knew Lynn's trials stemmed from my complaining about her to Tom, but I never spoke to Lynn herself, and I let everything go on as it was. Eventually, my guilt was more than I could bear. I decided it was well past time to confess my role in Lynn's unhappiness.

"May I talk to you?" I walked into her office with my heart racing. She had every reason to sever our friendship, and I wouldn't have blamed her. I shut the door and sank into the chair across from her desk. "This is my fault," I said. And I told her what I'd done.

The hurt in her eyes made me wince. "I take my laptop home every night. I work for hours, sometimes past midnight. I just wish you had spoken to me directly," she said.

"I know. I made it all about me, and I'm so sorry." Tears stung my eyes. What made it worse was realizing I'd trusted Tom, who wasn't the understanding leader he seemed.

But then she looked at me and said, "It will be okay. I didn't realize how you felt, and I understand why you spoke to Tom about it. Things will work out."

"But I ruined your life," I protested.

Then she smiled and shrugged. "What have you ruined, really? I still have my family and friends. What more do I need?" She walked around the desk and hugged me.

I clung to her, taking in the scent of her perfume and barely believing she could be so forgiving. "I won't do it again."

"It's fine," Lynn said. "I'll be all right."

Even so, I contacted Tom to tell him I was wrong, that I had complained because of my own selfishness. But the damage was done. A week later, Tom fired her. Lynn called her husband to tell him the news, and I listened as my tears welled. I'll never forget how Lynn's husband burst into the office, his face red and his shoulders set for battle.

"How could you?" He pointed at me.

"Leave her alone." Lynn touched his arm. "It's not her fault."

He didn't say another word. He just walked back to her desk and helped her pack.

Over the next year and a half, Lynn and I met for dinner several times and caught each other up on our future plans. She decided to open her own business, which had been her dream for the last twenty years. Later, I visited her at her new office and told her how proud I was of her achievement.

Two years ago, Lynn was killed by a drunk driver. I was grief-stricken and my guilt threatened to return. It wasn't fair — she'd finally achieved her dream, but she hadn't had time to enjoy it.

But as the months passed, I realized what a great gift she'd given me. When faced with the unexpected death of a loved one, I've heard people say, "I never got the chance to say I'm sorry." I was grateful that I had.

Lynn's graciousness expressed how wonderful she really was. Her family and friends in the community had their stories about what made her that way, and I had mine. Now whenever a friend confesses something to me, all I need to do is remember Lynn and how she showed me the beauty of true forgiveness.

— Mary Wilson —

It's That Simple

While we try to teach our children all about life,
our children teach us what life is all about.
~Angela Schwindt

"What's your 'Thing of the Day'?" I asked my fourteen-year-old son as he scooped a heap of mashed potatoes onto his plate. This is a question our four kids (and whichever friends are staying for supper) expect to be asked each evening at suppertime. Usually, it's followed with, "Uhh... Umm... We had pizza for lunch." And then I have to veto the response and ask for something significant—either something he learned or something that happened with his friends.

But, this day, my son surprised me as he went into great detail about how he had been honestly wronged by a couple of classmates and laughed at in front of the class.

I asked more questions and learned that the teachers were aware of the situation. The issue had been dealt with as much as the teachers and staff were able to. It was really just a matter of kids being mean and deciding to pick on someone.

I thought about the situation all night. I vacillated between contacting the teachers, contacting the parents of the classmates (who I know), and not doing anything since the story had been told to me in a matter-of-fact way—not overly emotional.

I waited until the next day after school. On the car ride home, I questioned my son.

"So, was it weird or awkward today after yesterday's situation?"

My son was honestly surprised that I brought it up again. "What? No, it's over, Mom. They're my friends. They were just being dumb. They apologized. Forgive and forget, you know? We're all good."

I was amazed at his ability to forgive and move on. I was worried that perhaps he was trying to hide his concern or sadness about the issue. But as I watched him over the next days and weeks, everything seemed "normal." I even secretly spied on the class when I was in the school volunteering. And he was right. They were "all good." Wouldn't it be great if everyone could live the "forgive and forget" way of life?

—Jesse Neve—

The Choice to Come Clean

Right actions in the future are the best apologies
for bad actions in the past.
~Tryon Edwards

My heart pounded as I stared at the screen. I re-read the message from my friend, Noelle. Someone had upset her by sharing her personal news, a recent development Noelle had shared with only a few people. She didn't know who let the word out, but she was hurt and disappointed.

I felt so guilty. I knew how the news had gotten out because I had been the one to tell someone beyond her immediate circle. Honestly, I hadn't realized she meant to keep it so close to home, but at the same time I'd known it wasn't a good idea when I started to tell it to someone else. I'd forged ahead anyway.

Did she really not know it was me? It would have been easy to come clean and apologize if her note was an accusation. But it read as though it had been copied and pasted to several people. Once again ignoring the right option, I chose the coward's way out.

"I'm so sorry that happened to you," I typed. "How awful that your confidence was broken."

I hoped that would do. Her reply came back within seconds: "Thank you."

Surely, that would be good enough. I didn't own up to my actions, but I'd expressed remorse and sympathized with her pain. And, really, that's what I would have done if I had confessed. It would be okay for me to remain anonymous as long as I was sorry, wouldn't it?

But, deep down, I knew I'd been the one to break faith and hurt her. I was ashamed, not only of my original action, but because I'd heaped wrong upon wrong by covering it up.

I felt miserable at church on Sunday. I abstained from communion. Watching others partake while I sat in silence was a painful experience — one I never wanted to repeat.

Later, the speaker challenged us to risk everything to find God's best. He asked us to examine ourselves and see if anything stood in the way of our relationship with God, and if so, not to let anything stop us until we cleared it away. Chancing it all — whatever we feared, whatever held us back — would be worth it to be right with Him.

I knew what stood between me and doing the right thing: my reputation. That's what I feared losing in telling Noelle the truth. Of course, she would be disappointed in me, but deep down I dreaded the possibility she'd tell others. It would be within her rights to do so. Yet what was my reputation compared to doing the right thing? To remain silent would make that reputation a lie anyway. Was I truly willing to risk it, as the speaker had phrased it, in order to receive the forgiveness I needed?

I went straight to Noelle after the service. I first confessed my sin of gossip and then how I had chosen not to come forward when I had the chance. I felt relief already, and then Noelle showed grace and forgave me. She told me why my actions had been so painful, and I won't soon forget the reminder to listen more closely to my conscience when speaking of others. We parted that day on good terms and are still friends. I never heard if she relayed my wrongdoing to anyone else, but even if she did, I know that telling the truth and asking for forgiveness cleared me of shame and set my heart free.

— E. Mifflin —

38

The Housemate from Hell

Do you think the universe fights for souls to be
together? Some things are too strange
and strong to be coincidences.
~Emery Allen

I had just started my new job in midtown and desperately needed a place to live. My buddy mentioned a vacancy in the Brooklyn brownstone he was renting. It would mean my sharing the upstairs floor (and the same bathroom) with an existing tenant.

The next evening, I knocked on the door of the brownstone and met my prospective housemate, Nori, for the first time. Nori was quite attractive, I must admit. She welcomed me with a big smile and gleaming eyes, and suggested we get to know each other over dinner and drinks. Next thing I knew, Nori and I were sitting in this romantic, little dining spot. Over candlelight, we talked for hours and got along famously.

It was past midnight when I escorted Nori back to her place. I realized I was holding her hand as we walked, which felt strangely comfortable considering this was supposed to have been a formal "meet and greet," not a date! As we reached the stairs of her building, Nori looked up at me with a sly smile and a flirty glint in her eye.

"So, do you want to see what the *other* bedroom on the floor looks like?"

I wasn't expecting that one at all. And I sure as heck wasn't prepared for it. My brain was whispering, "Say no, you idiot. This would be a disaster waiting to happen!" The rest of me wasn't quite so sure.

"Um… Nori… I really, really like you. But if we're going to be sharing a living space together, I'm not sure starting off this way is the best way to go, if you know what I mean."

To say Nori did not take the response well was an understatement. Her smile vanished, and that flirty glint turned to a dirty glance. And then, without uttering a word, she stormed up the stairs of the brownstone and slammed the front door behind her.

From that day forward, during the year I shared that upstairs floor of the house with Nori, pretty much the only words I heard from her were, "How much longer are you going to be in that shower?" and "Please don't take any of the fruit I have in the fridge." I dreaded those moments when our paths crossed on the staircase or on my way to the bathroom. I tried being sociable and pleasant. Nothing worked. Eventually, I just gave up.

Now here's the thing that made it especially confusing for me. With the other two occupants of the house, she was charming, fun and engaging. We should have been getting along great. And other than what I assumed were hurt feelings that first night, I could think of absolutely nothing I had done to cause her to treat me like the walking plague. But that moment of healing in our relationship was not to be. One day, I passed by her room on the way to the staircase and saw Nori packing up all her belongings. I decided to be brave and enter.

"You moving out, Nori?" I asked.

"Um, yeah. I'm going to give it a try moving in with my boyfriend." (Nori had met a seemingly nice fellow, a pharmacist, about a month prior, and they had been spending a lot of time together.) I wished her the best and told her I was sorry things couldn't have been better between us.

Nori didn't look up. She just nodded her head and continued her packing. I remember thinking to myself, *Sheesh! Good luck to her beau! Thank God I don't have to deal with her anymore!* And, yes, I'm sure she felt the same about me.

Fast-forward four years to a Saturday in spring. It was to be my first official date with a young lady I really liked. We were going to spend the day at the Brooklyn Botanic Garden. I wanted so badly for everything to go just right because I knew in my heart that this girl was somebody special. I picked up my date at her Manhattan apartment building on East 30th and First Avenue, and we started to walk toward the subway station. Suddenly, she stopped in her tracks.

"Hey, Gary, would you mind very much if I introduced you to somebody real quick?" she asked.

"I guess not," I replied somewhat hesitantly.

And with that, she took my hand and escorted me around the corner to the local pharmacy. As we entered, I heard my date ask someone, "Do you know if Nori is here today?"

Nori? I thought to myself. *Oh, my God, I can't believe there's somebody else in this city with that same name!* I shook my head and chuckled at the irony of it all. Thank God it wasn't going to be *that* Nori whom my date apparently wanted to "show me off" to! Except... it was!

In the distance, wearing a white pharmacy coat, was a woman who sure as heck looked like my Nori. And, as she got closer, I could see her eyes widen and her jaw drop in astonishment. My heart raced as I prepared myself for the epic embarrassment that would inevitably result from this looming disaster of an encounter. But, as she approached my date and me, a huge smile broke out on Nori's face. She pointed her finger toward me. "So... *this* is the guy you think may be The One?"

I turned to look at my date. Her face turned bright red in embarrassment.

"Um... you two know each other?" she asked nervously.

Nori and I looked at each other for an indescribably awkward few seconds. And then I decided to just man up to my date.

"Okay, look, here's the story. If I could have chosen one female on this entire planet that I would *not* want you to speak to about me, it would be this lady standing in front of us right now. Nori and I were housemates in Brooklyn a few years back, and the truth is she absolutely hates my guts!" My date just stood there in stunned disbelief, her eyes darting back and forth between Nori and me. Then Nori did something I wouldn't have seen coming in a million years. She clasped my hands in hers and looked me straight in the eyes.

"I don't hate you, Gary," she said. "In fact, I've always hoped I would have the chance to ask for your forgiveness."

Nori then turned to my date while still holding my right hand in hers. She took a deep breath before continuing. "Seriously, I was so screwed up back then. I must have made Gary's life in that house a living hell. Trust me when I tell you that you have found yourself a really great guy."

Nori went on to fill me in on her life. She had married that nice guy she had started to date back when we were living together. Together, they ran the pharmacy around the corner from the apartment where my date had been living that past year. It was a lovely conversation, and the healing that took place was palpable on both our sides. I walked out of that pharmacy feeling like the weight of the world had been lifted off my shoulders. But my date was not smiling. In fact, she was almost in tears.

"I can't believe Nori told you that thing I said in confidence!" I knew she was referring to the comment about my being "The One."

"I mean, we haven't even gone out on our first official date yet, Gary, and you have to hear something like that?" She started to cry.

But Nori's comment really didn't bother me much at all. And in case you're wondering, my date and I went on to have a lovely, relaxed and memorable afternoon. And we did decide to see each other again… and again… and again. A year later, we got engaged. And a year after that, we were married. Yes, my date on that crazy spring day was my wife of almost thirty-one years now, Dana!

As a former psychology grad student who wound up becoming a Wall Street analyst, I guess I can summarize my philosophy about "forgiveness" as follows: What holds true for stocks also holds true for us. In order to sustain a positive, long-term, upward climb, we must first "fill in the gaps." Well, let's just say in the case of my "Nori story," forgiveness certainly helped pave the way for what has been my most significant long-term gain!

— Gary Stein —

39

We Were Here First

Be at war with your vices, at peace with your
neighbors, and let every new year
find you a better man.
~Benjamin Franklin

We lived out in the country, ten miles from town. Originally, only my in-laws lived there. When they offered us an acre of their land, we jumped at the opportunity to raise our children in the country.

Shortly after my husband started work, he learned layoffs often occurred during the winter months. To compensate for the loss of income, he obtained a kennel license to raise and sell registered puppies, something he did throughout his teenage years. The kennel brought in the extra income we needed, and the children loved playing with the puppies. No one else lived in the area, so the occasional barking did not bother anyone.

After a couple of years, other families began moving in around us. Each had five acres or more. Quickly, we became friends and enjoyed various celebrations and picnics together, creating many happy memories.

The neighbor next to us came a year later. His brother's family lived across the street, and he was happy to be close to them. When they started looking for a spot to build their house, both his brother and my husband reminded him about our kennel. My husband showed him the location of the kennel building so they could find a place to build away from the occasional noise. In the end, they decided to build on a small hill overlooking our house and dog kennel, about 100 feet from our shared property line.

By the end of the first year in their new home, the neighbor began complaining about the dogs. My husband talked to him and explained the steps he was taking to mitigate the noise, which included moving some dogs and selling some. Unfortunately, nothing we did improved the situation for them.

Over the next year, the neighbor called the dog pound multiple times to file complaints, and he tried getting our kennel license revoked. Lastly, he called several times, telling us the dogs were now causing his wife's migraine headaches. All this conflict broke my heart.

I didn't know what to do — until the following Sunday. As I sat in church, listening to our pastor preach from the "Sermon on the Mount," my heart began pounding so hard I thought it might burst out of my body. He read the following Bible verses:

"Therefore, if you are offering your gift at the altar and there remember that your brother or sister has something against you, leave your gift there in front of the altar. First go, and be reconciled to them; then come and offer your gift" (Matthew 5:23–24 NIV).

It felt like the Lord spoke directly to me through those words, and I knew why. Like an old movie projector, showing slide after slide in rapid speed, pictures flashed in my mind of the ongoing dispute with our neighbor. Now, God was nudging me to apologize. "But, Lord, it wasn't our fault! We were here first," I whined to Him internally.

As we drove home from church, I told my husband I needed to call our neighbors to apologize that afternoon.

Once home, I tried to eat but couldn't. I prayed. I walked over to the phone, thinking about what to say. Then I walked away — too scared to call. Finally, with one last desperate prayer, I picked up the phone. With my hands shaking and my heart thumping, I dialed.

Thankfully, the neighbor's wife answered the phone. I apologized for all the problems arising from our business and for causing her headaches. I told her we sold several dogs to lessen the noise and moved some. We felt we had tried everything we could to mitigate the sound and make it less stressful for her. When I finished, she said, "I am so glad you called. I've wanted to talk to you, too."

She explained how she knew it was not all our fault. Her husband got overly concerned when she started getting sick. The dogs bothered her occasionally, but she knew they did not cause her medical issues or headaches. She apologized to me, too, for all the distress this situation had caused us.

After hanging up the phone, I cried, thanking God for the peace that was now restored through forgiveness.

The next day, I was even more thankful for this timely conversation because a "For Sale" sign appeared at the end of our neighbor's driveway. It stunned me. I had no idea they were selling their house. Our neighbor never mentioned it during our conversation.

What if I had not called the day before and apologized, as I felt compelled to do? Would my apology have sounded sincere if I had waited and discovered they were moving and then called? Would the conversation have yielded the same results? I doubt it.

Initiating the conversation challenged me, but it was worth the effort. Forgiving each other not only provided healing to our friendship, but it also led to the resumption of our neighborhood gatherings.

That lesson in forgiveness has stuck with me. Many times in life, challenges test our character, urging us to do what is right, not just what feels comfortable. Apologizing is often the right choice, even when we did not start the argument or cause the issue.

— Barbara J. Todd —

Chapter
5

Keeping a Marriage Healthy

40

The Joy Ride

When someone you love becomes a memory,
the memory becomes a treasure.
~Author Unknown

E very time the Navy transferred my husband to a new duty station, the small wooden cradle his father had made for our son moved with us. Yet whenever Mark brought up the subject of having another child, I refused.

"It was different when Brian was born," I said. "You were in training, and the Navy gave you a couple days off to coach me through labor and help with the new baby. Now you're on a submarine for months at a time. I'm not going to do it alone! I already feel like a single mother."

Mark knew it was no use arguing. He couldn't guarantee that his sub would be in port when I needed him.

The year Brian was nine, I turned thirty. A girlfriend sent me a Christmas card with a photo of her smiling kids. On the bottom of the card, she wrote, "I'm due again in June!" I felt a twinge of jealousy.

"Are you having second thoughts?" Mark asked. We were getting ready to move to Charleston, South Carolina, where he'd been assigned to a sub with a predictable schedule. "If you get pregnant now, I'll be home when the baby is born," he promised.

That's all he needed to say. We weren't even settled in Charleston when I found I was expecting. Mark missed the holidays, but knowing he'd be back for our baby's birth made it easier to live with. The days passed, and my abdomen grew round, as if I'd stuck Brian's basketball under my shirt.

A couple of months before the big event, my in-laws offered to drive down from New York and stay with Brian when it came time for his father to help me at the hospital. Mark returned from sea excited to hear his parents were coming. "There's going to be an overnight trip for fathers of the crew," he said. "It's the week after you're due, so my father will still be here."

I made a face. Brian had been two weeks late. What if this baby was late, too? But Mark's father had recently survived a heart attack. He might not be with us much longer. How could I say no? The chance of the two events coinciding was low.

Mark phoned his dad. "How'd you like to take a ride on a submarine?" he asked. Of course, his father said yes.

My in-laws arrived a few days before my due date, but a week went by with no sign of labor. The cradle and layette were ready, but apparently the baby wasn't.

On the day of the cruise, Mark and his father packed their underwear and toothbrushes while I waddled around the house uneasily. What if our baby chose that night to come?

"Don't worry," Mark said. "We'll be back first thing tomorrow."

The men kissed us all goodbye and left. That evening at dinner, my stomach felt queasy. I thought I was just upset about Mark leaving. But in the middle of the night, a strong contraction woke me. I began my Lamaze breathing and held off calling the doctor. After all, I was in labor fifteen hours with my son, and Mark said he'd be home in the morning.

The contractions shortened to a minute apart. I pounded on my mother-in-law's bedroom door and yelled, "This baby isn't going to wait for Mark!" She drove me to the hospital and stayed in the waiting room with Brian while a nurse listened sympathetically to my rants.

"My husband and I planned carefully so that he'd be home when our baby was born," I told her. "He promised me! And where is he now? Taking a joy ride on a submarine with his father!"

At 5:26 that morning, I gave birth to a baby girl and named her Emily. The doctor sang "Happy Birthday" as he cut the umbilical cord.

My husband had missed it. All the other times Mark had missed special occasions, I couldn't be mad. Going to sea was his job; it paid the bills. But this time he didn't have to go!

When the sub pulled into port, Mark received his mother's message that the baby had arrived. He and his father rushed into my hospital room as I was holding Emily. Mark kissed me on the cheek. "I'm sorry I wasn't here."

"It's okay," I lied. It wasn't okay at all. His parents were standing beside him, so I didn't tell him how abandoned I'd felt. I looked into my infant's big brown eyes, grateful that she was healthy and my labor was over.

Eventually, Mark retired from the Navy and took a civilian job. One day, our daughter came home from school and set her books down on the kitchen table. A sheet of paper sticking out of her English book caught my eye. I smiled when I saw the title: "The Story of My Life." Emily was only in fifth grade. Her life story so far had to be pretty short.

I pulled out the paper and cringed. In careful cursive, she'd written, "My mother has never forgiven my father for not being with her when I was born."

Oh, no! What had I done? More than a few times, I'd mentioned to Emily that her father had missed her birth, that she came later than we'd expected while her dad was on a submarine deep in the ocean with Grandpa. Mark's absence stood out from my memories of that day. Had I really said that I'd never forgiven him, or did she sense it?

I tucked the paper back into her book. That night, I explained to Emily how her father had always wanted another baby. Not being present at her birth didn't mean she wasn't important to him. Although I tried to sound forgiving, it was still a sore spot for me.

More years passed, and we lost Mark's father. At the funeral service, the minister asked my husband if he'd like to say a few words. Mark edged his way out of the pew and stepped up to the altar. Staring out at the congregation, he began, "My best memory of my dad was when I was in the Navy, and we went on a father-son submarine cruise."

My stomach tightened. It all came back: how he'd left me alone with his mother, and I'd gone through labor with a nurse. After all this time, I hadn't let go of the hard feelings.

"My father was the happiest I'd ever seen him," Mark continued. "He wanted to know how all the equipment that I operated worked. I could tell he was proud of me." He pushed tears off his cheeks. "I'd made something of myself without going to college." Mark looked in my direction. "And though I regret missing my daughter's birth, that cruise was the best experience I shared with my dad." His shoulders heaved with silent sobs.

Tears came to my eyes. Finally, I understood why that cruise was so important to him. When he sat down beside me, I pressed my hand into his. He squeezed mine back, and any lingering resentment melted away.

— Mary Elizabeth Laufer —

41

New Year's Eve Party

Forgiveness is not a feeling; it is a commitment. It is a
choice to show mercy, not to hold the offense up against
the offender. Forgiveness is an expression of love.
~Gary Chapman

I'm still not sure how I got talked into it, but one year I agreed to throw a couples' New Year's Eve party. It took me days to prep, especially with cleaning up after our toddlers.

Then there were the lists to be made and shopping to be done. I scurried through the supermarket, keeping the cart moving with one hand and funneling Cheerios into four open toddler hands with the other.

I would make lasagna, bread, salad, and cheesecake — the baking could be done while the kids napped. I quite enjoyed the baking. The smells of yeasty bread and tomato sauce lifted my mood until I glanced around the kitchen and realized I should have waited to clean until after I cooked.

The night before, my husband helped me set up tables. After the tablecloths were on, it looked like one long table extending from the kitchen island across the family room to the fireplace. I felt a growing sense of excitement. Even though I didn't like hosting parties, this could be fun.

The morning of the party, I woke to the sun shining. Everything was ready. It was going to be a lovely evening.

At 4:00 p.m., my mom arrived to pick up the babies. My husband would be home in an hour. I puttered around wiping up nonexistent spills.

At 5:00 p.m., I texted my husband. "Are you on your way?"

"I'm going to be held up here for a few minutes. Sorry."

"Oh. Okay. Everyone will be here in an hour."

"I know. I should be there, no problem."

At 5:30, I texted him again.

At 5:45, I called him.

"They will be here in fifteen minutes. If you leave now, you won't even have time to change."

"So sorry, honey. I'm still tied up. I'll be there as soon as I can."

The conversation that followed wasn't one of my finest moments. He was trying to get off the phone so he could get home sooner. I wanted a pound of flesh. This was my greatest fear — hostessing alone. I worried I'd be standing there with a room full of people not knowing what to say and wishing the ground would open up and swallow me alive. I hadn't even wanted to have the party and now I had to handle it by myself. It ended with me bursting into tears and slamming down the phone as the doorbell rang.

The first guests were early.

I wiped my face and threw open the door with a cheery smile, thankful the guests ignored the telltale signs of tears.

I kept texting my husband as guests arrived and time passed.

I tried to hide the panic and frustration from my guests at my plans going haywire. I felt awkward and unsure of how to proceed. By 7:30, stomachs were growling. His texts promised he would be home before dinner was done. So we all sat, with one empty chair beside me. Everyone said the food was amazing. I didn't notice. I tried to make conversation while I was terribly embarrassed by the empty seat beside me.

At 9:30, I hid in the bathroom. "This night was a disaster," I ranted to myself. In the other room, though, I heard laughter as the group set up *Taboo*. It was time to play as couples. And I was the only one without the rest of my couple — at my own party.

Then my husband called. "Honey, I never imagined this could

have happened. I know how uncomfortable you are being there alone. I am doing my absolute best. Please forgive me. I know it's not what you want to hear, but I'll be there by midnight — for sure."

By midnight? He was going to miss the entire party?

My husband continued to explain, "I know it won't help, but I promise I'd be there if I could. This is the first second I've had to call. Things are crazy here. The final numbers for year-end inventory must be in by midnight. Some imbecile wrote random numbers on boxes and boxes of parts instead of counting them. Now we have to recount them all. Everyone is mad at me because they have to stay instead of being at home with their families."

I realized what the night had been like for my husband. Up until that point, I'd been far too worked up to see his side. All I knew was that he wasn't home. But he was taking a lot of heat at work. He wanted to be at the party. And the icing on the cake was a wife who was being Host-zilla.

"Will you forgive me?" he asked again.

In that moment, I made a choice. I chose forgiveness. I also realized much of my crash-and-burn night had been in my control. While I couldn't control the circumstances, I could control my reactions. "Yes." I took a breath. "I'm sorry for being so impatient. Take your time. I'll see you when you get here. Happy New Year."

I washed my teary face, turned off my phone, and joined the game. The next two hours flew by as we yelled out answers and laughed until our bellies hurt. I almost forgot about my husband until I heard the garage door open. I looked at the time: 11:38.

A few minutes later, we watched the ball drop on TV, and my husband leaned over and kissed me. "Happy New Year."

"Happy New Year." As I said the words, I was thankful for a new year. New beginnings. I resolved to be more patient, understanding and forgiving in the coming year.

— Nancy Beach —

42

Another Chance

Without forgiveness, life is governed by...
an endless cycle of resentment and retaliation.
~Roberto Assagioli

My husband David and I loved our new son-in-law. We liked his sense of humor and his kindness toward others, and we accepted him as our own. But within months of the honeymoon, Jerry resumed acting like a bachelor with his old friends; gambling and other behaviors began to surface. Now we wondered if Shelley and Jerry could indeed live "happily ever after."

After two years, the birth of our first grandson brought joy into both families. We hoped this responsibility would improve our son-in-law's conduct. But deception, broken promises, and treatment programs became part of the marriage. Household items disappeared, and large gambling debts mounted.

When the marriage ended, I went to court with Shelley and watched her sit with a stoic face on the witness stand. While the judge decreed six years of marriage terminated, I cried silent tears in the back row.

Afterwards, we stopped at a coffee shop to "celebrate" Shelley's new freedom.

Over our treats, I said, "I thought you would be crying and upset."

"Mom, I don't have any tears left. I have cried and grieved for years. Now it's time to move on with my life."

And life did continue. Shelley began graduate school that very day. We participated in our four-year-old grandson's activities with special camera moments. Within the year, our son was married in a beautiful wedding, and Jerry brought our grandson into the back of the church for family pictures. While he stood across the room watching, I felt such sadness as I thought about Jerry and Shelley's own "perfect" wedding pictures.

Our ex-son-in-law's lifestyle spiraled downward with changed jobs and broken promises for visitations. His erratic emotional behavior became a concern for both families. One afternoon, I felt that I should pray for Jerry's safety and state of mind, but my prayers seemed insincere. How could I pray for Jerry without love and forgiveness in my heart? I didn't want to love him or have him back in the family. I just wanted him changed into a responsible father.

That day, I sobbed as I released the resentment that had wrapped around my heart. I chose to forgive Jerry. Silently, a divine alteration occurred. Suddenly I felt at peace, and for the first time in years, I prayed for his wellbeing without any bitterness. A few months later, he began a faith-based treatment program out of town, which lasted over two years.

Shelley raised her son and received no child support during this time, but we witnessed miraculous provisions for her school and living expenses. Our daughter also worked a full week, juggled graduate-school studies, stayed active in church, attended support groups, and ran a small home-based business. She ministered to other hurting women in painful relationships. Over the next months, Jerry apologized for many wrongs to her during their son's visitations. Through honest letters, deep emotional wounds began to heal. Seeds of love began to grow.

One fall day, David and I decided to drive the two-hour distance for Jerry's graduation ceremony and sit alongside his family and our daughter. We wondered how long this change of behavior would last as he publicly testified of his recovery. When he thanked Shelley with a verbal acknowledgment, we could see sparks flying between them. David and I looked at each other.

Driving home, my husband commented, "We didn't sign up for this again."

After Jerry's return to the city, the two attended an intensive marriage seminar for broken marriages with follow-up sessions. Our daughter learned to trust again and forgive her ex for the years of addictive behaviors and back child support she never received. The four of us met on several occasions, and a shallow foundation of trust began to form. But when we took our family picture for the annual Christmas card at Thanksgiving, we did not include Jerry. After all, he had not officially rejoined our family, and maybe their relationship would crumble again.

After Christmas, my husband and I were out of town when Shelley called us with the news. They had gotten engaged and wanted to remarry on their original wedding day in February. They wanted our blessings. Before returning home, David and I searched our hearts to release any residual bitterness we held. We decided to give Jerry another chance.

Five years after their divorce, my daughter and son-in-law remarried before friends and family who had been a part of their tumultuous journey. Our ten-year-old grandson escorted his mother down the aisle as the only attendant in the service. The wedding ceremony included marriage vows, but they also made a covenant promise to their son to never separate again.

When I thought back on it, I realized that eleven years earlier we had participated in a lavish *wedding*. On this afternoon, through prevailing love, we witnessed a *marriage*. Sniffles could be heard throughout the room.

Afterward, David and I, my elderly parents, and our son and daughter-in-law embraced Jerry as he re-entered our family circle. We took photos of the reunited family during the short reception. The couple drove away for their honeymoon, and a big bundle of joy arrived nine months later — a baby boy of restoration.

I often tell people, "I have two grandsons from two marriages and one set of parents."

Fourteen years later, their love continues to flourish. We have helped Jerry in his successful estate-sale business, and people stare in amazement after hearing our stories. Since their remarriage, many other couples in anguish have listened to Jerry and Shelley share about their divorce of despair and their remarriage through forgiveness. Forgiveness made room for love and another chance.

— Sharilynn Hunt —

43

How Love Works

*Life appears to me too short to be spent in nursing
animosity or registering wrongs.*
~Charlotte Brontë, Jane Eyre

I was seventeen and had just gotten in a huge fight with my boy-friend. I was crying in my room when my dad came in and sat down next to me.

"What are you going to do?" he asked.

I shrugged. "I'm not sure."

"If you're going to forgive him eventually, you may as well do it now. After all, it's Christmas Eve."

"But I'm really, really mad at him."

"I understand that. But if you know you're going to get back together with him eventually it's mean to wait and ruin his Christmas."

I sighed. "I do still care about him. I really don't want to end our relationship over this stupid fight. But I want to stay mad at him for a few days."

"Why?"

"To teach him a lesson."

My dad shook his head. "That's not how healthy relationships work. If you value the relationship, you need to make things right between you and the other person as soon as possible."

"But if I forgive him right away, he won't be as sorry as if I wait a few days."

Dad shook his head again. "Nope. You can't hold a grudge to

teach him a lesson. That's not how love works. You need to decide if the relationship is worth holding on to. If it is, you need to offer forgiveness immediately."

After my dad left my room, I called my boyfriend and offered him my forgiveness. We made up and enjoyed a lovely Christmas.

Less than a year later, we broke up for good. In hindsight, forgiving him wasn't the best move for my life. I should have seen the fight as the red flag it was and ended the relationship sooner.

Although getting back with him wasn't the best decision, I've never forgotten my dad's advice. I've carried it into every relationship I've had since.

My husband Eric and I have been married for twelve years. While we have a close relationship, we do argue occasionally.

One of our biggest arguments was on the day of our fifth wedding anniversary. It was on a Saturday, and by noon, when he still hadn't said anything about our special day, I knew he'd forgotten.

I was hurt and angry. A part of me wanted to pout and make Eric feel really bad for forgetting. I wanted to punish him to make sure he never forgot again.

But then I remembered my dad's words. *If you know you're going to forgive him eventually, you might as well forgive him now.*

Eric hadn't hurt me on purpose. He'd made a mistake, and it caused me pain. But he hadn't set out to do something hurtful.

I was upset, but forgetting an anniversary is obviously not a reason to end an otherwise-great relationship. I knew I would forgive him eventually.

So I had two choices. I could pout all day, ruin our anniversary, and forgive my husband a few days later. Or I could offer forgiveness right away and make the best of what was left of our special day.

It was tempting to hold the grudge, to make sure my husband realized that he'd messed up. But Dad's advice rang in my ears: *You can't hold a grudge. That's not how love works.*

We ended up having a pretty nice day. And Eric has remembered every anniversary since then.

In life, we all have to decide if our relationships — both romantic and platonic — are worth the effort we put into them. If someone is hurting us on purpose and they never seem truly sorry for the pain they've caused, maybe forgiveness isn't the best course of action.

But if we value the relationship and know that forgiving past hurts is the right move for us, we should never wait to offer it. Holding grudges isn't good for them. Or us.

My dad taught me to be quick to forgive when the hurt is accidental and the relationship is important to me.

Time with loved ones is valuable, and we don't want to waste it being angry.

Forgive quickly. It's how love works.

— Diane Stark —

Never Too Late

Remember, we all stumble, every one of us.
That's why it's a comfort to go hand in hand.
~Emily Kimbrough

My mother-in-law was only fifty-seven when she got the diagnosis. She didn't have long to live.

Soon, it was time for our family to make a difficult decision about whether to move in with her or put her in a nursing home. After enduring her attacks for years, I preferred the option of sending her to a nursing home. That way I wouldn't have her disrupting my marriage or my homeschooling life with our four children. *Send her to the nursing home and let someone else deal with her,* I thought.

We tried to move her to a nursing home, but it didn't work. One week, she made too much money. The next week, she made too little money. We gave up on the option of putting her in a nursing home, but I still didn't want to uproot our family and move in with her.

We lucked out. Her best friend stepped up, as she had always done. She put her life on hold to move in with my mother-in-law. She spent countless hours, days, and weeks taking Deb back and forth to the doctors, helping with in-home nurses' visits, bathing her, and so much more. Unfortunately, she couldn't stay long, so we had to make the decision we had been avoiding.

It was time for *me* to make the decision to move in with a lady I had never truly loved and usually didn't even like. Still, I was not willing. The love I have for my husband, though, tugged at my heart. All he was asking was for us to help him with his mom — the woman who had loved him, raised him, and thought the sun set on him.

It took us days to get moved in to my mother-in-law's house. We had bags of clothes and school supplies, small animals, and so much more. Our new normal would no longer include weekly field trips or runs to the library. The four kids and I would now be her sole caregivers. The kids were willing to take on this responsibility as their hearts were full of pure love for their grandma. Still, I didn't want to be there.

Little did I know that, in the weeks to come, I would get to witness a transformation. Deb began calling all those she had wronged and inviting them to come over. I would sit and listen as she expressed her sincere apologies for what she had done. She would ask for forgiveness in a way that was so heartfelt there wasn't a dry eye in the room. She told them she loved them and asked that they never forget how much they meant to her.

And then the day came. It was my turn to have the heart-to-heart talk with this lady I had tried to avoid at all cost. We sat in her living room as the kids played outside. She said that she wanted her son and me to renew our vows in her living room. She wanted it to be special and memorable. And she wanted me to know that she was so sorry for all she had done to me. She was proud of the wife her son had married.

At that moment, I fell in love with my mother-in-law. I no longer saw the past when I looked at her. Now I saw a beautiful woman full of love. And I continue to miss her and love her back.

— Shannon Cribbs —

45

Mud Pie and Coffee

*There is no love without forgiveness, and there is
no forgiveness without love.*
~Bryant H. McGill

The University Inn restaurant was packed that night. A waitress set two plates of mud pie on our table, flipped through her ticket book, and hurried away. I looked at Steve across the table, tall and strong in his red flannel shirt, and thought how comfortable I felt sitting with him. But his silence worried me.

I pushed the piece of mud pie around on my plate, prying crust away with my fork. "I'm glad you took my call. I didn't think you would," I said, glancing at him.

He stirred his coffee, tapped the spoon on the rim, and folded his hands in front of his cup. "Well, you said you wanted to talk." He seemed guarded.

Looking back, I realize how much was depending on that little conversation in the University Inn twenty-seven years ago — three amazing kids, four Golden Retrievers, twelve cats, seven different house mortgages, two major career changes, and an unwavering partner for life.

Now, after two decades of marriage, I know Steve loves me despite my faults. It was in the vows we took one January afternoon before God, family, and friends. If they didn't go like this, they should have: "Thou shalt love your wifey when she feeds your prized trout to the cats; honor her when she wakes in the morning with dried saliva glued to her chin; and cherish her when she throws her Super Nintendo controller in the garbage after losing four *Monopoly* games in a row."

Over the past two decades, we've both had to apologize, both learned to forgive, and both committed the same transgressions days later. To err is human. To forgive is true love. To forget is humanly impossible.

But before we were married, there were no guarantees to love for better or worse. Forgiveness was still optional. On that night in the University Inn, when we were both in college, Steve had a choice to make — to forgive me or forget me. It was the first real test of his love.

On that night in the restaurant, I unfolded my napkin, feeling ashamed. "Steve, about that note. I didn't mean for it to sound the way it did," I began, wishing I'd never written it.

It wasn't a big deal, really. Lara and I were studying in the lounge with some girls from the hall when Steve walked through the door. Lara nudged me and wrote in the margin of my notebook, "Steve's here. You okay with that?" (Lara was a psychology minor.)

Embarrassed, I scribbled, "That's fine, as long as he doesn't talk to me." I put a smiley face in the margin because I knew Steve loved to talk — not about himself, but about everything else. At that time, he was a real Phil Donahue, searching for subjects to ponder and debate — from computers, to ancient Rome, to dream houses, to how the world will end.

I opened a packet of sugar and poured it into my mug, listening to the clinking dishes and muffled conversation around me. "I wrote that note because I had so much to read. I was happy to see you," I said, "but I knew if we started talking, I wouldn't get my paper done."

Steve propped his elbows on the restaurant's table. He wanted more.

My cheeks burned. "I'm sorry if I hurt you, Steve," I continued, smoothing the napkin over my knee. "I think you're a great guy, and I really do love talking with you."

I knew Steve had seen the note the second he sat down next to me in the lounge. He didn't talk to me for a week after that. My roommate told me he'd written me off.

Steve sighed, then dug into his mud pie and asked, "Marianne, why didn't you just tell me you were busy? I'm taking twenty-one credits this semester. I know how it gets."

I looked at his flannel shirt, thinking how soft it'd feel against my cheek. Steve knew about my checklist — the one I ran guys through to see where they rated on my man from Snowy River scale. When I saw *The Man from Snowy River*, I realized that's what I wanted — a quiet, rugged cowboy who'd ride through storms to my rescue on his mountain steed. Steve failed the test: He was a marketing major, played computer games, and had only ridden a horse twice in his life. Somehow, I didn't care.

I nudged the maraschino cherry off a mound of whipped cream, rolled it across my plate through fudge, and stabbed the cherry with my fork. "I didn't tell you because I was afraid I'd hurt your feelings," I answered finally.

Steve smiled. "It'd take a lot more than that to hurt my feelings. I'd rather you just be honest with me," he replied.

I picked a crumb from the table and dropped it on my plate. Good Lord, how could I be honest with him? If I showed him who I really was — showed him the mound of dirty clothes in my closet, told him my favorite lunch was a bowl of raw Top Ramen, and that my favorite album was *John Denver's Greatest Hits* — he'd run out of my life forever.

A couple laughed suddenly from their table two booths down. Steve poured more cream into his coffee. "Well, I'm just glad you called me. I appreciated that," he said.

Steve was my man from Snowy River in his own way. He came to my rescue when I needed it — not in the gallant flurry of galloping hooves, but in other ways. The week before our wedding, he stood outside in a blizzard pouring fuel additive into the gas tank of my truck when it wouldn't start. When I found my black Lab dead on the side of the road, Steve buried her. When I lost my contact lens in the parking lot at Garcia's, Steve picked it up from the pebbles. When I was in labor with our first baby, he made me a bologna sandwich (even though eating a bologna sandwich was the last thing on my mind). When I wanted to finish my last semester of college as a nearly thirty-year-old mom of three, he told me I could make it — even when no one else thought I could. And later, when I thought my world had ended after the kids had grown and left, and the house grew quiet, Steve showed me how our life together had really just begun. He's been my man from Snowy River when I needed him.

After two decades of marriage, Steve and I have a history. We've learned to forget and sometimes forget to remember. But that night at the University Inn, everything was still too new. There was nothing solid to hold onto — and I pleaded for someone to save me.

"I'm sorry. I didn't mean to hurt you," I said, on the verge of tears.

Steve stared at me for a bit, and then pushed aside his plate. "Well, Marianne," he said, leaning forward on his elbows, "you're forgiven. Don't worry about it," he said. And then my future husband squeezed my hand, flashed me a warm smile, and poured us another cup of coffee.

— Marianne L. Davis —

46

The Un-Love Letter

Simply love your spouse better today
than you did yesterday.
~Aaron and April Jacob

s I opened the door, my two little girls squeezed past me, dropped their backpacks on the kitchen floor, and hit the fridge for their after-school snack. A tote full of research papers begging to be graded slumped from my shoulder onto the table. I was ready for my own pick-me-up, a cup of leftover morning coffee, before making dinner.

I turned toward the coffeepot. The morning dishes weren't in the sink, and the floor had been mopped. The pile of junk mail that usually cluttered the counter had been replaced by a single envelope with my name printed in my husband's familiar scrawl.

My heart fluttered. He hadn't written a love letter to me since he was in the police academy before we were married. Then I replayed the casual comment I had made on my way out the door that morning: "Since you're working evenings this week, it would be nice if you'd do something to help out around the house while you're home."

Instead of reaching for a coffee mug, I picked up the letter, anticipating an apology and his gratitude for everything I did as a wife and mother. But when I read the first line, my heart sank. It was not a love letter.

"I'm tired of being accused of not helping around the house. Yesterday, I washed the windows and cleaned the gutters. I serviced the lawnmower and sharpened the blades to get ready for summer. Did you notice? I also picked up your car from school and took it for an oil change. I bet you didn't notice that either, did you?"

I glanced through our now pristine windows at the mountain covered with spring green. No, I hadn't noticed the windows had been washed. Did he really take my car to the garage so I didn't have to waste a precious Saturday morning on vehicle maintenance?

The letter continued in the same tone — a little anger, a lot of hurt — and I deserved every word. It wasn't only what I'd said that morning that prompted his protest. It was a culmination of comments I'd mumbled over the past months: "I wish you would... You never... Can't you just..."

I wasn't completely oblivious to his household contributions, but instead of giving him credit for the tasks he did, I nagged him about the tasks he didn't do. The truth was, when he worked evening shift, I envied the solitude he enjoyed by day. He spent hours alone in a quiet house while I took on the parenting role for both of us at night — dinner, homework, baths, bedtime. Then I graded papers or made lesson plans before I collapsed into bed. Who had time for laundry? For dirty floors? For solitude? Not me.

But I also didn't have time to wash windows or mow the lawn, and I didn't have to — because my husband did.

I folded the letter and slid it inside the envelope to hide his words and my shame. I walked to my bedroom, opened my top dresser drawer, and tucked the envelope in the front corner so every time I opened that drawer, I would see it and remember.

I returned to the kitchen, pushed aside the research papers on the table, and snatched a pen and notebook from the tote. My hand paused above a blank page. Careless, hurtful words had tumbled so easily from my mouth, but these new words must be deliberate and meaningful, worthy of forgiveness. I wrote, "I'm sorry."

Our younger daughter, Randi, skipped to the table and leaned against me. "What are you writing, Momma?"

"A love letter to your daddy." *Filled with gratitude for all the energy he spends taking care of our family,* I added silently.

She covered her mouth and giggled. "Kelli!" she called to her big sister. "Mom is writing a love letter!"

She put her hands on her hips and looked straight at me. "Do you love my daddy?"

"Yes." I smiled. "I do."

— Karen Sargent —

47

Ten Words

I believe forgiveness is the best form of love in any relationship. It takes a strong person to say they're sorry and an even stronger person to forgive.
~Yolanda Hadid

'd waited all day in case he was planning a surprise. But disappointment was replacing hope now. "Do you know what day it is?" I asked as nonchalantly as possible. Instead of a romantic dinner at a fancy restaurant, plans for a getaway weekend, or a small token of his affection wrapped in beautiful paper, the surprise I received was a blank stare and a casual response of "Sunday."

My husband had indeed forgotten our first anniversary. Deep hurt bubbled to the surface of my unmet expectations and erupted in angry words hurled to wound him back. This wasn't our first fight, nor would it be the last.

Coming from a family that didn't manage conflict well, I was woefully unprepared for the inevitable disagreements that arose soon after wedding bells stopped ringing. Toothpaste brands, bedtime routines, how and where to celebrate holidays — the list of potential discord seemed endless in the early days of marriage. From the seemingly inconsequential to the extremely important, unresolved issues began to pile up.

As the fourth of five children, I grew up as a peacekeeper in my home. In the era of "father knows best," I never felt free to ask questions, talk about decisions that seemed unfair, or express my opinion.

Hating conflict, I found myself fluctuating between stuffing my feelings and overreacting to them because a healthy alternative hadn't been taught or modeled. One cannot give what one does not have, so I don't fault my parents. They also seemed to lack the knowledge and skill to resolve issues in a healthy manner.

My husband's family didn't manage conflict well, either. We muddled through the early years doing the best we could. With wounds piling up, we turned to our faith to find hope; we were not disappointed. Attending a conference designed to uncover the secrets to resolving conflicts, we discovered the power of ten ordinary words.

"I was wrong. I am sorry. Will you forgive me?"

We had said we were sorry to each other hundreds of times. Somehow, though, that didn't resolve the underlying issues of our conflicts. The hurt often remained, accumulating over the years as we dumped it onto the pile of past injuries.

During the conference, my ears perked up when I heard the presenter say, "It's not enough to say that you're sorry. You have to own the problem." That week, we learned to be brave, own the problem, and begin an apology with "I was wrong." We also learned that an apology without asking for forgiveness is incomplete, even arrogant in assuming forgiveness would be granted without actually asking for it. I couldn't ever recall anyone asking me for forgiveness, so it never occurred to me to ask. Understanding the power of releasing negative emotions and the freedom it brought to my soul began building a foundation for reconciliation.

Those ten words laid the groundwork for a win-win scenario when resolving conflicts. Ten words forming three simple sentences revolutionized my marriage. Once I experienced the liberty it brought, I wanted others to experience it, as well. It changed the way I mentor young women and how I teach students to resolve conflicts in the classroom.

Coercing children to say they are sorry is ineffective, especially if they aren't sorry. Forcing a repetition of the phrase "I'm sorry" often creates resentment, causing other conflicts, and invariably models lying if the child isn't truly sorry. The potential to avoid creating a pattern for "people pleasing" later in life inspires me to teach peacemaking skills to children. Speaking what others want to hear rather than the truth often causes more conflicts than it temporarily averts.

I teach children to own their behavior, avoiding resentment and false feelings from making children say they are sorry. Modeling statements like, "If you're sorry about what happened, now would be a good time to tell your friend," sets the stage for learning to ask on their own. Genuine sorrow can then be expressed without the forced, insincere "Sorry" that often accompanies childhood interactions. Taking the time to dissect the issue and working through the three parts of a true apology propel children into healthy conflict-resolution patterns.

In marriage, and in the rest of life, I've learned the power of those ten words: "I was wrong. I am sorry. Will you forgive me?"

— Cindy Richardson —

48

The Clean Record

Forgiveness is the key to action and freedom.
~Hannah Arendt

"Love doesn't keep a record of wrongs," the teacher said, and continued through the end of the Bible passage. I heard only the first words, and those words echoed in my head like a song on repeat. It was a Wednesday night Bible class, and we were studying the "fruit of the Spirit." We were on a familiar subject — love. I had thought that I knew about love, but that one sentence hit me like a battering ram.

A record of wrongs? I went through the rest of the class with a sick feeling in my stomach, the words playing over and over. But I couldn't put my finger on why they disturbed me.

We left class to go to the weekly devotional, and as we sat down, my husband turned to me. "Are you okay?"

"I'm fine," I said, ignoring the bustle about us as everyone found a seat. "Why?"

"You just seem really quiet."

"I'm fine."

And that was true — in part. But the verse kept playing in my head as I listened with half an ear to the devotional. I couldn't put my heart in it. Once the final prayer was said, I figured it out, as if I needed some quiet to sort everything out properly.

I was keeping a record of wrongs.

And not just wrongs, but perceived wrongs, too. Could I claim I loved her? The sick feeling in my stomach returned as we pulled out of the parking lot. "No."

I didn't grow up in Ohio. I'd only been there once before I got married and moved there to be with my husband. I'd only met my mother-in-law that one time.

She did a lot of things that bothered me during our first year of marriage. But the most painful one was assuming that I wouldn't be in the family pictures at my brother-in-law's wedding.

She told me to get my husband's place card while he was busy taking pictures. I remember staring sadly at my own card. It wasn't that she was trying to be mean; it really hadn't occurred to her that I'd be in the family pictures.

"Love doesn't keep a record of wrongs."

But surely I am justified in being hurt, I told myself as we pulled into the Toys "R" Us parking lot. I grabbed my purse and followed my husband inside. I barely saw the toys as I told myself again, *Surely, I have that right.*

Yes, the rational part of me said, *you can be upset. But you don't have to keep a record to hold over her head. That's worse than any of the things you think she's done — and how many of those are because you don't talk to her, either? How many are just ignorance you haven't corrected? It's not her fault she has no idea how you feel.*

The guilt pricked at me in the store and over the next few days. What could I do about it? I knew it was unfair and wrong. But my feelings had festered over the course of the year. I wanted her to understand the pain — even if she hadn't meant to cause it. But I knew it wasn't fair, and so I decided to act.

It took me a few days before I thought of something to try. I wasn't sure if it would work or even help. And even though I had a plan and had committed to following it through, it took me several more days to sit down and put my fingers on my keyboard.

I was going to write out the record of wrongs I had been carrying around in my head and heart.

It took days to scour my brain for every single thing that had bothered me — I wasn't going to miss one. Once my list was complete, it took me another week to get up the courage to do what I knew I needed to do next. But, finally, I sat down and pulled up her record.

I highlighted the item at the bottom of the list, said a fervent prayer asking God to help me, and pressed Delete.

I'd written down her record, and now I had to wipe it clean. Keeping it wasn't right or fair, and a lot of it was my perception, not her fault.

I moved on to the next one, highlighted it, and pressed Delete.

I had to stop a few times to pray and breathe. It was hard releasing all of the things I had held onto for so long.

But my hurt was just as much my fault as it was hers. It wouldn't hurt as much if I hadn't kept holding on to it. I prayed that as I deleted each item on the list, God would help me erase it from my memory.

I moved up the list. Highlight, delete, highlight, delete. After half an hour, I reached the top of the list.

Her blank record stared at me, clear of everything I had held against her.

Nothing changed right away except that my heart felt lighter. But over the next few months, the changes in myself became more obvious. I found that I was no longer looking for reasons to be upset with her, and I could think of things that I appreciated about her.

Her parenting style would not have worked for me, and there's nothing wrong with that because my husband wouldn't be the kind of man that I need him to be if it did. She provided the only thing that made the move worthwhile. And that makes her one of the best moms ever.

And her record? It's still blank.

—L. Y. Levand—

How to Find Forgiveness

49

Chicken Soup for the Soul

Letting Go

*Let today be the day you stop being haunted by the
ghost of yesterday. Holding a grudge and harboring
anger/resentment is poison to the soul.*
~Steve Maraboli, Life, the Truth, and Being Free

The faculty was shocked at the news. Our college was being
shut down due to state budget cuts. The dean had managed
to save two small units of the college: his unit and that of our
department chair.

I was tenured and had been promoted to full professor just weeks
earlier. I had recently completed a doctorate and had worked long hours
for seventeen years, teaching a heavy course load. This was about way
more than losing a job. It left me feeling that not just my work but
also my discipline were not valued by the university. Being the major
breadwinner in my family, my children would also be affected. I felt
like I had given the university my best years, only to be treated unfairly.

The next day, one of my faculty friends told me she had relayed
the terrible news to her revered, wise friend, Flo. To her shock, Flo
had said, "That's wonderful!"

My friend said, "No, you don't understand, Flo. Lots of people
are going to lose their jobs, and students will not be able to finish their
degrees. It's awful!"

Flo responded, "Change is always good. It will bring new opportunities." Well, none of us was convinced we should be happy about
this change, but these words stuck in my memory.

At first, I buried my feelings of loss by focusing on helping my students find ways to continue their studies elsewhere. Eventually, I did survive my layoff by moving into a department in another college of the university, but the scars of betrayal remained — in particular those inflicted by Fran, our department secretary. Fran had joined us a few years earlier in an exchange with another department that found her troublesome. She felt invincible because of her family relationship with a high-ranking member of the administration, free to announce her own edicts for our department.

I hadn't forgiven Fran for her role in the destruction of our department. I couldn't stand the sight of her. While she didn't do anything in particular to me, her malicious acts increased the pain and the impact of the cuts for other members of the faculty.

In the two years following the layoffs, Fran would try to talk to me when she saw me, but I wanted nothing to do with her and responded coldly. The sight of her brought back not only what she had done but the whole dishonorable way our faculty had been treated. One day, she said, "I never did anything to you." I didn't respond as I felt her lack of integrity was not worthy of my time.

One day, I went into a meeting, and I found I was sitting two seats behind Fran. I felt the tension rise in my body the way it always did when I saw her. I relived all the horror and unjustness of what had happened. My mood changed from upbeat to angry and depressed.

Fuming, it occurred to me suddenly that I was the one experiencing this misery. Holding onto this grudge took energy from me and made me, not her, feel dreadful. I was the one who was letting her make me miserable — and I could change that.

I decided to stop letting Fran's presence trigger that release of venom in my heart. I would remember consciously to take a deep breath, relax, and think about the advantages of my current career in my new department. I would not let Fran's presence remind me of the past or think of her as relevant to my life.

My new focus was on the advantages of my new position, remembering Flo's words about change bringing new opportunities. I enjoyed the challenge of teaching new types of courses and students with different majors. I forged new alliances and friendships that I would not have had if the change had never happened. For that I am grateful, as well as for the lesson of peace in letting go.

From that moment on, whenever I saw Fran, I would acknowledge her pleasantly. As I let go of the resentment, I felt a great sense of relief. I relaxed and no longer had the burden of stirring up negative emotions. Whenever I am tempted to hold onto resentment, I recall the misery it self-inflicts and Flo's advice that "change brings opportunity."

—Gwen Sheldon Willadsen—

50

Memories Worth Keeping

The moments we share are the moments
we keep forever.
~Author Unknown

We were five adults gathered in a sunny Arizona living room. We had come for the wedding of my brother Eddy's daughter.

Although we hadn't been together for two years, not since Mom's funeral, we quickly reverted to lifelong family roles. As the oldest, I tried to organize the gathering. Don Jr. inserted philosophical comments. Steve, the middle child, teased in his quiet way. Sue tried to keep our attention by making inane observations that had nothing to do with the conversation.

The baby — Ed to most of the world, but still Eddy to us — was almost forty. Eddy was the caboose, the "accident" who came along four years after Sue. He was never treated like an afterthought, though. In fact, he was Dad's favorite, although Sue claimed I was a close second.

I certainly didn't feel like a favorite when Dad screamed at me for burning the potatoes or when he dragged me away from my friends because I hadn't finished the ironing. Or later, when he berated me for staying out too late with the boy I married eventually — even though I was technically an adult at age eighteen.

We sat around snacking and talking about the wedding. Mom would have loved the ceremony, Dad less so. He didn't like weddings. But there were lots of things he didn't like.

Sue said, "Dad was just plain mean."

Eddy objected. "He had high expectations, but he wasn't mean."

The rest of us said, "Yes, he was!"

Unlike Eddy, we remembered the sting of Dad's belt on our backsides. And then there were the chores. As teenagers, Don and Steve spent long summer days baling hay alongside Dad, coming in from the field only when it was too dark to work. And before school, they awakened at four to milk the cows. Sue and I cooked and cleaned while Mom helped with the milking and Dad left to work in the factory. Eddy's primary chore was bottle-feeding the calves.

As youngest and favored, Eddy enjoyed other privileges, too. He sat in the front seat with our parents while four of us scrunched together in the back of the old Ford. Dad bought him a topcoat and hat that matched his and boots like the ones he wore to work. Occasionally, I was the recipient of a kick from those boots when I tried to steer Eddy where he didn't want to go.

As my siblings and I talked the day away, disagreements over childhood memories surfaced. We were merciless in teasing Sue, who brought up incidents that no one else remembered. We had differing accounts of childhood events, so I finally decreed that two of us had to remember the details for a memory to be deemed accurate.

Sue asked, "Do you remember Don shooting a tin can off my head with a bow and arrow?"

"It was a slingshot," Don contradicted, and Steve concurred.

"Do you remember Diana breaking the picture window when she threw a rock at Steve because he read her diary?"

"No," I corrected her. "He'd be dead if he read my diary. Don and Steve broke the window when they were wrestling. That was the first time Mom and Dad left all of us home alone. We gathered up our quarters, dimes, and pennies and put them on the table with a note, and then we hid in the attic."

"We got the idea from a *Father Knows Best* episode," Don said, "but it worked better on TV. Dad was furious."

"That was a bad day."

"Even on good days, he never acted like he loved us. He certainly never said so."

"He just didn't show it," Eddy said.

We talked a long time about the many ways Dad demonstrated he didn't love us. We harbored unhappy memories of his temper.

Eventually, our conversation turned to losing Mom. We wondered why she had put up with Dad's demands those many years. And we wished she'd intervened when he treated us unfairly.

We turned from discussing Mom and Dad's parenting to our own parenting mistakes. I said, "If I could do it over again, I wouldn't be so permissive. I guess it was a reaction to Dad's strictness." We all wished we could have a do-over to fix our errors.

The passing hours brought laughter and tears as we argued, reminisced, and disputed each other's memories. Old sibling rivalries faded as we shared regrets over things we'd done that we shouldn't have and things we should have done that we hadn't. The waves of emotion were exhausting as we shed tears of sadness one moment, tears of mirth the next.

As day turned into night and our time together drew to a close, Don said, "You know, in spite of everything, in spite of what we did wrong and our parents did wrong, we all turned out okay."

Yes, we were doing fine. Four of us went to college and enjoyed successful careers. Sue home-schooled her three girls and did volunteer work. We were all honest and dependable in our personal life and work life. Between us, we'd raised twelve responsible children.

"Mom was the fun-loving parent, but we learned some important lessons from Dad, too," I remarked.

"Dad taught us to work hard," Steve conceded. "He used to tell me hard work may or may not help me get ahead, but no one ever succeeded without it."

Don recalled another Dad-ism: "You can be five minutes early as easily as five minutes late."

Eddy quoted, "Protect your good name. It's something you can't buy."

Sue chimed in, "Your word is your bond."

We had spent much of the day criticizing Dad, but in the end, we acknowledged that we'd also learned some valuable life lessons from him. Dad wouldn't win a "Father of the Year" contest, but we recognized he'd done the best he could.

And we learned from his mistakes. We were generous with saying "I love you" to our children, wanting them never to wonder whether we cared about them.

The anger we'd felt toward our parents, particularly Dad, began to fall away that day. Five siblings talked through a lifetime of grievances. Our resentment dissipated, and we were finally set free of the past. We realized Dad must have loved us; he provided food, shelter, clothing, and education. He simply wasn't able to express his love in words. It was too late now because dementia had taken his voice. But it wasn't too late for us to love him.

We were adults, but it seemed that real maturity was achieved only when we were able to forgive the mistakes our parents made and accept their imperfections. Maybe that was also the beginning of accepting our own.

— Diana L. Walters —

51

Live Like a Pit Bull

The world would be a nicer place if everyone had the
ability to love as unconditionally as a dog.
~M.K. Clinton

W hen the rescue organization found Judah, he had been discarded by the only "family" he'd ever known, thrown away after a lifetime of abuse. Judah's jaw and teeth were broken, and his face was scarred, the result of a gunshot wound. He had been used to fight, and when he would no longer fight, he was used to breed. His ears had been "cropped" by a kitchen knife. His tail was brutally hacked off with an axe, and what remained of it was so infected it had to be amputated. Judah had a tremendous amount of healing to do, physically and emotionally.

Judah spent a year with the rescue. He attended adoption events, and we met at one of those events. I was in no position to adopt a third dog at the time, but I was drawn to Judah. The way he flopped onto his back, hoping for a belly rub whenever a new person approached, made me laugh.

Several months after our initial meeting, Judah celebrated one year with the rescue. People were asking why he hadn't been adopted yet, and I realized it was because he was waiting for me. So I submitted an application and Judah came home within days.

I adopted a Pit Bull — not just any Pit Bull, but one with baggage. A dog with a history of trauma. A dog who had been mistreated by dogs and humans alike. And I was bringing him into my home to live with my son and two other dogs. Was I out of my mind?

What I didn't know, and what Judah soon taught me, is that unlike people, dogs don't dwell on the past. They live in the moment. Although he has no reason to, Judah loves people. He is the sweetest, most loving, cuddliest dog I've ever met. He is so happy and grateful for the most basic things that people take for granted: a loving family, soft blankets, and nutritious food.

This dog, who scared away so many people because of his breed and history, has taught me the value of forgiveness. Of living in the moment. Of enjoying life's simple pleasures. What a different world we would live in if everyone acted more like my Pit Bull.

— Shannon Hanf —

52

A Close Shave

Mistakes are always forgivable,
if one has the courage to admit them.
~Bruce Lee

I n the 1920s, my nineteen-year-old uncle, Sebastian "Buster" Palmeri, proudly completed his apprenticeship under a master barber, John Martin, in our little coal-mining town of Pittston, Pennsylvania.

Mr. Martin promised Buster, "The next customer is yours, son." Eagerly, the young man mixed shaving soap in a ceramic mug, only to hear the customer shout, "No *kid* is gonna shave *me*!"

Despite Mr. Martin's assurance that the new barber was indeed qualified, the grouch bellowed, "I said, *no kid* shaves *me*!" Humiliated, the young man sat down and pretended to read the *Pittston Gazette*.

Fast-forward forty years. My uncle, now proprietor of Buster's Barber Shop, the most popular meeting place in town, visited a hospital ward to shave a friend.

Upon leaving, he spotted a gaunt, disheveled old man. Since everyone knows everyone else in a small town like Pittston, Buster recognized him. It was the grouch who had humiliated him decades ago. What poetic justice to ignore him now!

My uncle's upbringing triumphed, however, as he asked gently, "Mr. X, would you like a shave to make you more comfortable?"

"I have no money to pay you," whispered the sick man.

"This one's on me," Buster said, and gave him the royal treatment:

How to Find Forgiveness |

shave, talcum, neck massage, and pillow plump-up.

The old man's voice trembled. "I remember you. I wouldn't let you shave me when you were a kid."

"I don't remember that," fibbed my uncle. "I hope you feel better. God bless you." And he picked up his black leather barber's bag to leave.

Tears filled the dying man's eyes. "Buster... wait. Thank God there are men like you in this world. If everyone was an S.O.B. like me, we'd be in bad shape!"

—Sister Josephine Palmeri, MPF—

53

Forgiveness Beyond the Grave

Forgive, not because they deserve forgiveness,
but because you deserve peace.
~Author Unknown

Someone once told me that forgiveness is like grief. There is no "one size fits all" solution. It takes time to work completely through the hurt, and just when we think we're over it, something happens to stir up old feelings again.

My mother was angry at me when she died. She was so sick that she ended up in the ICU connected to machines to keep her alive, and that was something she never wanted. Her brother took her to the hospital, and I had no control over the situation. Still, I could see in her eyes that she blamed me for not getting her out of there. Soon after, she died, so we never got closure. Although I didn't feel guilty — she really needed to be in the hospital — it still haunted me that we never had a chance to reconcile.

I dealt with my feelings for a long time... or at least I thought I was dealing with them. When I signed up for a grief recovery class it was for a different loss. The counselor suggested that we go back in our lives and deal with an earlier loss first. She wanted us to learn how to use the tools for grief recovery without so many new, raw emotions attached. That way, we could apply them effectively moving forward. Once we worked on an old hurt and practiced the principles, we would be better able to deal with the recent loss. It was like building a house starting with the foundation and dealing with the roof later.

Part of the process involved writing a letter of forgiveness to the person we were grieving over — saying all those things we forgave them for, asking them to forgive anything we did to hurt them, and telling them all the things we didn't get to say while they were still here.

That made sense to me, so I searched my heart and found that hurt from the loss of my mother was still festering inside me. I thought about all the things I wished I could still say to my mother, both the things I was sorry for and the things that were not my fault and couldn't change. In the end, I wrote out all my feelings, both good and bad, about my relationship with her. It was a very emotional and draining experience, involving many issues that I needed to forgive.

My mother was a challenging woman emotionally. She was the baby of her family and was very spoiled growing up. In some ways, I became the adult early in my life and felt the need to take care of her.

She was a beautiful, talented, and fun person most of her life. I try to remember that part of her because she became unhappy and miserable after she and my dad divorced. She never recovered from that and turned to alcohol for comfort, which made her mean and sullen. She wanted to die for a long time before she actually did. I felt it was my job to keep her alive. As a young person and the oldest child, I saw that as the right thing to do.

My brother once told me in sort of a joking way, "If you'd quit dragging her to the hospital, she'd be dead by now." Later, I realized he was probably right. She really didn't want to be here.

I worked on my letter and read it to our little group. It was very emotional, but also released a lot of feelings I had been holding on to. I walked away feeling a lot lighter and had less pain. It started the process of forgiveness for me. I still work on it when old feelings pop up, but it's not so frequent or intense now.

On her birthday and Mother's Day, I can think of her fondly and without so much regret. If she is looking down on me and can understand how I am feeling, I hope it gives her comfort, too.

After lots of introspection and tears, I came up with my own how-to for incorporating forgiveness into my life:

- The other person doesn't need to know you forgive them. In fact, it's sometimes better to stay away from the person who hurt you, rather than go back for more.
- While writing a letter of forgiveness can be beneficial for you, you should never send it to the other person. I burn my letters so they are released to the universe, and no one else can ever read them.
- Reading your letter out loud is part of the healing. Find a trusted person and a good listener, maybe someone who doesn't know the person who hurt you. Tears will come, but that can be healing, too.
- Reconciliation is not necessary. No one needs to keep being hurt or abused by another.
- You can work on your forgiveness issues even when the other person passes on.

Forgiveness can be a process rather than a quick fix. I learned that it was worth persistence and hard work because of how much better I felt in the end.

— Stephanie Pifer-Stone —

54

The Text

We change the memory of our past
into a hope for our future.
~Louis B. Smedes

My father was a hard man to love, but I loved him nonetheless. He'd always had a bad temper, and he took out his frustrations on me when I was a boy. He yelled at me often. He called me nasty names. He did other things that were deeply damaging to my self-esteem. But in spite of those things, I still loved him.

After not having spoken to my dad for two years (ever since a blowup at his house on Thanksgiving), I was ready to forgive him. I *needed* to forgive him. But I couldn't. I didn't know how to forgive him. I'd spent forty-five years on this planet and, I'd finally come to realize, I didn't really know how to forgive at all.

"If only he would apologize to me, I'm pretty sure I could do it…" I told myself.

For months, I waited, hoping he would call to tell me he was sorry. He knew I was angry with him. He had to have known. I never responded to his texts. I ignored Father's Day. Ditto for his birthday. For nearly two years, I'd been pretending he didn't exist. I'd been pretending I didn't even have a dad.

And then something happened that made the whole matter more urgent.

My best friend passed away. I'd spoken with my friend on the phone a few hours before he died — a phone call that happened purely by chance. It was, to my knowledge, the final conversation of my friend's life. There was nothing bad about the conversation; it was a regular, run-of-the-mill phone call between good friends. But if I'd known it would be our last conversation, I would have said other things. I would have expressed my deep appreciation for my friend, for all the wisdom he'd imparted to me over the years, for all the fun times and laughter we'd shared. I'd never told my best friend what he'd meant to me, what he'd meant to my life. And now that he was gone, I would never be able to tell him. It was a piece of business that would forever remain unfinished.

I resolved that I couldn't leave another piece of business unfinished.

I needed to forgive my father.

"If only he would apologize, I'm pretty sure I could get over the hump...."

One day, it occurred to me that my dad was never going to apologize. He wasn't ever going to take responsibility for any of the harsh things he'd said or done. He just wasn't that kind of person. But I still had a deep need to forgive him.

It was a simple decision. There were no fireworks, brass bands, crooning angels or parting of the heavens. I simply decided to forgive my father. I forgave him for the Thanksgiving blowup and for every other thing he'd ever done to me. So many painful memories. So much damage to a boy's soul. But I needed to do it. Any day, my dad could pass away unexpectedly, just as my friend had. I couldn't leave this important business unfinished any longer.

It was a simple decision that I felt in every part of my being, in every cell of my body. I didn't tell anyone what I'd done. I silently forgave my father and I went about my life feeling unburdened. I had it in the back of my mind to call my dad and tell him that I'd forgiven him, but time got away from me. I forgave my father in my heart and told no one about it.

A few days after I'd made that decision, I was having dinner with a friend when my cell phone started vibrating in my pocket. The phone did its thing for at least a minute, but I ignored it, choosing instead to keep my focus on the dinner conversation. After my friend got up to use the restroom, I took out my phone and checked the screen.

Immediately, I noted the missed call was from my dad. It was interesting that he'd tried to call — he hadn't tried in quite some time. Then, a second later, I noticed the long text he'd sent, which the phone had broken up into several segments. It wasn't like my dad to send long messages. I knew he'd only left the text because I hadn't picked up his call.

In the lengthy, multi-part text, my dad apologized to me. He apologized for every harsh thing he'd ever said or done to me. He apologized for being a bad father. And he asked for my forgiveness. Of course, he didn't know that I'd already forgiven him a few days before. He didn't know because I hadn't told him. I hadn't told anyone.

For what seemed like an eternity, I stared at the screen choking back tears. I read through my dad's text a couple of times. When my friend returned from the restroom, I read the text aloud to him.

"Your dad sounds like a pretty good guy," my friend commented.

I cleared my throat. "He's not a bad guy," I said. "He's done some bad things, but he's not a bad guy."

"Did you ask for that apology?" my friend inquired.

"No. Well, I guess in my mind I did. But not out loud."

My friend smiled wistfully. "You're lucky to have your dad, you know. My dad died a long time ago. I still miss him. I wish I had a text like that from him."

I nodded slowly, still holding back my tears. "It's always amazing to be reminded of how the universe really works," I muttered.

I had nothing else to say about the matter at the moment, but soon after leaving the restaurant, I contacted my dad and arranged to visit him. I hadn't seen him in two years, and I missed him. Actually, I missed him a lot. My dad and I had a lot of catching up to do. And the way I saw it, we weren't going to be able to do that through a text.

— Anthony Clark —

55

The Path to Forgiveness

Forgiveness is an act of the will, and the will can
function regardless of the temperature of the heart.
~Corrie ten Boom

As a counselor for the past thirty years, I have encountered many people who struggle to forgive because they don't feel like their offender deserves to be let off the hook. After experiencing chronic physical abuse at the hands of my own mother, I can understand those feelings.

It wasn't until I recognized that my resentment had me on the hook that I began my journey toward healing. Bitterness kept me trapped in anger, negativity and self-pity. Finally sick and tired of being sick and tired, I cried out to God and asked Him to free me from the burden of bitterness that was holding me hostage.

A few weeks after I sent up my desperate prayer, a gentle-hearted lady named Iris came to share with our small group at church. Iris opened up about the sexual abuse she sustained from her father and declared, "Forgiveness doesn't make your offender right; it just makes you free." Her words stabbed me awake that evening. Up until then, I felt like I was anything but free. Choosing not to forgive my mom made the abuse worse as I endlessly ruminated on her offences.

That truth was brought home a few days later by, of all things, a TV show. A lesson on forgiveness was the last thing I expected as I wandered through the living room that evening. My kids were watching one of those shows where a crew of actors plays pranks on people. As I sat down on the sofa to watch with them, I saw him on the screen — a large man with tufts of dark hair and a belly-roll hanging over his belt in front. If he had a name printed on the back of his belt, it would have read, "Bubba."

The show host described the set-up. A sign was posted on the cash register in a convenience store declaring, "We don't make change." A camera was hidden to record the responses of customers. First, a middle-aged woman walked in and laid a few items down on the counter. The show host, posing as a cashier, rang up thirteen dollars and some change. The lady gave him a twenty-dollar bill, and the mock store clerk put it in the register and closed the drawer. Rather annoyed, the woman informed him, "I believe you owe me change."

"Hey lady, read the sign," the cashier remarked. "We don't make change." At that point, the censors had to beep out the irate lady's protests.

Then "Bubba" shuffled in. His purchases came to five dollars and some change. He, too, presented a twenty-dollar bill. The quasi-clerk once again placed the twenty in the register and closed the drawer. Continuing to breathe through his mouth, Bubba uttered, "Uh, I think you owe me some money."

"Read the sign, buddy. We don't make change."

Then Bubba turned on his heels and started to walk out of the store. The cashier moved from behind the counter and went after him, tapped him on the shoulder and inquired, "Hey, we owe you money, a decent amount of money. Why are you just walking away?"

I will never forget Bubba's response. With his hands in his pocket, fumbling with his keys, Bubba declared, "Uh, I decided a long time ago that I don't rent space in my head to nobody."

In that moment, I realized that I was renting far too much space in my head to way too many people for far too little results! I was continuing the abuse as I nursed and rehearsed my resentment over and over again. Later, I learned in recovery that "resentment is me drinking poison and hoping you die." Choosing to let go of my offences didn't legitimize my mother's behavior. But it did free me from drinking from the toxic well of bitterness and self-pity.

I wish I could say that my life played out like a made-for-TV movie, my mom and I restored our relationship, and everything was peaches and cream after that. My mother didn't change, but I did. And because of that, we were able to have a few polite visits before she died. The last time I saw her, I told her I loved her and meant it.

At the time, I didn't know the lessons my pain would teach me. That didn't come until much later when I was counseling a woman from my church whose life of abuse and neglect made my story sound like a picnic in the park by comparison. As Sarah Ann poured out her story, with tears streaming down her face, she looked up from her Kleenex and made a remark that totally took me back.

She said, "I'm so glad you've had pain in your life, Linda."

"Excuse me?" came my weak reply.

"I'm glad that you have had pain in your life because I know that you can understand what I've been through. I've never been able to share any of this with anyone before. But I can tell you all of this crazy stuff because I know you get it."

After she left, for the first time in my life, I got on my knees and thanked God for the lessons I learned from the hurt in my life. I thanked Him for the empathy I had for Sarah Ann and so many others because I did get it. And I thanked Him for the blessing of helping people find healing on the path to forgiveness, which fills my life with joy and purpose every day.

— Linda Newton —

56

Face to Face

Genuine forgiveness does not deny anger
but faces it head-on.
~Alice Duer Miller

"He's so cute! What's his name?"

"Stevie," I answered proudly.

"Like Stevie Wonder?" the woman asked.

"No, like Steve Laube, the literary agent," I replied.

I scooped up Stevie and walked toward my SUV. I'd lost count of how many times someone had asked me if I'd named my dog after the popular singer from my childhood.

"Maybe I should start calling you Stevie Wonder Dog Wootan," I told Stevie as I secured him in the front seat of my car.

The truth of the matter is that Stevie was anything but a wonder dog. My husband and I had driven four hours to pick him up, only to discover a puppy that looked nothing like the picture online. At four months old, he was tiny, shook uncontrollably, and had excessively dry, flaky skin. Against my better judgment, I paid the lady, and we were on our way. We were less than halfway home when he got carsick all over me.

This dog and I were off to a shaky start, and it didn't get much better. Soon, I discovered that not only did the dog have an ear infection, but he had severe food allergies; he couldn't eat or drink anything without gagging. Antibiotic ear ointment and expensive dog food did the trick, but I wasn't sure how to handle the dog's apparent fear of humans.

I felt ill-equipped to handle the commitment I'd made to a dog with so many special needs, especially one who didn't seem to like me. There wasn't a lot of bonding going on. I suppose that's why the dog went unnamed for more than two weeks.

"We can't keep calling him Dog," I told my husband, Joey. "We need to decide on a name."

Since I spent the most time with the dog, I got the majority vote. Stevie it was.

My phone rang. It was my friend Tesi. She wanted to meet for lunch.

"I'm at the park trying to socialize the dog," I told her. "Let me run him home and I'll meet you in half an hour."

I arrived at the restaurant to find the small parking lot mostly empty. Tesi was nowhere in sight, and I decided to wait for her in my car.

A car pulled up to the front of the restaurant. I didn't pay it much attention until I saw a man and woman emerge from the vehicle.

Oh, no! I reached for my purse so I could call Tesi and tell her not to come. I pulled down the visor and crouched in my seat, hoping the couple wouldn't notice me. My brand-new cell phone was nowhere to be found, and I suddenly remembered that in my rush to leave the house, I'd left it on top of Stevie's crate.

I watched as Tesi's truck entered the parking lot.

"No! Don't do it!" the voice inside my head screamed as I watched my best friend park right next to the couple. Tesi emerged from her car and waved in my direction.

"Tesi? I thought that was you. How are you?" the woman asked. Immediately, Tesi dropped her hand, but it was too late. All three of them turned toward me and stared.

I sat up straight and tried to pretend I hadn't been hiding. I managed a weak wave and took a deep breath before getting out of the car. I walked up to the trio as Tesi mouthed, "Sorry."

"Hi, Mom. Hi, Dad."

"Hi, Sissy. It's good to see you," my dad said.

It was the first time in over two years anyone had called me Sissy.

I hadn't answered to that name since I'd become estranged from my family, and I was surprised at how much comfort it brought me in that moment.

"What have you been up to?" they asked.

"I got a dog," I blurted out. It was an awkward, tentative exchange — one I hadn't bargained for when I woke up that morning. "He's kind of a dud, but he's pretty adorable," I rambled on nervously.

I had yet to transfer my pictures to my new phone, and I still carried my old iPhone 6 around as a photo album of sorts. I whipped it out and pushed some buttons. "Here he is!" I said as I thrust the phone in my parents' direction. They agreed with me: What Stevie lacked in personality, he more than made up for in cuteness.

"Maybe we'll get to see him in person one day," Dad said.

"Well, you could come over now — after you eat, of course. I mean, if you want to." No sooner had the words escaped my lips than my heart began beating wildly in my chest. Where had that come from? I knew I was called to forgive, but did I really have to do the forgiving face to face?

I called Joey when I got home. "Babe, my parents are on the way to the house right now."

"Our house?" he asked, confused.

"Yes!"

"Well, good," Joey answered. "It's about time y'all made up."

The thing is, I didn't want to reconcile with my family. Things had been said and done that had hurt me deeply. I hadn't seen my parents in over two years, and I had no problem letting it go another two... or longer.

"You know, Melissa, you're all at fault. You've said and done things, too. At least give things a chance and see where it goes," Joey said. "Do you really want to spend the rest of your life worrying you are going to run into them every time you go out?"

I knew Joey was right, but it didn't make it any easier.

I held Stevie on my lap as I waited for my parents to arrive. "Alright, Stevie, you are going to meet your grandparents for the first time. Perk up your ears and don't act terrified when they come in." I was one to talk; I felt more than a little terrified myself.

My parents sat on my living room sofa and *oohed* and *aahed* over Stevie for more than an hour that day. The conversation didn't deviate much from the dog, but I was fine with that. I didn't know if, or when, either of us would reach out again, but three weeks later my dad called and invited Stevie and me over for a play date with his dogs.

It might help socialize Stevie, I reasoned, so I went.

Two months later, I reached out to my mom and dad for a puppy play date.

I continued spending time with my parents, and eventually I no longer needed Stevie to act as a buffer. Things didn't return to the way they were before our falling out, but then again I wouldn't have wanted them to. Face-to-face forgiveness wasn't so bad.

As for Stevie… he's quite social these days, and I'd have to say his most amazing feat is singlehandedly building a bridge of reconciliation with those adorable little paws of his.

Turns out Stevie Wonder Dog Wootan is quite the wonder dog, after all.

— Melissa Wootan —

57

A Few Simple Words

An apology is the super glue of life.
It can repair just about anything.
~Lynn Johnston

K ate and I met in college. I was a junior, and she was a freshman. We were roommates and hit it off right away. Our inter-
ests were identical. We loved the same music and movies. Our
clothing styles were borderline edgy and comfortable. We
spent a lot of time together that year. Afterward, we went our separate
ways, though we stayed in touch.

One day, several years later, I received a call from Kate.

"I'm getting married!" she shrieked into the phone.

"Congratulations!" I shrieked back.

"I want you to be a bridesmaid," Kate said, and she told me all of
the details that she'd already worked out with her fiancé.

"Can you come up here to have a bridesmaid meeting?" she asked.

"Sure," I said. "I have to work that night, but I'm sure I'll get out
a bit earlier than five. We don't usually stay that late on a Friday."

Sadly, this was one day when my boss went on a rampage and
wouldn't have liked to see me sneak out before precisely 5:00 p.m.
As soon as I could, I hopped into my car and made the ninety-minute
journey north to the get-together. I liked to drive, so I didn't mind.
I was in a good mood until I got off on the wrong exit. The evening
went downhill from there.

"Where are you?" Kate demanded.

"I don't know," I admitted. "I'm not familiar at all with this area."

I kept making attempts to turn myself around, but in the days before smartphones and GPS apps, I was in too deep to get out.

A phone call further deflated my mood.

"Never mind," Kate said, clearly unhappy. "Everyone wants to go home; it's too late."

Great, I thought. *Now I get to drive another ninety minutes home after spending forty-five minutes trying to find the place.*

I stopped on the way home to grab a coffee. When I got back, I found a scathing e-mail from Kate.

The words "selfish" and "inconsiderate" were thrown around liberally. My most significant error, in her eyes, wasn't just getting lost in a part of the state where I had no previous experience driving, but that I hadn't left earlier than 5:00 p.m. like I said I might. She effectively ended our friendship through that one e-mail.

"I don't want you in the wedding," she concluded. "I can't have your disregard for others getting in the way of planning."

My only response was "Okay."

I could have fought harder, but I was in no mood, and pride is a fickle thing.

I boxed up the books she'd let me borrow and sent them back the next morning.

The whole experience left me angry and bitter. We unfriended each other on social media and didn't speak again.

One day several years later, I found myself lonely and divorced, living in the same area where I'd been lost on my trek to locate the bridesmaid party. I'd been thinking about Kate a lot. We had enjoyed fun times together, and our shenanigans had been something to behold. We had laughed until we cried on more occasions than I could count.

Finally, I put aside my pride and sent her a message.

"I miss you," I started. "I am not sure if you're still up here, but I've moved to the area, and I could use a friend. I want to apologize for everything that happened between us."

My heartbeat rang in my ears as I hit Send and awaited a response, even though I didn't expect one at all.

Almost immediately, I received a response.

"I miss you, too! I am the one who should apologize!"

And so it went that after years of the silent treatment, with a few simple words we put aside the ridiculous fight and picked up where we'd left off. It was that simple. Kate had also divorced recently, and she became my favorite partner in crime. I couldn't have survived my first year as a divorcee without her.

The best part? I no longer felt that gnawing feeling in my gut when I thought about her or my time at college. I didn't feel the pang of sadness at losing a close friend. Now, I had room for my roomie in my heart, and a feeling of loving warmth spread throughout my life.

— Eilley Cooke —

Chapter 7

Forgiving Yourself

58

The Best Day

All we have to do is forgive ourselves wholly
and completely for ever thinking
that we are not good enough!
~Jodi Aman

I pull up covers, tuck blankets tight, gently kiss foreheads, and flip light switches. Bedtime is a sweet ritual that begins with pulling on PJs, brushing teeth, and reading a story. It is that moment of the day when we reconnect, and the house finally falls silent. Another day is behind us.

I pad down the stairs quietly, my multitude of parenting duties complete for another day. But before my foot even hits our last step, rather than treating myself to a deep breath, I begin reviewing the day. I'm tallying my failures. At a time when I should be reveling, I'm mentally listing all the ways I think I've fallen short as a mommy.

It feels like I spent the whole day yelling and fussing about picking up toys, refereeing emotional sibling injustices, and demanding that screen time be balanced with backyard play, drawing, building, or creating something. And goodness, I allowed entirely too much sugar: syrupy pancakes, a couple of Oreos at lunch, an afternoon Popsicle, *and* a bowl of mint-chocolate-chip ice cream after dinner. Good grief, I tried and failed once again at feeding the kids less sugar.

I'd not made time to have them read to me or practice those yet-to-be-mastered multiplication tables. I'd envisioned starting to read a book aloud during breakfast, but hadn't followed through. When water spilled at dinner, I'd groaned and sighed. Toys are scattered around the house, and I checked off very little from my to-do list. I'd been obviously grumpy when my husband came home. Had I laughed at all? Why couldn't I be more fun? Did I look any of them in the eye? Was I cherishing every moment and making their childhoods magical, as all moms should? Everyone else is better at this.

Instead of enjoying a well-deserved rest, I'm judging myself—unfairly, as I'll learn.

A little voice interrupts my thoughts. "Mom?" my youngest daughter calls to me. "Momma, this was the *best* day. I love you."

Wait. Today? The best? What about all my fussing?

I turn toward her room, asking why she thinks the day was good. Her response: "We got to play all day, and you really took care of us. You are such a good mommy." The sleepy opinion of my four-year-old catches me off guard, immediately diminishing my inner critic's authority.

I climb back up the stairs, sit down on her bed, and say, "I'm so happy you had a good day. Wanna do it all over again tomorrow? I'm sorry I fussed so much."

"It's okay, Mom. We were kinda crazy. I loved today, though."

Her generous opinion of me, how she looks right past my flaws, causes me to pause to reconsider the day.

She deserves my apology, but as I start down the steps once more, I realize that I might need an apology, too. Maybe I am being stingy with grace for myself. Maybe I've been listening to a harsh voice that I should be ignoring.

I need to forgive myself for having unreasonable expectations of my kids and myself.

I need to forgive myself for comparing myself to the curated social-media feeds of other moms.

I need to forgive myself for believing in an inflated caricature of the perfect mom.

I am intentional about teaching grace to my kids. I offer it to them and encourage them to pass along that same offer of forgiveness. But how much more effective might it be to lead by example?

On that ordinary evening after tuck-in, I laugh at myself, beginning a gradual shift in how I think about myself as a parent. Though it takes me some time to fully recognize mommy guilt for what it is, I feel lighter immediately, knowing that my kids see our days differently than I do. I can set down some of the mental burdens I have been carrying.

It's time for a daily dose of grace in the morning and probably another at night. Letting go of unreasonable expectations would be so freeing. I need to stop inviting in false stories spoken by my inner critic. Who is setting these expectations anyway?

The next day, I wake up reminding myself that I am going to start moving toward forgiving myself more, acknowledging in advance that I'll mess up, and lightening up. It is time to end this season of parenting self-doubt and start learning to be okay with the messy beauty of our ordinary days. I need pep talks, prayer, and less failure tallying.

Later, I take a moment to look around the breakfast table at the faces of little people who love their mommy and don't notice every flaw. Their tendency to shower me with grace floods me with gratitude and a serving of hope. So, after I pour milk in cups, I sit down beside them and declare, "It's going to be the best day."

— Rebecca Radicchi —

59

Pop

Gratitude bestows reverence, allowing us to encounter
everyday epiphanies, those transcendent moments
of awe that change forever how we
experience life and the world.
~John Milton

When I was seventeen, Dad gave me a compliment. I remember it because I think it was the first one. Until that point, nothing I had done seemed good enough for Dad.

When I was young, he would take us — his seven sons — down to help with his janitorial business at St. Thomas Grade School, the same school I attended. The other students lived in big houses, but our family of nine lived in a three-bedroom duplex. I always thought we lived in half a house.

One night at the school, Dad threw his keys at me and said, "Damn you! Look at all the spots you missed! Why don't you wake up? You're not going to amount to anything!" And I wondered what he thought he had amounted to. He was the one cleaning toilets.

At seventeen, I wrote and performed a show that was a huge success. It sold out the high school theater two nights in a row. Dad said, "Paul, I've never been so proud in my life! Nothing John did could compare to this." John, my older brother, was the star of the family — football hero, MVP. John even called our father "Pop," another thing that made me feel he was much closer to him than the rest of us who called him "Dad."

Why did he have to bring up John? Why couldn't he just acknowledge me? I decided that my father couldn't even give a compliment the right way.

For years, Dad was a disappointment. His Hallmark birthday cards were too generic, as if he wasn't even willing to celebrate with me or show he cared. Meanwhile, I was paying a therapist so I could talk about him. I wanted an apology for the times he had yelled at me.

I find it easy to apologize to most people. I pride myself on it. In fact, years ago when I was teaching, my seventh-grade students got sick of me apologizing to them for losing my temper. I never understood why they would tell me there was no need to apologize. Maybe they thought it was appropriate to lose one's temper when students throw things at you.

Up until I started teaching, I had always seen anger as wrong and Dad as wrong. Period. But while teaching and experiencing a classroom of crazed adolescents, I finally understood what it was like for my dad to be dealing with seven sons. My anger wasn't a mistake — it was part of the passion of wanting to make a difference in their lives. And, yes, it was a fear of losing control, of not being respected. In his commitment to me, Dad risked being enraged and disliked. I was out to be better than him; he was out to make me better. Beneath his temper was an intense concern for what he thought was best for me. We all have good intentions, but not always the best delivery.

When I turned thirty-nine, I decided I needed to forgive him. He had been doing his best, and again... seven sons! So, I went back to my old school where he had berated me.

As I stood outside the window, I realized that Dad was not who I had to forgive. I needed to forgive myself for all the years I had bottled up my anger toward him. I was so critical of myself that I couldn't enjoy my life.

I couldn't view anything in a positive light. Rarely did I permit myself to enjoy a movie or a ballgame without a nagging sense that I should be doing something productive. Sunsets stood for disappointment, showing me that the day was over and I hadn't gotten enough done.

As much as I wanted Dad to apologize, I realized I owed him an apology for the anger I had carried for so long. His anger occurred in occasional outbursts; my anger was rooted deep. Apologizing to him was extremely difficult: I'd be changing who I was. When I apologized to the class, I was honoring my ideal of never losing my temper. But apologizing to Dad would mean letting go of what made me better than him. It would mean seeing myself for the self-righteous jerk I had been.

The next time we had breakfast, I told Dad that I was sorry he had to deal with the chip on my shoulder. He said I didn't have to apologize for anything. I told him it meant a lot to me after he saw my first show in high school and said he had never been prouder in his life. For the first time, thirty years after he said it, I let the words in. It moved me deeply.

"Well, I knew how much it hurt you that year not to get a chance to play quarterback," he added.

As he said that, I realized why he had brought up John in his compliment all those years ago. He knew how devastated I was not playing quarterback. He wanted me to know that football wasn't as important as my writing and performing. It wasn't that Dad couldn't give a compliment right; I was the one who had taken his compliment the wrong way and turned something nice into something insulting.

I began seeing past the slights I kept collecting to realize that this man — a stranger to me for so many years — was my biggest ally. Dad was never against me; the world was not against me. My world was dark because I kept turning out the light.

My mom's love was always obvious, pure and simple. Dad's love was clumsy, complicated, critical. His love snuck up on me like an avalanche. We have a lot in common, especially our faltering, expanding hearts.

I looked up at Dad, the man whose features I have inherited: his strong nose, pale pink skin, blue eyes and thinning white hair. Even our crooked smiles matched.

"Well, there is something I do have to say." And as tears welled up, I said, "Thank you, Pop." And he has been "Pop" ever since.

— Paul Lyons —

60

The Hard Road to Self-Forgiveness

There is no sense in punishing your future for the
mistakes of your past. Forgive yourself,
grow from it, and then let it go.
~Melanie Koulouris

"What do you think of my eyebrows?" Jean asked. "I'm sure you approve of them now." Baffled, I stood there in silence, with a clueless expression on my face. I was attending my ten-year high school reunion, and Jean, a girl I had never known that well in high school, was asking me about her eyebrows. Had I missed something?

"Kent told me about the time at work when you wanted the other employees to tackle me and hold me down so you could wield your tweezers on my bushy brows," she said, glancing at Kent, who stood next to her.

Please, God, I begged silently, *find me a rock to crawl under now.* I hadn't thought of that day in ten years, and I'd completely forgotten I'd ever worked with Jean or Kent. The memory rushed back, flushing my face bright red. The way I remembered it, another employee had said those words — words Jean never should have heard.

Dumbfounded, I stuttered, "I didn't say that, did I?"

Kent laughed. "You did. Don't you remember?" At that moment, the dinner bell rang, and I slid into the shadows where I hid for the rest of the night. I had been so flustered I hadn't even offered Jean an apology.

Disgusted with myself, it sickened me to know that I'd hurt a person so much that she'd actually changed her physical appearance on my account and still remembered me a decade later. What kind of high school monster had I been? Jean was a talented artist with a bubbly personality, and I'd always admired her, even if I didn't know her well. And yet, whenever she groomed her eyebrows she thought of what I'd said behind her back.

My husband once told me I collect guilt the way people collect stamps. In fact, I wrote a Chicken Soup for the Soul story called "My Guilt Collection" where I mentioned my problem. Over the years, I've made some strides, but I still find self-forgiveness one of the hardest roads I've ever traveled. My past wrongs always come back to haunt me. That night, I tossed Jean in with the others I'd hurt inadvertently over the years — people I never realized I'd harmed until later in life.

One day, in an effort to atone for my guilt, I decided to search for my victims online, write them an apology note and be done with them forever. I removed a few names, which brought me peace where those people were concerned, but failed to find the others.

Frustrated and unable to let these memories go, I ended up sharing my woes with a close friend and fellow Chicken Soup for the Soul writer. I told her what I had done to Jean and how I'd searched the Internet, but couldn't find her address. My sweet friend knew how important this was to me and offered to help. She found Jean's address, and I sent my apology off in the mail. In my note, I told Jean she did not need to write back, but she did.

Dear Jill,

Thank you for the letter that you sent. I have to admit your name did not ring a bell in my mind, so I dug out the yearbook, and I do remember you.

I actually do not remember the conversation about my eyebrows.

However, I did have some major hairy caterpillar brows.

I feel bad that this comment weighed so heavily on your mind for so long. At that age, all sorts of things get said. Please do not let this worry you anymore.

Thanks again for your note.

Jean

Her words blew me away. I'd spent over thirty years berating myself while picturing Jean in front of her mirror each day, reliving my words. Yet Jean had gotten over it long ago. It hit me hard — if Jean didn't remember me or what happened, maybe no one else I'd felt guilty about did either. Perhaps they'd forgotten, forgiven, and moved on. I could only hope.

Now when I'm tempted to visit my guilt collection, I think of Jean. Her much-needed response earned a prominent place on my writing desk as a reminder to keep striving to let my past mistakes go. I'll admit, it's an ongoing battle for me, but I won't give up. If I can master the art of self-forgiveness, I know it will be one of the greatest gifts I will ever give myself.

— Jill Burns —

61

The Wave that Set Me Free

Forgiveness is for yourself because it frees you.
It lets you out of that prison you put yourself in.
~Louise Hay

It had been a year since Mom had passed away. Why was I still grieving as if it were yesterday? Guilt.

We'd found Mom a cute ranch house close by where I could bring her meals each day and spend time with her and her little dog, Kati. As her Alzheimer's progressed, however, Mom began to wander from home. Other times, she hallucinated that a child was staying with her or that she was somewhere other than in her own home.

My three brothers lived in other states, depending on my husband John and me to care for Mom as we'd promised. A decision needed to be made before something terrible happened. My brothers flew in one by one, agreeing that it was time to find a place where Mom could be supervised and safe.

During one of these visits, my youngest brother and I argued. Growing up, he'd been my best friend. We'd ridden mini-bikes throughout the countryside, carried a puppy or kitty home without asking first, shared secrets, and spent countless hours swimming and fishing. We were the ones who were there when our daddy died at a young age.

We both knew Mom needed to be in a safe place. We'd just gotten downright exhausted from trying to figure it all out… from trying to understand the horrible disease rapidly stealing our mom from us.

Eventually, John and I found Mom a lovely facility where she would be comfortable. The kind staff even agreed to take in Mom's dog. But it was still painful watching our mom locked behind the doors of a memory unit, unable to come and go for a breath of fresh air or to walk Kati. On her good days, Mom would reassure me she'd made the right choice in moving to be near us. I visited her every day, wheeling her outdoors to "cloud hunt" or watch the children play at the playground across the street. Leaving her each evening broke my heart.

Two days before my birthday, I held Mom in my arms as she took her last breath. For months, I relived those precious moments, wondering if I could have done anything more for her.

Here it was a year later, and I couldn't help wondering if I'd ever get over my grief.

"We need to get away for a while," John said one evening. "Want to go to your happy place?" My happy place had always been the mountains. I adored watching the eagles soaring overhead, seeing the mountain ranges at sunrise, watching night envelop the forest like a soft blanket…

I closed my eyes, picturing the Blue Ridge Mountains and cascading waterfalls.

"I need to visit my little brother in Florida," I heard my voice state from somewhere deep inside. John looked at me silently before nodding in agreement.

"That would be a good thing."

We called him that evening, letting him know we'd be arriving that weekend. He sounded excited that we were coming. The weather was beautiful when we arrived on Merritt Island. I'd been apprehensive about our first greeting since the funeral.

"Lord, help us to forgive each other!" I prayed.

No words were needed, however. We held on to each other like there was no tomorrow.

The following day, my brother and sister-in-law invited us to visit Cocoa Beach. Together, we walked along the beach, gazing at the beauty of the white sand and the water sparkling like diamonds. Without a word spoken, my brother knew I was still suffering inside.

"Come on," he said. Taking my hand, he led me to the water's edge.

"Did you ever ride a wave? There's something about it that makes you feel so free inside."

"I didn't bring a suit," I said nervously.

"Doesn't matter. Come on." He took my hand in his. "Now just hold on until we reach that huge wave out there. When I tell you, I'll let go of your hand, and you'll just reach out and ride that wave."

"Let it go, Sis," he added. And, just like that, I knew what my brother was getting at.

Together, we ventured farther and farther into the ocean, our toes sinking into the sand, my heart beating faster as an enormous foaming wave barreled in our direction.

"Now!" my brother shouted above the roar, releasing my hand. I raised my arms, catching the wave as it lifted me into the air and then rolled me back down and up again... exhilarating, commanding, freeing.

I watched my brother in the distance, riding wave after wave, smiling as he released all his worries and the tensions of the week. Suddenly, I too felt as free as a bird. I watched another enormous wave headed my way. This time, I had no hesitation. I released all my cares, picturing myself soaring to the heavens, to the place where our mom now happily resided, completely well.

Laughing, I felt my brother's hand in mine. Together, we headed for shore.

— Mary Z. Whitney —

If Only

Forgiveness is really a gift to yourself—
have the compassion to forgive others,
and the courage to forgive yourself.
~Mary Anne Radmacher

Ever since childhood, my older brother Todd's favored coping mechanism was running away, literally and figuratively. When that stopped working, he opted to build a wall and distance himself from our family and his past.

The perplexing thing was that his reluctance to face his personal vulnerabilities was never a hindrance to his many professional successes. His ability to compartmentalize only increased my antipathy about the ease with which Todd turned his back on us.

Moreover, I became enraged at his seemingly cavalier ability to dismiss our mother who, despite enduring immeasurable heartache, remained steadfast as the guidepost for her five young children. My resentment turned into contempt and finally into an unyielding resolve to forget that he existed.

After a few years of self-imposed exile and some mea culpas, Todd attempted to reconcile with my mother and a couple of my siblings. However, my loyalty to my mother kept me from forgiving him for his devastating actions. I refused to even acknowledge him.

Blinded by the ignorance of youth and a black and white worldview, it never once crossed my mind that Todd might have had altruistic reasons for abandoning the family for a while. In retrospect, I realize that leaving our hometown was the only way he could allow each of us to heal on our own terms. He genuinely believed that his presence was too emotionally toxic. If he remained, it would only add to our mother's grief.

Fast-forward to a cold and gray January evening in 1999. I still see my mother standing stoically in the foyer of the tiny, split-level apartment I had recently moved into upon my graduation. It was quite out of character for her to show up unannounced, but I was not overly concerned.

"Todd is dead. He took his own life."

I don't remember much else. "He took his own life" repeated on a loop for what seemed like hours but was likely only minutes. I do remember screaming, "Mommy, I am so sorry."

That was the end of the independent life I had envisioned for myself. I moved back home to live with my mom. I was filled with guilt, anger, and regret, believing that it was my fault — that my rejection of him was the reason he felt so alone.

My mother never blamed me or anyone else. Instead, like always, she carried those burdens alone, refusing to subject her children to more suffering.

I never stopped believing that if I had set aside my pride and welcomed him back, it might have been enough. On the other hand, my siblings and mother had welcomed him. They had kept the door open to him the whole time he was absent. Todd was the one who opted to keep it locked from the inside.

His goodbye letter offered little comfort. While Todd's last words provided a bit of clarity as to the actual catalyst for this act of desperation, there are no real answers.

Anyone who has experienced the brutality of a senseless loss will say that searching for complete reconciliation is a useless exercise.

Apart from losing my mother, having my sibling die at his own hands is the most painful thing with which I have been tested. It surpasses the death of my father when I was a little girl and the breakdown of my marriage shortly after the birth of my son.

Almost a year after Todd died, I was offered a job in London. I hated to entertain the thought of moving away.

"Only cowards leave" repeated in my head.

However, my mother insisted I go, so I agreed begrudgingly to give it a chance.

In hindsight, I know that this single decision saved me and continued to do so for the entire decade I remained abroad, as well as the years that followed when I finally returned home.

The irony of it was born from the epiphany that the same choice — to leave — that fueled my anger toward Todd was the lone act that provided *my* ultimate salvation.

The so-called "cowardly escape" afforded me the freedom of anonymity. No longer was I shackled by the constant reminders of the past. I had a clean slate.

Becoming a mother only continued to strengthen my journey toward forgiveness.

Actively participating in my son's development and growth these past ten years, I am able to understand that I can tell him he is loved, show him he is valued, and share with him the wisdom of experience.

But he alone will have to navigate the path his life takes. He has free will, and I can only hope that I continue to provide him with the necessary tools to cultivate a happy, fiercely independent life. In the end, he will be in charge. And I hope he will not be cowed by anything.

This quest for absolution has been an arduous but enlightening fight. I do not expect to achieve full inner peace about Todd. However, I have forgiven my twenty-year-old self for her flawed dedication to her family. And I forgive Todd for finding peace in his own way.

— Lucy Alexander —

Acceptance

*One day, I decided that I was beautiful, and so I
carried out my life as if I was a beautiful girl. It doesn't
have anything to do with how the world perceives you.*
~Gabourey Sidibe

A heap of clothing sat discarded on the bench as I wiped my
reddening eyes. "I hate my body. I hate that I'm bigger than all
the other girls. It isn't fair," I cried in the dressing room. I was
only thirteen, but I was tall and plus-size so my options were
very limited. I never fit in the clothes the other girls could wear, and
I often ended up having to wear clothes that seemed matronly to me.

I couldn't fit in any of the dresses I had brought into the changing
room in the juniors department. I loved all of them, but they were
designed to fit lean young girls.

It wasn't just my weight. As my mother had explained, we were
descended from peasant stock. This meant we had wide hips and broad
shoulders and were built for labor. I had never been small or delicate,
and deep inside I hated myself for this.

Staring at the mirror, I glared at my round belly and thick thighs.
I hugged myself, trying to cover my fleshy upper arms.

I didn't understand how this could happen to me; I ate the same
amount as the other girls. I wasn't athletic, but I wasn't lazy. I worked
hard and kept active in other ways. Yet, on more than one occasion,
I'd heard the other girls whisper "fat" and "cow" behind my back.

Standing in my underwear and bra, I continued to sob as I re-hung all the pretty dresses.

Thirty years later, a more adult version of myself stood admiring myself in the mirror in my bedroom. The black mermaid dress fit perfectly and clung to my ample curves. Clothing had most definitely evolved to include fuller-sized women. This dress made me feel glowing and vibrant.

I thought of the girl crying in the fitting room all those years ago.

I've made peace with my body over time. This body has borne two children. My thick thighs were their pillows, and my breasts nursed them.

This body survived abuse. This body carried me during the heaviest of trials. During a natural disaster, it showed me how much it could do as I lugged and heaved furniture and boxes from the bottom floor of my house, salvaging what I could of my family's belongings. My arms toiled as I ripped up carpet and repaired what I could.

My wide shoulders have lugged hundreds of pounds of soil, woodchips and plants, and toiled for hours as I transformed my yard from all sand to an urban homestead.

"I'm so sorry I didn't believe in you all those years ago," I apologized to my older self in the mirror. "I didn't know how beautiful you were back then."

—Nicole Ann Rook McAlister—

The Road to Forgiveness

We must be willing to get rid of the life we've planned,
so as to have the life that is waiting for us.
~Joseph Campbell

From the deck of my rented condo, I watched the Swallowtail butterfly frolic in the air. Almost as big as a Warbler and lemon yellow in the sunlight, he was easy to follow as he dipped and climbed, fluttered and floated. If a butterfly could feel joy, this was the most joyous butterfly I'd ever seen.

Or maybe I was seeing the joy in everything because I was so full of joy myself. It was a beautiful spring morning. The air was cool, but held the promise of summer-like heat later in the day. I had a cup of cappuccino, a dish of yogurt and berries, and hours before I needed to be anywhere. I looked around, and it occurred to me that I loved my life. I loved where I live, the friends that I've made, the work that I do, and the cat curled up by my feet. I loved the hobbies I had and the opportunities I'd created.

It wasn't always this way.

A year and a half ago, my life was very different. I lived in a different province. I had a different career. I drove a different vehicle. But the biggest difference of all was that I had a husband who abused me. I'd been married for almost twenty-five years, and while the physical violence didn't happen every day, the threat of it was always present alongside the emotional abuse.

The years had taken a toll on me. I was overweight and had

multiple health issues. I was filled with bitterness and resentment. I didn't care anymore if I lived or died. And I blamed him.

One January morning, everything changed.

There was no warning. His anger came suddenly, ferociously. By the time it passed, I was left bleeding on the floor.

My eighteen-year-old son helped me to my room, sat me down and said, "Mom, this has got to stop."

Finally, I agreed.

Despite my fear of the many obstacles we would face, we walked out the door that day, empty-handed, and never went back.

The road was long and hard. The challenges we faced as we sought to build a new life were daunting. At night, I would toss and turn, cry, and wonder if it was even worth it. I had to find a way to get beyond the pain so I could move on with my life. A voice inside my head told me I needed to forgive. But how?

How could I forgive a man who had robbed me of so much in my life? A bitter taste came with every one of life's moments that should have been sweet — our marriage, the birth of our children, every Christmas and birthday for twenty-five years — all marred by the taste of his anger. If I were to forgive him, wouldn't I be saying that what he did to me, to our family, was okay?

I spent a lot of time thinking about forgiveness. How to give it. How to ask for it. I did a lot of searching, both online and within. Then one day, I realized that forgiveness didn't mean I needed to condone the actions of my husband. All I needed to do was say, "It's in the past. It doesn't matter anymore." And I needed to believe it.

That's it.

Once I had taken that step, I could stop being the victim and start living the life I was meant to live. But there was one more thing I had to do: learn how to forgive myself. In many ways, that was harder. It was easy to blame him for everything. The truth was that I needed to accept responsibility for my own part in it. If I had left the first time he hit me, I would have been in control of my own life, and none of it would have happened.

But that's in the past. It doesn't matter anymore.

I wake up in the morning, look in the mirror, and say, "I forgive you." I made mistakes. But for every mistake I made, there was a second chance, and I'm doing my best to make the most of it.

Some of the smallest things that most people take for granted are a source of wonder and joy to me because they were denied to me for so long — and that makes me grateful.

— Sally Quon —

Seeking Forgiveness

Life can only be understood backwards;
but it must be lived forwards.
~Søren Kierkegaard

O n the Fourth of July, thirty-four years after graduating from high school, I found myself sitting at a picnic table in the park with some of my former classmates. We had come to town for an all-school reunion in honor of our town's 125th birthday.

Being the intense introvert that I am, this impromptu social event was a challenge for me. I started out nervous and tense, but I felt myself relax as our conversation centered around funny things that happened back in the day, and what our classmates were up to now.

Eventually, the conversation came around to a classmate, Janelle. Jill said, "Has anyone been in touch with Janelle?" I was surprised. It hadn't occurred to me that my classmates thought about her, too.

Diana said, "I tried to contact her for our last reunion. She was one of only three people who never responded."

Jill's face was sad as she said, "I've always felt bad about how she was treated." There was a general murmur of agreement around the table. "I called her a couple of years ago. I wanted to apologize. Janelle's voice shook when she told me she wanted nothing to do with anyone from our town. Then she told me never to contact her again. I felt terrible."

I understood where Jill was coming from. Like many people, I look back at my school years with a medley of emotions. Amazement that it was so long ago; regret about some of the choices I made; and relief that I somehow survived that difficult time.

Everyone knew everyone in our small, Midwestern town of 1,000 people. There were only forty-two kids in our grade, and we went to school with Janelle from kindergarten through our senior year of high school. Unfortunately, Janelle, or more specifically, how I treated Janelle, is one of the regrets I mentioned earlier. I wish I had made a different choice in how I acted or reacted to the situation, and I still think about it.

It had started in elementary school when Danny, a popular kid who was always looking to be the center of attention, caught a glimpse of Janelle picking her nose. Unaware that she was being watched, she slipped her finger into her mouth. Quickly, Danny nudged Rick next to him, pointed at Janelle, pantomimed gagging and said loudly, "She ate her boogers!" By the time Rick nudged Mike to tell him about it, Janelle had turned toward the boys, wide-eyed, curious to see what was going on. The boys still had the "grossed out" look on their faces. Danny pointed and exclaimed, "THAT is SO disgusting."

During recess, Danny began the taunt that was repeated by every boy on the playground. "Booger eater, booger eater, Janelle is a booger eater." Poor Janelle! I can still picture her in my mind, head down in shame. By 3:30 that day, everyone in our class knew Janelle's new nickname. By the end of the next day, everyone had called Janelle "booger eater" at least once. Granted, some of us were more reluctant to join in, but somehow we did it anyway.

"Janelle never did anything. She just kept her head down and looked sad. Unfortunately, no one else did anything either. I wish I'd had the wisdom and foresight to do something kind for Janelle back then. I wish any one of us, or all of us together, had stood up for her," said Jill. Everyone around the table agreed solemnly.

Sitting at the picnic table, I felt terrible as I realized how angry Janelle must still feel today. Why wouldn't she?

Remorse. Regret. Guilt. Sadness. Shame. I felt all of these emotions and so did my former classmates.

That conversation with my classmates played over and over in my head in the days that followed. It was obvious we all felt bad. We all wanted to ask Janelle for forgiveness. We had all thought about her through the years.

One night, out of the blue, I noticed Janelle's brother Joe on Facebook. I messaged him and explained how some classmates and I were wondering how Janelle was doing. The conversation went like this:

Joe: "Janelle is divorced, has two fantastic kids and one grandson. She is doing okay. She really doesn't want anything to do with our hometown."

Me: "I can understand that. We were all cruel to her."

Joe: "We all did stupid things when we were young." Joe went on to tell me a few details about Janelle's family and where she was living.

Me: "If the opportunity ever comes up, please tell Janelle we talked, and we are truly sorry!"

Joe: "Will do."

As I mourned my dream of making amends with Janelle, I realized how much I had enjoyed spending time with my classmates, and I had an idea.

That night, I contacted several of my classmates. "I really enjoyed seeing everyone on the Fourth. Can we get together again soon?" Five of us met at a central location a month later. We laughed, reconnected and shared fun memories. After lunch, while lingering over dessert, I shared my conversation with Janelle's brother.

Each of us shared a time when we were reminded of Janelle over the years. Jill shared how her own daughter was bullied in school. Diana shared how her son came home from school and told her about his classmate being bullied, and they talked about how he could stand up for the child being bullied. I shared how we teach acceptance and kindness in my school. Several of us had tears in our eyes as we talked. We all regretted the part we played in the bullying. When it was time to leave, Jill smiled and said, "When can we get together next?" We scheduled the next date.

Diana said, "I want to believe that, even though we cannot make amends directly to Janelle, we can at least forgive ourselves. Let's make a pact going forward to do small acts of kindness in Janelle's honor."

We hugged each other tightly with damp eyes and agreed.

I said, "I'm glad something good came out of that negative experience that happened so long ago. Although forgiveness didn't occur the way we wanted it to — with Janelle, rekindling our friendships — forgiving each other and forgiving ourselves feels good." Everyone nodded in agreement. "We can't change the past, but we can forgive and move forward."

— Debra Lynn —

Making Amends

*Getting free from the tyranny of past mistakes can
be hard work, but definitely worth the effort. And the
payoff is health, wholeness and inner peace.*
~Steve Goodier

I had achieved almost nine months of sobriety when I prepared for my ninth step — the making of amends to those I had hurt as a result of my drinking. Making amends could take the form of a simple apology over the phone or in a letter, rather than in person. I decided to take care of a particularly difficult apology over the phone. I wrote out a script so I wouldn't forget what to say. I wanted to be sure I didn't veer off my mission if he angered me or triggered me to put up my defenses. Two people who have shared an unhealthy marriage have so many dysfunctional patterns, and I didn't want to fall into any of those. I wanted to complete my mission as assigned.

However, when he answered I abandoned my script and spoke from the heart. I drew strange comfort from the sound of his voice, perhaps because it had been a mainstay in my life for so long. I still don't understand why the sound of his voice soothed me when we never shared intimacy. I knew nothing about his inner life.

I understand now I attracted this type because of the family I had grown up in. They had never met my need for emotional support and connection, so I found a spouse who neglected my emotional needs in the same way. His family did, too. So, I went from one dysfunctional family who ignored my needs to two — a double portion of suffering I brought on myself through psychological programming I had been powerless to control.

I began speaking straight away, avoiding the requisite small talk at the beginning of a conversation. I wanted to get this over with and minimize the humiliation and disappointment when he refused to forgive me.

"I wanted to tell you I'm sorry for my part in the marriage breaking down. I didn't know how to control my emotions, which caused a lot of problems for us, so I wanted to take responsibility for that."

The tears came now out of sheer humiliation. I was so tired of working this step in the program and felt misled by the promise that it would change my relationships. I waited for another non-response, the silent shrug, as I revealed further evidence of my lack of mental soundness, giving ammunition to the people who had the power to hurt me most.

"Well, I do, too," he said. What? I sat up. "I take responsibility for my part, too. There's a lot I could have done that I didn't, and I regret that, too." And then the kicker, "You know I've always thought very highly of you, and that hasn't changed. It takes a big person to apologize."

I sat stunned because he was the last person I believed would give me credit for anything. To be fair, he had the most reason of anyone to mistrust me. I was an alcoholic, after all, and I had done plenty to hurt him, at least as much as he had done to hurt me. Where he had hurt me through lack of attention, I had hurt him through too much of it: complaining and demanding to be heard. It was my parents' relationship all over again, and probably his, too. I thanked him, and we talked about the kids for a few more minutes before we hung up.

The next week, he took our daughter for an orthodontist appointment and texted me to ask if it was okay for her to get braces on her teeth. We knew she'd need them, but didn't know when. I said fine, and when I asked how much they cost so I could pay half, expecting a monthly amount, he said he'd taken care of it. "I gave them the whole amount in a lump sum to avoid paying interest," he said. "So, don't worry about it."

I considered how to make amends to my daughters, too. It would be easy to apologize to them; I did that often now, as I embraced humility and earned their trust. I worried, however, that I might harm them by dredging up the past and creating a heavy atmosphere when they were beginning to enjoy a sane and sober mom. I remembered amends need not be an apology. I decided that, rather than words, I'd use actions to earn their forgiveness — by nurturing them in a special way.

We had two bathrooms on the upper floor of our townhouse, both with bathtubs. I announced they were getting a spa treatment and ran the water in both bathtubs at the same time, pouring scented bubble bath into each one. They lapped up the attention as I travelled between the two bathrooms, lathering shampoo into their little heads, scrubbing tiny toes with pumice, applying face masks, and providing reading material while they lounged in their respective bathtubs after their treatments.

I had never seen them more relaxed or happy, and the serene faces reflected children doing their best to behave like adults — real ladies at a spa. It cracked me up. The power of a simple act of love that cost nothing made me realize these children needed little more. Each act stacked on top of the other creating a child with confidence because she believed she mattered. Primed to receive love, they forgave readily without realizing anything needed forgiving.

The wordless amends to my children gave me intense pleasure, and I experienced, for the first time, the honor of taking care of them rather than the burden. Being their mother was not a sacrifice or something I had to do at the expense of myself. Caring for them gave me a life mission: to love them unconditionally, without fear or expectation. My jobs or personal goals no longer mattered as much as making sure these children knew they were loved.

Having grown up with an emotionally abusive mother, I had concluded that loving one's children must be very hard — a choice between one's self and them. Only one of our needs could be met, and motherhood meant sacrifice on a Mother Teresa scale. But I knew now that mothering was a noble calling. If my children felt loved and reasonably happy, it would be the greatest accomplishment of my life.

— Laura Connell —

Getting All the Facts

67

Now I Get It

*It is the highest form of self-respect to admit our errors
and mistakes and make amends for them.*
~Dale E. Turner

After my mother died, I had an irrational hope that I would find a note in her journals saying she loved me. As I sorted through her accumulation of eighty-four years of living, I did find journals, but there was never a mention of me. Her writings were all about my brother, who had been the primary focus of her attention.

I grieved her death deeply, but I was also a pathetic woman in her fifties still craving her mother's time, attention, and approval. Her death meant I would never have those, and I would need to find a way not just to accept, but to forgive my mother. I had no idea how to forgive someone who was no longer alive, but I knew I must find peace with the relationship.

I was the third of four children, a quiet, mousy child whose only attribute seemed to be keeping quiet and not making trouble. I wasn't the pretty one, the smart one or the one with special needs. I felt invisible. My brother was born almost five years after me. Although it wasn't obvious at first, it became apparent eventually that my brother had intellectual disabilities. His needs superseded all else as we circled the wagons to take care of him.

David became the family focus, and I tried to become the best sister possible by teaching him words, taking him places, and sacrificing so he could have whatever he needed. In my mind, I became more than his sister; I was his protector and caregiver. I loved my brother sincerely, but in the back of my mind was an unsaid hope I might win approval and attention from my parents if I became the perfect sister. It never happened.

My life was intertwined with my brother's in a way that exceeded the normal sibling bond. When I left for college, I packed up my clothes and a bag full of guilt. I longed for the freedom college promised, but I worried about how David would deal with being the last child left at home. He had been raised with three sisters and all their friends and activities; it was going to be a quiet, lonely house now. I was entering an exciting time in my life, having experiences my brother would never have. My joys in life were always tempered with concern for my brother. My freedom was limited, closely tethered to my brother.

My brother's life became more difficult as he became an adult. He was plagued with increased physical pain and a diagnosis of schizophrenia. Having aged out of the public-school system, he faced a void. There was no plan for adults with intellectual disabilities in our community. He began acting out violently, and I was often the recipient of his physical anger, sustaining a black eye, sprained ankle and numerous bruises during several outbursts. As a mother with young children, I distanced myself to protect them, but also because the entire situation was becoming increasingly unpleasant.

My children rarely had their grandmother's attention, and although I was an adult and should have been beyond it, I still wished I had a mother who wanted to spend time with me. I envied friends who had mothers with whom they shopped and lunched, mothers who were their friends. I especially wished my children had a grandmother to dote on them. I fantasized about the fictional Norman Rockwell family holidays. Instead, our family get-togethers were rife with stress and, as always, centered on my brother. Would he become enraged and hit someone? Would he stuff himself and then throw up violently? Would my mother spend the entire holiday catering to my brother's every whim? The answer was almost always "yes" to all of these scenarios. I longed for normalcy, unaware it exists only in fiction.

When my mother received the diagnosis of pancreatic cancer, she knew her time was limited. As with most parents of children with disabilities, her first concern was her son. Although he was finally happy — living in a home where he had a job, friends and twenty-four-hour care — my mother cushioned his life with frequent visits, weekends home, endless phone calls and gifts. She worried about who would love and visit him, and what he would do on holidays. Would he understand she was gone, or would he feel abandoned?

I assured her I would do my best to step into her role, but why would she believe me? I had done very little to help in the last twenty years. I had barely acknowledged her struggles as a mother of a child with special needs, selfishly fixated on what she wasn't giving me instead of asking what I could do to lighten her burden. She transferred legal guardianship of my brother to me, and explained tearfully but calmly to David that she was dying. She died two days later.

I took over the guardianship role somewhat begrudgingly, just going through the motions. In the beginning, he called too many times a day. One day, it was twenty-two times! I put a smile on my face and made the visits, taking him to Walmart, and out for lunch and ice cream. Soon, I learned limits would need to be set, boundaries my mother never had with David. I set a budget of twenty dollars for each shopping trip, and he adapted well to the challenge. I also didn't want him to eat until he threw up, which seemed reasonable to me, but it was a limit my mother was never able to set. As trivial as it seemed, the endless phone calls were an irritant, and we reached an agreement that he would call me once every evening unless there was a problem. Setting boundaries eased the tensions for me and allowed me to begin enjoying time with my brother.

In the ten years since my mother died, he and I have grown considerably closer. What started out as an obligation has become a pleasurable experience as my brother and I find new ways to reconnect, and I learn what it means to be "his person." The years have flown by, and the distinction between being his sister and his mother has begun to blur.

I understand my mother more fully now. She did love me, but the needs of my brother were overwhelming, and her limited resources had to be allocated where they were needed most. Like a triage physician, she tended to the most wounded first and assumed those who weren't visibly traumatized were fine.

I wish I'd been a better daughter during those tough times, but until I walked these years in her "mother" shoes, I couldn't understand the burden she was carrying or the deep love and responsibility she felt for David. I hope she hears me now when I say, "I love you, Mom. Not only do I forgive you, but I understand!" I can't undo the past, but through loving my brother, I think she hears my message loud and clear.

— Diane Morrow-Kondos —

68

Reframing Road Rage

*What wisdom can you find that is greater
than kindness?*
~Jean-Jacques Rousseau

Most of us know that on any well-traveled highway there's a chance we'll encounter an unexpected stretch of bumper-to-bumper traffic. I'd just passed Olympia on my way to Seattle when the backup began. No flashing lights, no fire trucks, no police to explain the cause.

I was in the far left lane when I saw the sign that read: "Left two lanes closed ahead due to road construction."

Slowly, drivers in my lane begin merging to the right. When my turn came, I tried to edge into the right lane, but a large, white SUV would have none of it even though everyone else had been politely alternating.

I moved closer to the cones marking the end of my lane, this time putting the nose of my car ever-so-slightly into the other lane as if to say, "I'm not really asking." The driver in the white SUV moved up again, preventing me from merging, and gave me the finger. I responded with a gesture I like to offer drivers who fail to share the road — two thumbs-up and facial expressions that make it clear this is sarcasm. The driver responded by lowering his window.

I knew I wasn't supposed to engage. What if he had a gun? But I rolled down my window anyway. I encouraged him to move along as I was sure I'd find a nicer driver behind him. He pointed and yelled at me to get in. My response was sprinkled with expletives. He yelled again and commanded me to get in. Conscious of the scene we were performing for the drivers behind us, I moved my car reluctantly into his lane.

I took some deep, calming breaths, reducing the disturbing level of heat on my face. I drank some water, turned up the radio, and then realized that this lane was going to end, too. Refusing to risk another incident, I found an opening and merged right. But guess who didn't? I glanced over at the doomed lane to my left and saw — him.

A wave of anxiety washed over me as I wiped my sweaty palms on my jeans. Next thing I knew, he was rolling down his window.

Were we going to do this again? I worked quickly to generate the proper selection of witty yet insulting replies to whatever offensive remark he would throw my way. I rolled down my window. I imagined the drivers around us who had witnessed our last encounter rolling down their windows too, braced for a worthy spectacle, their phones set to video mode.

Before I could launch into our inevitable F-bomb volley, he cut me off with these words: "I'm sorry."

My guard lowered and my shoulders relaxed as my eyes focused on an attractive man in a white SUV who was apologizing for his behavior.

"I've been driving since California, and I'm so tired. I'm really sorry."

"I am, too! It's such a frustrating situation. I'm so sorry I over-reacted," I said.

We smiled at one another for that frozen moment — me amazed by the courage it took for him to express himself so openly, and him for recognizing my sincere appreciation for this unexpected moment of humanity we were privileged to share.

I gestured for him to go in front of me.

"Oh, it's okay. Go ahead," he said, still making amends.

"No, really — your lane's about to end. Come on in."

I waved once more as he moved into my lane, still reeling from the profound impact of the experience. The tightness in my muscles and the throbbing pressure of the blood moving through my body were replaced immediately with peace and a restored sense of hope that just maybe a future exists where we live up to the term "humankind."

— Shari Getz —

69

The Mean Girl

Everyone has untold stories of pain and sadness that
make them love and live a little differently than you
do. Stop judging; instead, try to understand.
~Author Unknown

I was standing in my dad's biology classroom after school, looking at a list of students being considered for Camp Skyline. Skyline was a special yearly retreat that only certain students got to attend. My oldest brother had gotten to go, and I desperately wanted to follow in his footsteps. Unfortunately, it was my senior year, and I still hadn't been nominated.

"Ew, why is Kayla on here?" I asked, my face scrunched up like I'd just tasted prune juice.

Dad's response to my question was perfectly legitimate: "Why are you looking at a private list that doesn't belong to you?"

He had me there. I grumbled something about the list being out in the open where anyone could see it, and then sat down to start my calculus homework. After a minute, Dad seemed to take pity on me.

"Skyline isn't just for academically gifted students, you know. It's also a place for people to clear their heads and sort out the issues in their lives. There are lots of reasons students get selected besides good grades."

I grunted and kept working. I already knew grades alone didn't get one into Skyline. If they did, my 4.0 GPA would've earned me a nomination years ago.

"It's an amazing experience," Dad added wistfully. As a staff member, he'd attended the camp numerous times. "Michael was lucky enough to go. I always hoped you would be, too."

That makes two of us, I thought. But, apparently, once again, I hadn't made the cut. I probably wouldn't have felt so bad if I hadn't seen Kayla's name on the list.

I'd known Kayla for almost four years. We took many of the same honors-level classes. Aside from being smart, Kayla was also pretty. Her mixed racial background gave her long, dark curls and smooth, mocha-colored skin. She definitely wasn't hurting for friends, either. A loud crowd of laughing groupies seemed to follow her no matter where she was headed, whether it was the cafeteria or the bathroom.

Being intelligent, beautiful, and popular would've been enough for most people, but not Kayla. She had to be one more thing on top of it all: The. Meanest. Girl. On. The. Planet.

She always seemed to be making fun of my friends and me — what we were wearing, how we talked, what "dumb" expressions we happened to have on our faces at any given moment.

Her cruelty wasn't limited to my social group, either — or even the human species. One time, during German class, a bird smashed into the window and died. While everyone else stood there horrified, Kayla started laughing because the bird "looked stupid when it hit the glass."

That's just who she was.

Or so I thought.

About a month after spotting the Skyline list, I was once again working in my dad's classroom after school when Kayla walked in unexpectedly. Quickly, I ducked my head, hoping she wouldn't say something mean. Thankfully, she ignored me and headed for the phone in the corner. I wondered if she had permission to use it, but wasn't about to draw her attention (or wrath) by asking.

As I sat by the stinky turtle tank, outlining my AP English paper, Kayla made her call. I'm not sure what it was about. I was honestly trying my hardest not to eavesdrop.

But blocking out the conversation became impossible when the woman on the other end of the line started screaming at Kayla so loudly that I could hear every syllable.

Kayla tried to reason with her, but the screaming continued. Mean words. Nasty words. Words Kayla herself had said many times about my friends and me.

Stupid. Dumb. Idiot. Loser.

I tried to make myself deaf and invisible at the same time. When the call finally ended, Kayla rushed from the room without looking in my direction. Her cheeks were red, but I don't think she was crying. I would've been.

While I attempted to go back to work on my English paper, the phone call haunted me. I kept wondering if the screaming woman was Kayla's mother. My own mother never would've said those words to me, no matter how badly I screwed up. I felt something I never thought I'd feel for my archenemy — pity.

Quickly, I shook away the thought. No. This was Kayla. The Mean Girl. After all the snide comments and haughty looks she'd thrown my way, she didn't deserve any emotion except contempt.

A few weeks went by and I'd mostly forgotten about the phone call. I was walking to lunch one afternoon when I spotted a spiral notebook lying in the hallway. There was no name on the cover, so I decided to take it to the office.

I'd only walked a few feet when a piece of paper slipped out and swooped to the floor. The page had a short paragraph typed on it, and a single name jumped out at me from the text: Kayla.

I knew I had no right to read it, but Kayla's latest disparaging remark was still fresh in my mind. Apparently, only "hicks" wore overalls. Well, maybe "hicks" also read papers that were carelessly left out in the hallway for anyone to find.

Smirking, I began to read.

In just a few short words, Kayla described how she felt about being of mixed racial heritage. She was black when she was with her black friends and white when she was with her white friends, but she never really fit with either group. I was shocked to learn that her skin color, which I had always seen as beautiful, was actually a source of isolation, confusion and low self-esteem for her.

Carefully, I slipped the paper back into the notebook.

I didn't know what to do with the information I'd just learned. Kayla, the girl who never went anywhere without an entire posse, felt alone in a way I could never possibly understand.

As I walked down the hallway, Dad's words about Camp Skyline came back: "It's a place for people to clear their heads, sort out the issues in their lives."

For the first time, I realized what he meant. Skyline wasn't a prize to be won. It was a haven for kids who needed help. Kids who were confused or sad. Kids whose mom screamed nasty words at them. Kids like Kayla.

Instead of resenting her for stealing my spot, I suddenly found myself actually hoping she'd get selected. Maybe it would heal the wounds those nasty words had left on her. Maybe she'd finally find a place she truly belonged.

As high school drew to a close, Kayla and I weren't exactly friends, but she did start being a little nicer, and I stopped calling her my archenemy. Looking back now, I don't even think of her as "The Mean Girl" anymore. I think of her as the girl who taught me one of the greatest lessons of my life: It's easy to judge other people. To write them off as mean, stupid, lazy, incompetent. It's much harder — and far more worthwhile — to try to understand them.

— Gretchen Bassier —

70

My Mother the Alcoholic?

*The eye sees only what the mind
is prepared to comprehend.*
~Henri Bergson

My mother, an alcoholic, disappeared in 1969 when I was twenty years old. Divorced from my father and losing custody of my two younger brothers, she left town abruptly with a man she met in a bar.

She left behind five children and an accumulation of angry and bitter memories. It took a crisis in my adult life to get me into therapy. There, I could finally admit to myself and others how growing up in an alcoholic home had affected me.

Quickly, I discovered that although my mother had disappeared, many of the behaviors our family had developed during her drinking years had not. I learned to identify those behaviors. I learned about the disease of alcoholism. I began to attend workshops for adult children of alcoholics. For the first time in my life, I felt a part of something positive. My life went from being crisis-oriented to serene — something I had never experienced before.

In 1985, sixteen years later, I received a call from a social worker in Florida.

"We have found your mother!" he said.

It seemed my mother had been found unconscious in a deserted building.

Suddenly, I was face-to-face with my newfound beliefs on alcoholism.

It was one thing to accept alcoholism as a disease when the alcoholic is no longer in your life. It is quite another to confront the alcoholic. Before she left, my mother had been verbally abusive and embarrassing. Could I live with that again?

On the phone, the social worker gave me the facts: homeless... living on the streets... found in that deserted house... alone ... unconscious... dirty... rats! My serenity began to disappear as panic moved in.

I recalled what my mother had looked like before her disappearance. Her complexion had been pasty, her abdomen extended by liver damage. She had looked old and haggard.

I debated with myself. What were my obligations to a mother who had chosen to stop being a mother to me? One minute, I pictured her as the angry drunk; the next minute, I was remembering a different person, the one she was before she became a victim of alcoholism.

I did have good memories from my early childhood, but I had shoved those into the recesses of my brain, refusing to see any good in a person who would choose alcohol over her own children.

The social worker gave me more facts: without a family member involved, she would be lost in the system... placed in a group home... she could wander out... become homeless again. She had no other connections, no money, no place to live... She didn't even have a pair of shoes.

I turned to others for advice. My brothers wanted nothing to do with a mother who had deserted them. My sister was supportive and agreed to help me in whatever way she could, but she was dealing with a new baby. My husband said, "Do what is best for you." What was best for me? I had spent years hating my mother, feeling deserted, practicing dysfunctional behaviors that I had learned as a child growing up in an alcoholic environment. I thought I had finally come to accept the past. But had I? There were still missing pieces. Where had she been for the last sixteen years? Why had she never tried to contact us?

I knew that despite my fear of seeing my mother again, the only way to put an end to the past was to face it. I flew to Florida.

Suddenly, the answers took shape. I discovered that two years after leaving home, my mother had collapsed in Florida and been rushed to a hospital. At that time, she had undergone brain surgery to remove a tumor. The removal of the tumor had caused her to lose her long-term memory. Upon her release from the hospital, she lived with the same man who had been with her when she disappeared. She believed she was married to him and used his last name. They had lived together in poverty until her care became too much for him, and he deserted her. The social worker had tracked down the man through an old letter. From him, she learned where my mother's family lived and started making calls. My oldest brother was the only one still living in our hometown and referred the call to me.

Doctors' reports explained that the type of brain tumor my mother had removed had probably been affecting her behavior for seven years before her disappearance. I realized then that much of the erratic behavior we had blamed on alcoholism had, in fact, been the result of the tumor.

She could remember nothing that had happened after the formation and removal of the tumor. She believed she had four children, not remembering the birth of my youngest brother. She thought her children still ranged in age from seven to nineteen. She had never tried to contact us because she didn't know where we were. I left the social worker feeling stunned and sad for all the wasted years.

I was also scared! I had heard all the facts, but I still hadn't faced my mother. And as much as I understood the facts on an intellectual level, I was having a difficult time differentiating between my mother the victim and my mother the angry, abusive drunk. I still pictured her as an overpowering person who had total control over my feelings.

I ran up a $200 phone bill getting support from my Al-Anon friends back home before I finally found the courage to go to my mother.

She was not the angry, abusive woman who had disappeared sixteen years before. Neither was she the alert, interested mother I could remember vaguely from my early childhood. She was an old woman. She cried when she first saw me and held out her arms. As I moved into them, I realized the past was over. Alcoholism had prevented our family from identifying the signs of a brain tumor in my mother. Alcoholism had split our family for sixteen years. Alcoholism had done enough damage. It was time to move on. My mother was no longer capable of hurting anyone. She needed to be cared for, and I had to make a decision — not as a lonely, scared child, but as a competent adult.

I made that decision and flew home with my mother. She lived in a nursing home close to my house for another sixteen years before she passed away.

She was confused often. She never remembered those years of alcoholism, and I am glad for that. She was not the mother of my childhood, but I did come to love her again, and I cherish the final years we had together.

—Judith Hackbarth—

The Man with the Mohawk

The unlikeliest people harbor halos beneath their hats.
~Author Unknown

Springing from the driver's door of the old dually pickup he had parked, a man in his twenties trotted across the street toward me. "How you doin'?" he said. He was shirtless and tanned, clad in shorts and work boots, with his hair cut in a Mohawk. He had several other guys with him.

"Great," I said unenthusiastically, despite thinking, *What the hell do you want?*

Moments earlier, blaring music announced the slow-rolling truck coming around the bend at the wrong time to suit me. Yes, I judged them, with no reasons beyond my state of mind, their bad timing, and my fifty-year-old bias against their appearance. That day, at that moment, these strangers were the last thing I wanted to deal with.

Our neighborhood was on a peninsula jutting into the Back Bay of Biloxi, Mississippi. We didn't fare well when Hurricane Katrina brought thirty feet of water across it. Since moving back onto our lot to live in a tent a couple of weeks after the storm, we had watched the tourists roll through, gawking at the debris strewn where upscale homes stood no more. We'd smile and wave, say "thanks" for their good wishes, and then get back to work trying to find anything salvageable.

This day, as I dug through the rubble, my mind was on old family photographs. A half-hour before the truck pulled up, I recalled one picture in particular. Its disappearance deflated me, occupied my mind, and disrupted my progress. It was a single snapshot on Disneyland's Main Street in 1984: my beaming mother standing arm-in-arm and cheek-to-cheek with Mickey Mouse. Maybe the park employee portraying Mickey struck that pose a hundred times each day, but the pure joy on my mother's face showed the once-in-a-lifetime thrill it gave her. She died two years after that photo was taken.

Remembering that lost image brought a rush of memories of other pictures I'd never see again. I was standing there engaged in my self-pity and reflection when the man in the Mohawk walked up to me, extending his hand for a shake.

"Hello, sir, my name is John." I exchanged his firm grip as he stared directly into my eyes.

I didn't introduce myself in return. Coldly, I asked, "What do you need, John?"

"Well, we were just driving around looking for a way to help and saw you out here working. We're here to work for you!"

Seemingly every day, someone stopped by with requests ranging from taking our debris to sell as salvage to asking boldly for money. While there were literally hundreds of legitimate people who helped, those unofficial offers made me grow suspicious.

"No, thanks, I'm good." I kept sweeping the section I'd been working, hoping he'd just go away.

"You sure? We'll do anything you need."

"Yeah, I'm sure. I'm good. Thanks." It was perhaps the lamest lie ever told. At that moment, a look around our lot explained better than words the true depth of our needs. John's face showed he knew I was full of it, but he didn't challenge me.

"We just got in after driving down nonstop from Pennsylvania. We're looking for anyone we can find who needs help."

"Pennsylvania?" I cast a doubtful look at his license plate, only to confirm the registration. The distance they'd traveled wasn't what caught me off guard. It was what came next.

"Yes, sir. We've been watching the news almost constantly since Katrina hit. We saw on TV what happened here, and we wanted to do something. Our church began collecting food and clothing, but we felt God drawing us here to start helping people now. So, my buddies and I piled into my truck and left. Drove straight through all night. Here we are!"

I felt horrible that I had originally treated these men less honorably than they deserved. Like everyone on the Coast, I needed more help than I could ever find.

"No, thanks. I really appreciate it, I do. But I'm sure you'll find somebody pretty quickly who needs a lot more help than me."

I looked at the other fellows in the crew cab and bed of the truck, about six guys, seeing them in a much different light than moments before. Originally, I had misinterpreted their eager stances as a bunch of guys looking to party. Now, I saw it was actually their eagerness to spring into helpful action. Still feeling horrible about myself, I declined their offer one last time. There was resignation in John's face.

"May I ask your name, sir?" he asked. I told him. He reached his hand toward me again for what I assumed to be a goodbye handshake. When I grabbed it, something was in his palm. I flinched. He clasped our hands, holding them together with his free hand.

"Mr. Livingston, God loves you. He wants you to have this, and He wants to remind you of the blessing of our meeting. We are all blessed to have met you, sir. Please know that we'll be praying for you." Paper pressed between our hands, and I suspected it was money. I let go and looked to see what he'd given me: a one-hundred-dollar bill. "Have faith. God will get you through this."

"No, John, I can't… I can't take this," I stammered, believing he and his boys needed the money much more than we did.

"Please, take it. It's not much, I know, but it's from our church, please."

"No, John, no. It's a wonderful gesture, really, but…"

"Please, sir. If you won't let us work for you, use this toward a chainsaw or gas for your generator. You'll find a good use for it." He began walking away, already waving while I stood there, dumbfounded. "Know that it comes with all our prayers for your recovery. God bless!"

I collapsed into a folding chair, physically and emotionally spent by those few minutes in a way I've rarely known, for reasons I've never fully understood. Before I learned his last name or how to contact him, they were gone.

Few moments through our Hurricane Katrina experience touched me like my encounter with John that day. Fourteen years later, our meeting lingers with me still. There were many angels like John who came to help us. I learned about the goodness of strangers, but more importantly, I learned not to judge someone based on appearance and my own biases.

—Alan Livingston—

Replacing Blame with Gratitude

We cannot embrace God's forgiveness if we are so busy
clinging to past wounds and nursing old grudges.
~T.D. Jakes

Twenty-six years ago, my husband and I were engaged when I found out I was pregnant. It was a complete surprise that we welcomed with open arms. We moved up the date, had a beautiful wedding, and began planning for the arrival of our baby. We both had careers and a nice place to live. Life was perfect.

I went to my first doctor's appointment when I was nine weeks along. He was recommended and seemed to be a good doctor. It was a very difficult pregnancy. I gained ninety-one pounds, had eclampsia, gestational diabetes and bleeding stretch marks from a rash that started late in my pregnancy.

When Chris's blue, lifeless body was pulled out of me, he was floppy and did not cry. The diagnosis: cerebral palsy.

I was twenty-two years old, and I was angry and wanted vengeance. My search for an attorney was on. In 1993, there was no Google so all my research was done at the library. I also sought word-of-mouth recommendations. Soon, we signed a contract with an attorney, and that began an eight-year journey during which I constantly relived my pregnancy and the birth of my son.

There was deposition after deposition. Doctors, nurses, and hospital staff were interviewed. They called in my son's current doctors and dug deep. After eight long years, it couldn't be proven that my doctor mismanaged my pregnancy and caused the cerebral palsy. We felt defeated and disappointed. Right or wrong, I wanted this man to be held accountable and to suffer like my family had.

It took me a while to come to grips with the verdict and the final meeting with our attorney was very emotional. As the attorney returned all the boxes of charts and files to me, she told me a fact that she had withheld. My doctor had a daughter with severe cerebral palsy. The lawyer knew that this information might have altered my decision about moving forward with the lawsuit.

I was shocked and in complete disbelief. This man was dealing with the same thing I was!

One thing became crystal clear: I needed to let go of the past eight years. For complete closure, I needed to dig deep in my heart and completely forgive the doctor. It was a process, but it needed to be done.

After three months of reading my Bible, prayer and research, I found myself sitting in my car in front of the doctor's home. I sat there and cried, and I asked God to forgive me for what I had put this man through. Then I found myself actually thanking this doctor for helping to bring my biggest blessing into this world.

Immediately, I felt at peace. I let go of my anger and instead felt gratitude for my son. This was so different from forgiving a friend for something hurtful; this came from deep in my heart. Whether that doctor had a daughter with special needs or not no longer mattered. Even if he hadn't been in the same position as we were, I realized that I wanted to forgive him for any mistakes he might have made.

— Gina Insinna-Rice —

73

What She Couldn't Remember

What mental health needs is more sunlight,
more candor, more unashamed conversations about
illnesses that affect not only the individuals,
but their family as well.
~Glenn Close

She was cruel. She was scary. And she was my mother. At nine years old, one doesn't understand a lot. And like most families in the 1960s, we didn't talk about mental illness. So whenever my mother lost touch with reality, or descended into a horrific psychotic episode, my parents would blame it on something. By the time I turned nine, the blame fell regularly on me.

I was often terrified to alight from the school bus after a day of learning because I never knew which mother I'd be greeted by. Some days, she wouldn't talk to me; other days, she'd scream and cry and call me horrible names — accusing me of getting up to all sorts of evil and dirty things. Much of the time, I had no idea what she was talking about, but she told me I was bad, so I must have done something wrong.

On other days, she'd bake cookies or a pie, or make my favorite dinner. She'd go to parent/teacher nights and come home beaming and proud of my achievements. Life with my mother was an emotional roller coaster, and whenever there were good times, I learned they wouldn't last.

By the time I was fourteen, my mother had long stretches when she didn't know who I was. During one chilling telephone conversation when she was in hospital, she told me I wasn't her daughter. I bawled my eyes out, trying to convince her that I was.

Turns out, my mother suffered with schizophrenia and what doctors then called manic depression (now called bipolar disorder). They were fancy, convoluted words for a kid to comprehend. She was in and out of psych wards from the time I was eight until I was sixteen. I became a nomad, bouncing around the homes of friends and relatives, never really feeling welcome or at home. Meanwhile, I only knew that my mother was the meanest person I'd ever met, and my hatred for her was fueled by fear.

Never in a million years did I think I could ever forgive my mother for taking away my childhood. I left home as soon as I was able; I attended college in another city so I didn't have to see her. I flip-flopped between avoiding her and showering her with gifts and tokens of affection. After all the pain and trauma inflicted on me, I still pined for my mother's love.

Over the years, I spent a lot of time and money on psychotherapy in an attempt to decipher my own feelings and hurts. I knew I needed to heal in order to move forward and build a healthier relationship with my mom. By the time I hit my thirties, my mother's psychotic episodes were muted and far less frequent. But when her illness was unleashed, it was impossible to reason or negotiate with her. I was still frightened of her, and I was still unable to forgive.

After much hesitation and apprehension, I decided to confront my mother. I needed to share with her how much she'd hurt me. Whether I was looking for closure, deeper understanding, or even retribution, I wasn't sure. I knew I didn't want to hurt her, and I was counseled to be very cautious with my approach.

One day, I invited my mom to my apartment. I brewed some tea, and we sat together on my sofa. I was absolutely terrified as to how to start.

"Mom, do you remember when I was a kid, and you were sick? Do you remember the things you did and said to me?"

She stared at me. Shuddering with fear, I kept going.

"Those names you called me? Even in public, in front of people? In front of my friends?"

Her expression was blank.

"How you threw things at me and hit me? How you'd attack me when I'd come home from school?"

Her eyelids dropped, her gaze focused on the floor.

"You told me I wasn't your daughter! Do you know how much that messed me up? I was terrified of you!"

I searched her face for some recognition, even a smidgen of recall. Nothing. We sat in silence. I was lost.

Finally, she spoke. "I… don't."

How could I continue with the confrontation given that answer? I hadn't considered that I might not get the satisfaction or the closure I thought I deserved.

"You don't remember all those awful things you did to me when you were sick?"

She sat, staring off into space. "No… there's so much I don't remember… I had shock treatments, so many. I was so sick. I really…"

Seriously? I thought. *She can't own up to her actions even now?* I realized that all my expectations for this conversation, this breakthrough, were dashed.

Then my mom began to speak, slowly and carefully. "I would never, ever hurt you. How could I hurt you? You're my daughter, and I love you forever."

"Mom, you hurt me. All I wanted was for you to love me, and instead you were unbearably cruel."

I wanted her to know that I swallowed a handful of her pain medication. I slept for two days straight, and she didn't notice. I thought of showing her the scars on my wrists from the times I had tried to let out the pain. I wanted to tell her that I was so embarrassed and afraid of her that I could never invite friends over. But I realized that to do so would be as cruel as she'd been to me. I was lucid and well, whereas she had been mentally and emotionally ill.

She turned to me, and her brow furrowed. "I do love you. I love you more than anything in the world. But somehow… I… I don't remember. I don't know what I did. I'm sorry. So, so sorry."

I gazed into her eyes, and I saw her confusion. She was owning up in the only way she could — by apologizing for the impact of things she couldn't even recall. There was no terrifying monster mother here. Instead, there was deep sadness and resignation that something had gone horribly wrong.

I realized that this incomplete resolution was all I was going to experience. And I had to learn to forgive what I still couldn't fully comprehend. My mom and I came to a quiet understanding that I could never forget what she'd done to me, and she would never remember.

But there's a world of difference between forgiving and forgetting. I forgave my mom that day, and while I can never forget, I learned to appreciate where she'd been and how frustrating it was for her — a bright, creative, funny woman fighting an illness that can kill relationships, families, and everyone who suffers with it.

Twenty-plus years later, my mom was eighty-seven and dying. I had fallen asleep at her bedside when I awoke to shouting.

"Cat!" my mom yelled. I jumped in shock. "Cat! I love you!"

When I was a child, my mother shouting at me would have frozen me with fear. Instead, I laughed. "I love you, too, Mom. Thank you."

— Cat Jerome —

74

Rock-Solid Apology

*A child seldom needs a good talking
to as a good listening to.*
~Robert Brault

I looked around the crowded waiting room at the hospital and sighed. Would the doctor be able to see my eight-year-old son next? I tried steadying the icepack over his forehead, but it was no use. I couldn't stop shaking. The gash in his forehead was deep, but at least blood wasn't pouring from the wound anymore. I pushed his damp hair back where drops of dried blood had matted his bangs.

Luke said, "It's okay, Mom. I can hold it myself."

His face streaked with tears, he seemed really brave for his age.

"Are you sure?" My voice cracked. I fought back the urge to cry.

"Yes." He nodded. "It doesn't hurt as much."

I handed him the icepack, and he covered his forehead with it. He was doing a much better job than I had.

We were at the hospital because another child had thrown a rock at Luke during recess as he was running around the corner. His teacher called me, and when I picked him up, I found him in her lap. His teacher was caring for his wound, trying to keep him calm. She felt terrible about what had happened, but I knew none of it was her fault.

Luke received four stitches and didn't cry once throughout the whole ordeal. For the next two days, his eye was swollen shut and black and blue. I felt like I'd had a mini nervous breakdown. Every time I tried to sleep or tend to housework, horrible thoughts crept into my mind. What if he'd lost his eye? What if he'd had brain damage? His doctor assured me he was going to be fine, but the what-ifs kept coming. Fear had taken over, and then the fear turned to anger. I was angry with the child who'd thrown the rock. I just couldn't shake it. What was she thinking? She should've known better.

Luke's principal and teacher called me that evening to see how he was feeling. His principal gave me their insurance information for the medical bills and told me Katie felt terrible. She assured me that she'd spoken with Katie and her mom. They were heartbroken over what had happened. She said Katie was really a good kid, and she'd never been in trouble before. She asked me if there was anything else she could do.

"Well, just make her understand that she can't do that," I said. "Remind her of the dangers of throwing rocks." She agreed that she would speak to her again, which made me feel better.

I noticed that as Luke started to heal physically, I wasn't as angry. After a few days, even though he still had stitches, he was almost back to normal. The swelling was gone, and the black-and-blue coloring under his eye was fading.

I thought about Katie and Luke. I wanted to stand up for my son, do the right thing, protect him, but I didn't want to mistreat Katie in order to do that. I knew her because I substitute teach, and Katie really was a nice kid. She'd explained to the principal how she'd seen the rock sticking up out of the ground and was afraid that other kids would trip over it. So, without thinking, she picked it up, hoping to throw it out of the way, and that happened to be just as Luke was running around the corner.

When I was Katie's age, I was playing around and threw a rock up into the air just as a car came down the street. It hit the roof of the car. The driver stopped suddenly and was furious. I tried to explain that I hadn't meant to hit their car, but he wasn't buying it. It really was an accident. I would never damage someone's property. I had been impulsive and wasn't thinking. I was lucky he didn't tell my parents. I would've gotten into a lot of trouble. I felt terrible about it, and even worse that he hadn't believed me. He thought I'd done it on purpose.

This was different, because I truly believed Katie.

Luke's teacher stopped by to see how he was feeling and dropped off a get-well card that Katie had made. It said:

Dear Luke:
I'm so sorry for what happened. I did not mean to hit you. I promise if you knew me, I would never do anything like that. I've been so worried about you. I hope you are ok. I'm so sorry, please forgive me!
Sorry,
Katie

Luke and I read it several times, and I couldn't help but feel a little choked up. It was a sincere apology.

I wanted this to be a teachable moment for Luke. I wanted him to learn about forgiveness, not holding grudges, or holding onto anger. I wanted to let go of my own anger, too. I also wanted Katie to understand that mistakes happen, and it's good to own up to them like she did. I asked Luke if he was ready to forgive her. After all, his opinion counted the most. He thought about it for a moment, smiled and said, "Yes." He knew she hadn't done it on purpose. Children are so resilient, so honest. They don't hold onto resentment like adults do sometimes. Their hearts are pure, so we wrote her a letter together.

Dear Katie:
We really appreciated your get-well card and apology. We have to admit when it first happened, we were upset and scared, but we know you never intentionally meant for it to happen. Who knows? Maybe something good can come out of this. Maybe you and Luke's story might prevent other children from getting hurt. Please don't feel bad about this anymore. This one incident doesn't define who you are. I bet you do 100 good things every day, and your parents are very proud of you. We're not mad at you. We know it was an unfortunate accident, and you were just trying to remove the rock so no other children would trip on it. We forgive

you, and we hope you forgive yourself.
God bless,
Mrs. Knight and Luke

Luke's teacher called me the next day after talking to Katie's teacher. She said that after Katie read our letter, she was so relieved and happy. She was glad that Luke was feeling better and healing. Luke and Katie both learned that mistakes do happen. We can learn from them and become better people. Forgiving someone is a part of healing and releases anger. The next time I substituted at Luke's school, Katie gave me a big hug. I hugged her back. We didn't have to say anything else; we both knew forgiveness was the most important step in healing.

—Terri L. Knight—

Ex-Spouses
Ex-Enemies

75

You Take Him with You

If we forgave for as long as we hold grudges, the world
would be a healthier and happier place.
~Charmaine J. Forde

I was so angry with my ex-husband that I felt my blood pressure shoot up every time I thought about him. Years ago, we said "I do" and "I love you," but whatever we meant by that wore thin in nearly twelve years and came to an abrupt end. But we'd had two sons together and, like it or not, by the rules of our separation agreement, I saw him on a regular basis when he picked up the kids. And, let's rub salt into the wound, he took them to the new home he'd made with his live-in girlfriend.

Seeing him walk into what used to be our home made me mad all over again. Only a deep desire to protect the boys from more angst and confusion kept me marginally civil during our brief interactions.

And when my ex-husband wasn't around, I still went on and on about him, not only to my friends but to anyone who'd listen — including our local librarian and my hairdresser. He'd been a liar! A cheater! I'd been hurt to the core when I'd learned the truth. My family and friends were kind and patient. Sometimes, though, when I began ranting about "the betrayal," and "what an insensitive jerk he was," and "how life's just plain not fair," they let me know by the glazed look in their eyes that they'd heard my story at least once too often.

"You may want to let go of some of that anger," my best friend Pat said one day over lunch. "You might as well still be married to the man. You take him with you wherever you go."

Her words resonated in me. *She's right,* I thought. *I do take him with me wherever I go. My anger's a prison, and my ex-husband and I are locked in it together. I've recited my story of betrayal and outrage so often that even I'm bored with hearing it. And by doing so, I keep the anger fresh and alive inside me like a dark, toxic cloud.*

That was the moment I decided to forgive him. I'd lived with my anger long enough. It was time to move on.

I forgave my ex-husband—although that did not mean we became friends. Too many disappointments had passed between us for that. But he's the father of my sons. They love him, no matter what, and are entitled to the best relationship they can work out together. Frankly, I still don't like the guy—but after I forgave him by letting go of my anger, I felt light and buoyant, as though an emotional weight had been lifted off me.

How strange. Nothing changed. We're still divorced. I'm still a single mom, doing the work of two people. Nothing really changed except me, but that seems to have made a world of difference in my life.

—Lynn Sunday—

76

The Kids' Dad

Make a positive difference in your children's lives.
Act and speak about your co-parent
with respect and integrity.
~Allison Pescosolido

A couple of months ago, I was having lunch with a dear friend. We've been friends for years, and she has seen me at my worst and best and every stage in between. She's the kind of friend with whom I can discuss the funny things my kid did yesterday and the current political climate.

It was no surprise then when she picked up on the fact that I always refer to my ex-husband as "the kids' dad." Sweetly and jokingly, she asked if I just didn't like saying his name. "Is this like referring to the current president as 45? Or Voldemort as He Who Must Not Be Named?"

I laughed.

I have a thing for names. I took my last name back after the divorce because it means something to me. Also, Lindsey Light is just a cool name.

My family and close friends call me Linz. My dad calls me #1. A favorite professor called me LL, and a current professor calls me L-squared. I've been called someone's girl, mama, prof, and teach. I love them all.

And when I like a guy romantically, he gets a nickname. There is something about a nickname that is intimate. Sometimes, it has to do with the season ("Scrooge"), and sometimes it's to point out obvious flaws ("A Red Sox Fan").

But when said romantic interest falls from grace and becomes a former flame, he gets demoted from nickname to an acronym. For example, one ex is now simply referred to as HWMNBN — He Who Must Not Be Named (which is part of the reason I chuckled when my friend mentioned it).

Names mean something to me.

So, as I started to ponder why I refer to my ex as "the kids' dad" and not "ex-husband" or "was-band" or "the exhole" (which might have been his name in my phone for a hot minute during the divorce, whoops), I decided it was a strategic move to re-position.

The kids' dad and I did not work as a couple. Our marriage failed, and that is unfortunate. No one goes into a marriage hoping it ends in divorce court. During our time together, though, we created some pretty spectacular, red-haired, blue-eyed human beings. And, boy, do they make my heart grow just like the Grinch's does at the end of the movie. It's a love so big it hurts.

So while I could remember my ex in the least flattering ways imaginable and could continually drudge up every bad memory we have together, I don't want to. I chose forgiveness a long time ago, even though it was neither easy nor immediate. But I keep choosing it because it frees me from a burden that I shouldn't have to carry. So, when I refer to him as "the kids' dad," I remind myself that this story ceased being about me a long time ago. His relation to me is no longer important, but his relation to them is everything.

No matter which way I spin it, he will always be the kids' dad, and I hope he's the best one he knows how to be.

— Lindsey Light —

77

My Ex-Wife

Keeping baggage from the past will leave no room
for happiness in the future.
~Wayne L. Misner

I guess I wasn't taught forgiveness growing up. My mother, now in her late seventies, is still telling stories about things her mother did or didn't do. Just the other day, she was telling the familiar story about how her mother wouldn't let her have a puppy. She sure can hold a grudge.

When I was in my early twenties, I fell in love with a man who had been married previously. Every weekend, his ex would drop their kids off with us so she could go out and have fun. She didn't want to be with her ex-husband, but she didn't want him to be with anyone else either. She attacked me physically, spread lies about me, and even called my mother on the phone to cause trouble for me.

Eventually, he and I married, and in doing so, I inherited an ex-wife. My interactions with her were frequent since there were children involved. We rearranged our schedules often to accommodate her. Eventually, we discussed things with a lawyer and were assured that we had a good chance of getting custody of the children. Her address, at that time, was in prison. After we won the case, she accused us of paying off the judge. Which, of course, we did not do.

The resentment I developed toward her festered until it grew into a kind of twisted obsession. I'm sad to admit that I spent considerable time gossiping about her to anyone who would listen. I would often daydream about bad things happening to her. Sometimes, in my daydream, she would apologize, and I would launch into a long lecture. Other times, I would leave her to suffer. Once, I imagined sneaking into her house and chopping off her hair while she was asleep!

When my husband's grandfather died, she was at the funeral. I was nearly ten years into my hateful grudge by this time. My husband's grandfather had been divorced from his first wife, my husband's grandmother, for decades. My husband's grandmother was in the back of the funeral home fuming about her ex-husband's girlfriend sitting in the front of the room, and I was in the front of the room fuming about my husband's ex-wife sitting in the back. I couldn't understand why she was there and why my in-laws and husband weren't mean to her. When I saw my father-in-law hug her, I almost went into a rage.

At one point, I confronted my husband about why he wasn't retaliating for the things she had done and continued to do. A man of few words, I will never forget his response: "It doesn't matter what other people do; I'm going to do the right thing." I knew he was right, and I loved him even more for it. I realized what a treasure this loving family was. They were teaching me about forgiveness, and I wanted to follow their lead. I just didn't know how to make it unconditional. I was still withholding my forgiveness until she jumped through the hoops of acting the way I thought she should, apologizing and showing remorse. I was close, but still not quite getting it.

I partially forgave and then took it back, and continued to intermittently gossip and fantasize about revenge for another five years or more. I knew I should forgive, but I couldn't figure out how.

One day in my car in the parking garage at work, I was listening to a radio program about forgiveness. The woman on the radio was explaining that forgiveness is like pushing the Delete button on your computer. Once it's done, it can't be undone. Finally, I understood that forgiveness is an act that is independent of the actions of others. I made up my mind right there in the car to forgive her no matter what she did or did not do — apology, good behavior, remorse or not.

Not long afterward, I received a phone call from her in which she told me that she was sorry "for every mean thing" she ever did to me.

It was a life-changing moment for both of us, but especially for me. She probably doesn't know how obsessed I was with hating her all those years or how I struggled with forgiveness. But in response to her apology that I had waited so long for but never expected, I was able to say simply, "Apology accepted. I forgive you." I cried like a baby when we got off the phone because something powerful had happened. The apology was like a fancy bow on a beautifully wrapped gift.

Because of the power of forgiveness, we were able to get through the teen years of the children. We didn't always see eye to eye, and I still got angry with her at times, but it never turned into the kind of venom that had coursed through my veins from those years that I held a grudge. Now the children are adults, and I rarely ever see "my ex-wife." I will never forget how my life changed for good because of her. It took me years, but I learned how to forgive.

—S. Kling—

78

My Rwanda

Blame keeps wounds open. Only forgiveness heals.
~Thomas S. Manson

"What is your favorite garment and how does it make you feel?" asked our pastor in his sermon on the book of Esther, who — along with Mordecai the Jew — had put on royal robes that made them feel honored. The message to the congregation was that we should clothe ourselves with compassion, humility, and kindness. But I couldn't stop thinking about his question. I fingered the soft cloth around my shoulders and thought about how it came into my life.

Forty-five years ago, Carl, the father of my two children, entered my life. He had just returned from a tour in Vietnam, and I had just released myself from an abusive relationship. We both needed something and someone to calm our minds and hearts and we found that in each other. In 1973, we married and moved the following year to start a concrete construction company in a boomtown surrounded by coal mines. Rather than continue my teaching career, I became the company secretary/bookkeeper. It was a struggle at first, but eventually we moved to the house on the top of the hill. We were doing well. Amy was born in 1975; Christopher in 1977. We had friends, parties and fun.

Then it all began to fall apart. I started my own furniture-refinishing business, which failed after two years. Carl was experiencing problems with his concrete-paving business and decided to move it to Arizona. I had just received a teaching contract and did not want to move. After eleven years of marriage, I asked for a divorce. We tried counseling, but my stubborn mind was made up. I was convinced there was someone with whom I would be more compatible waiting in the green grass on the other side of the fence. The divorce was unpleasant, and the following years were filled with turmoil and heartache — for us and our two children.

Ten years later, I married my current husband, Mike. I had matured enough to know that the perfect man did not exist. Life was good. We were happy. Christopher, now in junior high, was living with us. Amy was in high school in Arizona and living with her father.

On my daily trek to the elementary school where I taught, it became my morning ritual to pray as I approached a short bridge spanning railroad tracks. On one particular day, as I was thanking God for the blessings he had given me, I was moved to ask him to also bring happiness and peace to Carl. The prayer was forgotten until later in the week when I received an unexpected call from Carl.

"The strangest thing happened to me the other day," he related. "I was driving along and heard this voice say, 'You need to forgive Penny.' I drove a little farther, and it said the same thing again. So I guess I need to tell you that I forgive you, and… well… to ask you to forgive me, too."

When my voice box finally decided to work, I replied, "Carl, I forgave you a long time ago. But thank you for forgiving me. That means a lot."

"When did this happen?" I asked. But I really didn't need his answer because I already knew it would be on the same day at the same time that I had uttered my prayer.

In future times when we did get together, the interactions were pleasant. Mike and Carl got along well, as did his wife Carol and I. So when my daughter-in-law suggested that we invite them to our house for Christmas, I did not hesitate. "It has been years since my two kids have been with both of their parents at Christmas time!"

It was a typical Christmas with active grandkids and holiday smells of baked cookies and roast turkey. I was a bit nervous when it came time for the exchanging of gifts. Together, Mike and I have five children and fourteen grandchildren, so our giving budget is limited. Our presents to Carl and Carol were far from elaborate, and when I opened their gift to me, I knew I had been right in my apprehension.

"It's beautiful," I said, as I pulled out a colorful piece of material from an immaculately wrapped package. I took it out of its wrapper and unfolded it gently. "It's a shawl! And so incredibly soft!"

"It's a ruana," Carol said.

"A Rwanda?" Obviously, I'd never heard of a ruana.

"No, it's called a ruana. It's another name for a shawl."

"Thank you so very much," I replied, smiling as I wrapped the fleecy fabric around my shoulders. "I love my Rwanda!"

To me, it will always be my Rwanda (probably because the name of the country is stuck in my stubborn head, and maybe also because I like to be silly). As I looked down at it covering my arms in church, I knew that it was my favorite garment. In Texas, I take it everywhere because I freeze in air-conditioned buildings.

However, my Rwanda does much more than keep me warm. When I put it on, it makes me feel safe and loved, and most of all, forgiven. Covered by the Rwanda, my arms are unencumbered, just as Carl and I are released from the bitterness and hurt of the past through the blessing of forgiveness. We are now free to enjoy the beauty of our children and grandchildren — together.

— Penny Radtke Adams —

79

My Ex-Husband's Last Gift

*It's not an easy journey to get to a place where you
forgive people. But it is such a powerful
place because it frees you.*
~Tyler Perry

"Is there a green terrycloth bathrobe among your dad's personal belongings?" I asked, trying to sound nonchalant.

Patrick and I had been divorced for more than three decades. Truthfully, the only thing we shared during those years was our son, Zachary, who was by then a thirty-something man himself.

"Yes, there was a green bathrobe lying on his bed," Zach answered, a bit confused, as we stood in the living room of his late father's home. Zach had inherited the small brick ranch where Patrick had lived alone for a decade, disabled and on an oxygen tank, rarely venturing out. I had gone there to help my grieving son dispose of his dad's possessions.

Our boy had spent his growing-up years being juggled between two devoted but divorced parents. From the time he was a baby, it was back and forth for weekends, holidays, and summer vacations. As a financially struggling single mom, I would routinely pack Zach's overnight bag when he was small. He would watch with excitement, eagerly anticipating an outing with his father, which made me feel left out and unappreciated.

Patrick and I fought frequently during those early years, battling over child support, visitation days, and almost everything. Our immature love for our youngster was like a tug-of-war with both of us constantly trying to attain the position of his favorite parent.

Patrick never married again, and neither of us had any other biological children, so Zach became the whole world for both of us. To outsiders, my ex-husband and I certainly didn't appear to like each other. Our emotional skirmishes continued into Zach's adolescence, but something began to change when faith became an important part of my life. I laid down my weapon of bitterness and picked up God's call to forgive. I realized that in order to be forgiven for my own mistakes and failures, I had to forgive others. Soon, our mutual forgiveness produced special moments of kindness between us.

For instance, Patrick diligently tried to meet my requests for whatever Zach needed, and he also used his mechanical talents to fix my car whenever it broke down.

But the generous gift of the red leather boots touched my heart most. Sometimes, I would admire those boots while shopping with Zach, but I accepted that, as a single mother, I could never afford them. One day, my adolescent boy came home from visiting his father grinning from ear to ear. Patrick stood in the background, also smiling with satisfaction as Zach proudly presented the box with the boots to me as a present for graduating from my first Bible college.

Another memorable moment is from the Christmas when Zach was fifteen. My then fiancé and I had broken up eleven days before our planned church wedding with hundreds of expected guests. I was heartbroken and humiliated. Then Patrick showed up in the department store where I worked with our teenage son at his side. He helped Zach purchase a flowery red dress and some sparkling rhinestone earrings from the store for a Christmas gift to cheer me up.

Ultimately, the years washed away the memory of our heated arguments. After Zach became an adult, forgiveness even transformed us into good friends forged by the necessary teamwork parenting had created. With time, our misguided and destructive "young" love grew into a peaceful "old" friendship of two individuals who had navigated the challenging journey of raising a child together.

When Zach was twenty-one, I remarried. My husband Larry grew to be quite fond of Patrick, and he came to care for Larry as well. It was a terrible shock when Patrick died in his sleep at only sixty-four years of age. I guess it shouldn't have been a shock because he had been ill for a long time, struggling for each breath even with the oxygen. But when Zach called with the sad news, I was grief-stricken.

In my devastation, I said a prayer with two requests. First, I asked God to help me acquire a photo of Patrick and me together in younger, happier days. I didn't have any pictures of us as a couple. We were married only months, and our little wedding had taken place in my mother's living room without formal photos.

Second, I prayed to find the green terrycloth robe — the one I would wrap around my huge belly when I was expecting our baby boy. Patrick had left it to comfort me after we separated and he went out west to work. I wore the bathrobe for months, hoping he would return and things would get better. He did come back shortly before Zach was born, but we were never to be a couple again. With the divorce, I relinquished custody of the terrycloth robe and my dream of being a family. I hadn't seen the bathrobe for almost thirty-five years.

As for a photograph of us together, I was surprised at the funeral home when my ex-sister-in-law showed me an old Polaroid snapshot of Patrick and me on our wedding day. I'm in a borrowed flowered maxi-dress with baby's breath in my hair clutching a homemade bouquet of daisies. Patrick's arm is wrapped protectively around me. He's dressed in a beige polyester suit with a wide brocade flowered tie. It wasn't a happy day, though, because there were already too many problems to make our marriage work.

We didn't make it at marriage, but my ex-husband gave me the most precious gift of all: our son. Sometimes, I unexpectedly catch a glimpse of Patrick in Zach's broad shoulders and mischievous smile, which he inherited from his dad.

But back to the green bathrobe… After Zach said he had seen it lying on his father's bed, I raced to the vacant bedroom. It was faded and worn, but it was there. I had prayed Patrick would leave it for me, understanding that I would need its comfort again, just as I had all those years ago when I was pregnant and alone.

I was grieving for my son losing his father, and for me losing a dear friend. When the grief lessened, I started to recall joyful memories and even laughed at the outrageous fights my ex-husband and I once had. Now I keep Patrick's robe hanging in my closet. Love does change, but when forgiveness has been applied, it lives on forever.

— Christina Ryan Claypool —

80

Redemption in a Red Plastic Cooler

Before we can forgive one another,
we have to understand one another.
~Emma Goldman

After my parents divorced when I was twenty-two, my dad built a house on the property he retained in the settlement. His new house was right behind my mother's house.

He moved in with his new wife and her three teenagers. My mom and I were the only ones living at home then. My brothers and sister had already moved out to create lives of their own.

My dad and I didn't talk, which wasn't unusual because we never really had. Almost everything I knew about him I learned from day-to-day conversations he used to have with my mom over our kitchen table, or things I heard him say to friends and relatives who came over to sit and drink coffee.

But I saw him sometimes as I walked out the back door to feed the cats or take out the garbage. His lone figure paced under the pecan trees that lined the edge of his yard while he looked toward the house where he had raised four children.

Like most men in his family, he was short, wiry and thin. And even though the distance hid features of his face, my mind's eye filled in the familiar. His forehead and eyes creased with lines etched from working construction jobs in the hot sun. Straight, dirty-blond hair with a cowlick swirled at the crown of his head. His nose bumped out like the tip of a cheerleader's baton, and his ears, like his dad's, stuck out from the side of his head. Although my brunette hair was the same color as my mom's, I was shorter and thinner. Surely, he could tell it was me. I'd see him stop pacing, raise his hand, and wave. I waved back before going about whatever I was doing.

One day about a year after he took up residence behind us, my mom and I came home from shopping and found a plastic sack full of tomatoes on our front steps. I recognized his handwriting on the note with it. "I had some extra Early Girls," it said.

There was a time when my dad had been famous around our small town for the tomatoes he grew. Plump, juicy Early Girls and Louisiana Creoles were his favorite varieties. He had carefully tended two rows each spring and summer for years, bagging up our overflowing bounty and dropping them off at the homes of relatives, friends, and neighbors. Then he abandoned gardening for the bar room.

Now tomatoes started showing up on our doorstep once a week, always placed there while we were out. Apparently, he was gardening again. One day, we were unloading the tomatoes onto our kitchen counter when we discovered a package of fish at the bottom, fillets frozen in water so they wouldn't spoil before we arrived home. Magic marker labeled them as sac-au-lait.

My dad had also once been known for catching sac-au-lait, a flaky, white-fleshed fish that takes skill to pull from Louisiana's muddy bayou waters. Sometimes, he'd bring in fifty or sixty after a morning out in his boat, and I remember how he'd kneel patiently by the hose in our yard, scraping off scales before gutting and filleting each fish. After the fillets froze, he would set out to deliver them around town. But he had quit fishing around the same time he quit gardening.

Shortly after my mom and I unloaded our package, the phone rang. "You got the fish?" my dad asked. When I told him we had, he said, "All right then," and hung up. After that, he started calling every now and then. And even though we were only half a football field away from each other, the distance let him say things I imagine he couldn't admit while sitting across the table from me.

"I quit drinking," he told me once, saying he knew it had caused him to lose the love of his life, and he didn't want to mess up again. "I'm sorry for everything I did to y'all," he said another time, knowing he covered a lot of ground with that statement. Another time, he said, "I love you," as we were ending our call. All along I had been certain that he loved me despite his actions, but I didn't remember him ever saying the words before. I realized I had never said them to him either.

"I love you, too," I said, and felt myself letting go of a sadness I had held for a long time. Soon after, I walked the field that divided our homes to sit on his porch and talk while sipping coffee. My brothers and sister sometimes visited, too. In the ten years that followed, we grew our relationship one phone call, porch sitting, bag of tomatoes, and package of fish at a time.

And when he died suddenly of a massive heart attack at age fifty-eight, my brothers, sister, and I sat around our mom's table and told stories about things we remembered about my dad. We smiled at the good memories and chuckled at the bad, shaking our heads as if to say, "Can you believe he was like that for a time?"

His wife gave me the soft-sided, red plastic cooler he used to stack his packages of fish in when he would go out to deliver them, saying, "I know he would want you to have it."

I think of that cooler as my inheritance, and I have used it well these past twenty-six years. But every time I pack it with ice and layer in food for a picnic, I think of the true gift I received from my dad. He showed me that when we need to seek forgiveness, and we don't know the words to say, sometimes we simply need to start with a small gesture, like a bag of Early Girls left on a doorstep.

— Cindy Hudson —

81

Time Heals Even as It Leaves Scars

*When I stand before thee at the day's end, thou shalt
see my scars and know that I had my wounds
and also my healing.*
~Rabindranath Tagore

The headlights of the derelict pickup truck grew larger in my rearview mirror. Before I even realized I had been run off the road, I found myself in a copse of trees. The rusted Dodge pickup truck squealed away in a cloud of oily soot.

This wasn't road rage. It was revenge.

At first, I was numb. Then, pain pulsed in my left wrist, which had taken the brunt of the impact. I tasted the salty blood trickling from a cut on my left temple.

After wallowing in self-pity, I took an inventory of my blessings. First, my daughter hadn't been in the car—thank heaven. Second, my cell phone was—for once—charged.

The tow-truck driver dropped me off at the emergency room. As I sat waiting to have my broken wrist set, I wondered, *What next?*

Being run off the road by a virtual stranger was just one of dozens of tactics my husband had used to dissuade me from my bid for custody of our daughter.

The entire debacle had begun the previous year with a threat from my husband.

"Maybe I'll shoot you and bury your body in the cornfield," he had said. "I'll tell everyone you ran off with some guy you met on the Internet."

This was not his first threat, but this time I believed him. Violence was no stranger in our marriage. The beatings were growing increasingly frequent and intense.

The next day, I noticed his gun case had been opened. Our four-year-old daughter, who had witnessed this latest fight, was terrified. A little voice in my head kept repeating, "Get out. Husbands kill their wives all the time."

While he was at work, I packed whatever would fit in the car. Tears blinded me as I drove away from my marriage. My daughter dozed in her car seat, exhausted from the stress. Two introspective days later, we arrived at my parents' home in Tampa, Florida.

"Maybe you should have stuck it out — for your daughter's sake," I recall my mother saying as we settled in.

Could I feel any lower? At the time, I doubted it.

A week later, the sheriff served me divorce papers. A friend called to tell me that "the other woman" had taken my place in the family home. There was officially no going back.

We lived in Florida for eight months before being summoned back to Illinois. It was November as we made the return trip. The farther north we went, the colder it got. The weather reflected the desolation in my soul.

Upon return, the judge ordered me to turn over our daughter to my estranged husband and his "fiancée" for a six-week visit. Images of him using our daughter to get revenge haunted me as I searched for a place to live.

The lawyer was a huge financial albatross around my neck, and I feared my "hostile divorce" would last longer than my bank account. Still, the tiny apartment above a printing press was a harsh slap of reality. The dead mouse on the bathroom floor drove me to despair, but I had to conserve money. Before my daughter's return, I scoured and painted. It wasn't much, but it would have to suffice.

The next day, the phone roused me from an ever-increasing lethargy.

It was my lawyer.

"Your husband wants sole custody," he said. "If you don't agree, he's going to order a psychiatric evaluation and try to have you declared an unfit mother." I was never so terrified.

The evaluation was a family affair, consisting of interviews, personality tests and observations. During our first communal session, the psychiatrist asked us to cooperate in drawing a picture of our home. My husband refused and stormed out. Though I didn't realize it at the time, his temper tantrum had convinced the psychiatrist that I should be granted sole custody.

Later, when the judge read the recommendation, I couldn't help but smirk at my husband, who had shelled out a couple of grand for the evaluation. I would pay for that smirk, and dearly.

Several days later, I took my daughter to the park. Within moments, a woman with two children appeared, seemingly out of nowhere. Soon, her children began harassing my daughter.

Sensing danger, I took my daughter's hand and attempted to leave. We made it about fifty feet when something hit me with the force of a freight train. A sharp pain in my right kidney dropped me in my tracks. When I tried to rise, the woman pounded my nose and cheekbone to a pulp. My daughter screamed in terror as blood gushed from my broken nose.

A van pulled up, and a man yelled to the perpetrator, "Hurry, get in!"

Before leaving, she said, "That was a gift from your husband, b----."

Eventually, she would be charged with aggravated battery, but it was no big deal. The assault merely added color to her extensive rap sheet.

Miraculously, I made it in one piece to the divorce trial, where I was painted in the worst possible light. Never have I felt as weary and ready to die as I did sitting in the courtroom listening to a fictional account of my life.

There was no real sense of victory when the judge awarded me full custody of our daughter. There was only sadness that someone I had once loved had tried to destroy me.

And though I was awarded custody, we would not be allowed to leave Illinois until my daughter turned eighteen. I would have to drive her 200 miles every other weekend for her visitation with her father.

When my daughter turned nine, my ex remarried, and she was no longer welcome in their home. For me, it was a relief. For her, it was devastating.

We celebrated my daughter's eighteenth birthday last year. Though she had been estranged from her father for nine years, the pain of loss never faded.

As we were leaving the auditorium following her high school graduation, a man approached and congratulated her. She smiled and thanked him, but obviously did not recognize him. Neither did I.

Then I took a good look at the graying stranger and froze. The years of my marriage — the good and the bad — flashed before my eyes.

"It's your father, Justine," I whispered to my daughter.

They hugged, hanging on for dear life. The years fell away magically, and I remembered his joy the evening she was born.

"This is the best day of my life," he had said, tears streaming down his face.

I found myself smiling. At one time, I had loved this man enough to create a child with him. Yes, I could finally forgive, if not forget. Time does indeed heal all wounds, even as it leaves scars.

— Rose Hojnik —

82

Where Have You Been?

We derive immeasurable good, uncounted pleasures,
enormous security, and many critical lessons
about life by owning dogs.
~Roger A. Caras

Maggie was our first and last dog. As a family, we had our share of unfortunate pets. A rabbit that kicked up shavings in great plumes as it scurried away from our daughter's hands. A cat that sulked behind the kitchen cabinets, and a desiccated goldfish that we scraped off the dresser, discovered a weekend after its tragic leap for freedom. However, my wife Katherine never gave up hope that somewhere, out there, was a pet that suited our family.

After reading an advertisement for a sweetly tempered rescue dog, Katherine traveled up a winding mountain road in the verdant hills of western Virginia to fetch her. Unfortunately, that sweet dog had a temperamental stomach. When she traveled back down the winding mountain road, she vomited the entire way.

Katherine would often surprise me with an impulsive adoption. Maggie was no exception.

"She didn't cost anything, Bill," Katherine said.

"A pet is an investment," I countered. "Nothing is free."

To say that Maggie was sweet-tempered may have been a marketing ploy. When I met her, she cowered, her black-and-tan body shivered, while her tail retreated between her legs. She stood eye level with our daughters, whom she would run from, scared silly by a pair of girls, ages six and four.

We fretted over another poor pet choice. It was clear that Maggie had been mistreated by her previous owners, and we worried that she might never recover. We decided to give her a week.

In the cool of the morning, I would sip my coffee, watching Maggie dart to the far corner of the yard and tremble beneath the girls' trampoline. I'd crawl underneath and tug on her collar, and she'd crouch down as if she could somehow disappear into the dirt. "Come on, girl." She would peer into the den, where the girls were playing, and when they looked at her, she'd scurry, nails clawing to get a purchase on the hardwood floors.

As the end of her probation week approached, Maggie must have sensed that her fate would soon be sealed. She placed a paw next to me on the sofa. I looked at her timid, brown eyes and patted the cushion. "It's okay, girl. Come on." Slowly, cautiously, she inched a paw forward and then another. It was a Herculean effort, as she wiggled her body, her legs shaking, one leg up, one leg down. Then, she placed her head on my lap.

"There you are," I said while rubbing her soft head, and looked over at Katherine who was wiping her eyes.

From that point on, her metamorphosis was astonishing. When sunset's glow painted the walls orange, she waited by the front door for my workday return, and when the girls placed a homemade newspaper hat on her head and draped a scarf around her neck, she sat still, looking quite miserable. Other times, she would playfully chase the girls around in a circle, crouching down on her front legs with her rump high in the air, her tail curled up into a C — Miss Maggie the Courageous. When she caught them, she would lick their faces while they laughed uncontrollably.

"Maggie, stop!"

We were shocked the first time we heard her bark, a deep woof that echoed. When the girls were playing softball in the front yard with a group of neighborhood kids, Maggie situated herself in front of our elder child, acting as a canine speed bump to trip the boy who was running toward her.

On our annual trips to the beach, I'd take curves gingerly to keep from upsetting her tender stomach, but invariably, she'd start puking. Each of us was so in love with her that we stomached the stench of vomit so that she would never again smell the inside of a kennel.

When I accepted a job in Massachusetts, after the company I worked for in Virginia went belly-up, we called for Maggie, "Come on girl, let's go!" Up she jumped into the van, good girl. One morning she was in Virginia and the next, she was sniffing a frozen, foreign yard. Her adjustment was far smoother than ours. Maggie's love remained steadfast. Our marriage crumbled.

The move shifted something I had buried deep inside, making me temperamental and depressed. Seven hundred miles and twenty-odd years was enough distance for the aftermath to bubble up. Katherine discovered that, like it'd been the case with Maggie, my previous owners had mistreated me. I came out to my parents when I was nineteen years old, revealing to them the true nature of the beast. But, they pushed me back into the closet, forced me to obey their religious rules. After two decades of marriage, Katherine rescued me.

"Bill, I have to ask you this now, or I may never. Are you gay?"

"I've tried not to be."

"Oh God," Katherine muttered. "I told myself to be ready for the answer. After all these years, how do I give you up now?"

When Maggie and the girls left me and returned to Virginia, I slunk into a basement apartment, a cheap rental in Waltham, Massachusetts. Many nights, I would come home and shout, "Maggie, I'm home," before reality struck me. The empty spot by my outstretched hand yielded not a soft head to rub, but a hollow emptiness.

Still, a piece of me was in Virginia with the girls. Maggie acted as my surrogate, the one who let their heartbroken tears roll onto her warm hide and nuzzled their sweet faces; the one who listened without judgment or reproach. When I visited, Katherine would stand motionless in the doorway, holding on to Maggie's collar, until she wiggled free and bolted toward me. I'd crouch down, letting her lick my face, and she'd whimper, as if to ask, *Where have you been?*

As with grief, there are stages of a divorce: denial, anger, hate, bitterness, indifference, and acceptance. We experienced them, much in the way we had collected ill-fitting pets with their nasty yellow teeth and a bite that induced pain and regret.

We fought over the mundane and argued about money. We were petty with our insults and name-calling. We became cold and distant. When my phone rang and Katherine's number appeared, I braced for another round of bitterness, another nasty bite.

"Bill, Maggie's sick."

That was what it took to shift us into the acceptance stage. I wrote a check for Maggie's final care.

Shortly after that call, I returned to Virginia, traveling up and down those winding mountain roads to fetch my daughters for Christmas. When Katherine opened the door, I crouched down before I remembered, and as I glanced up, in the gloaming winter light noticed the empty spot next to Katherine's waist. I rose and then slowly, cautiously, placed my head on her shoulder.

"There you are," Katherine wept. "Where have you been?"

Our investment in Maggie matured, and so had we.

— William Dameron —

83

The Yoga Cure

Yoga is the journey of the self,
through the self, to the self.
~The Bhagavad Gita

The overhead lights were dimmed, and candlelight flickered in the mirrors that made up one entire wall of the yoga studio. Instrumental music played softly through speakers placed in each corner of the room, and a faint scent of incense wafted through the air. "Welcome to twilight yoga," the instructor, Michelle, said to the handful of women gathered together on that cold winter evening. "Please silence your phones and make yourselves comfortable on your mats."

I removed my shoes, rolled out my thin rubber mat and sat facing the mirrored wall cross-legged.

"This is an introductory class," Michelle continued. "For the next six weeks, we'll cover the foundations of yoga practice. Let's sit straight and tall and put our hands in heart center position." She pressed her palms together and held them so that her thumbs touched the middle of her chest. Everyone in the class did likewise. "Now close your eyes and focus on what I'm saying."

She reminded us that this was a special day — December 21st, the winter solstice, when darkness lasts longer than on any other day of the year. The season when we spend so many hours indoors should be a time of quiet and inward reflection. *Hmmm*, I thought. *Maybe this yoga class wasn't such a good idea after all.* Most of my inward reflection involved anger toward my husband, who'd recently and unexpectedly told me he wanted a divorce after more than thirty years of marriage. *Perhaps I should have chosen kick-boxing instead of yoga.*

Michelle went on to explain that yoga seeks to create synergy between body, mind and spirit. "We'll stretch and strengthen our bodies," she said, "and we'll learn to breathe slowly and deeply. But we'll also concentrate on quieting our minds and learning to be only in this moment and no other."

Hmmm, I thought again. Clearly, Michelle didn't know I'd forgotten to put my grocery list in my purse, and I was frantically trying to remember all the items on it. And that I needed to gas up the car and drop off some overdue library books on the way home. Or that a load of dirty laundry awaited me when I got there. How in the world was I supposed to quiet my thoughts?

But as Michelle led us through some basic yoga poses — cat-cow, child's pose, warrior one, baby cobra, bridge and downward-facing dog — I stopped thinking about my to-do list. Many of the poses were challenging, and my breath sometimes went out when it should have been coming in, but I quickly forgot about everything but yoga. After forty-five sweaty but peaceful minutes, I felt wonderful.

"We're going to stop a little early tonight," Michelle said, "so you can ask questions."

My hand shot up. "Will you explain karma?"

Karma was the real reason I'd signed up for yoga. I didn't know much about it except that it was somehow related to revenge, which had become the major focus of my life lately. My husband had squandered our money. Been unfaithful. And lied about a million different things. All I wanted was to get back at him. Since I couldn't do that myself, I hoped karma would take over.

Most of what I knew about karma was based on Facebook memes. They were clever. Funny. And they made me feel just a little bit better about my situation. "My dream job is driving the karma bus," one of my favorite memes said. I also loved "Karma never loses an address," and "Dear karma, I have a list of people you missed."

"Let's get in butterfly pose to talk about this," Michelle said. She put the bottoms of her feet together and rested her hands on her knees. "In simplest terms, karma is the idea that we reap what we sow," she said, "but it's a little more complicated than that. Karma teaches us to think positively and act positively. We're all part of the fabric of the universe. What's inside of each of us flows out into the world. That's why it's so important to focus on the good."

Wow. That certainly wasn't what I wanted to hear.

I'd hoped that karma would cause my husband to experience financial ruin (after my half of our estate was secure, of course). That he would contract some horrible disease from his girlfriend. That he would be lied to by every single person he trusted.

But I wasn't really surprised I didn't get that answer. "If you plant an acorn, you get an oak tree," Michelle said softly. "If you plant a rotten seed, you get nothing." Then she pressed her palms together with her thumbs touching the middle of her chest. "We finish every class with our hands to heart center, the same way we began. Then we close our eyes, bow our heads and say the word 'namaste.'"

My hand shot up again.

Nicole smiled. "Namaste simply means the divine spark within me honors the divine spark within you. We're all one when we live from the heart."

Thus, my very first yoga class came to an end. On the way home, I gassed up the car, dropped the library books into the after-hours slot and bought groceries. I did those tasks mindfully, one at a time. I didn't hurry, and I didn't obsess about what was next on the list.

Later that night, while waiting for my washing machine to finish the spin cycle, I pulled my phone from my pocket and tapped the Facebook app. Amazingly, the very first post I saw was a meme. And, amazingly, here's what it said: "Be kind. Be fair. Be honest. Be true. And all these things will come back to you." That was a karma definition I could understand. And try to live by.

I won't pretend that the tremendous hurt my husband caused was instantly healed in that moment. Or that yoga, which I continue to practice on an almost daily basis, has been a cure-all for my troubles. But I do know that my first-ever yoga class, held on the darkest day of the year, helped lead me toward the light. Though it's unlikely I'll ever forget what my ex did, I have forgiven him.

And, every day, I strive to honor the divine spark within every living creature. Him included.

—Jennie Ivey—

Resetting Expectations

84

Etch-a-Sketch Mindset

Some people would not be practicing some things
if they had not preached them.
~Mokokoma Mokhonoana

Working closely with someone doesn't necessarily create closeness. Like magnets, the closer one pushes non-connecting magnetic forces together, the greater the repelling force between the two emerges. This was how it went between a colleague and me for a few years. Each interaction only made my frustration with him compound, and I did not hide my displeasure. My commitment to truth had always made me terrible at tact. My openly expressed frustration toward him caused his resentment for me to rise. The more we collided, the more divided we became.

One day, I gave a speech to my varsity boys' basketball team at Los Alamitos High School about having an "Etch-a-Sketch mindset." I gave each player his own Etch-a-Sketch as I went over the metaphor of shaking away whatever doubt or worry was on his mind and moving forward with a clean slate, full of confidence to succeed. Then I made the teaching about more than basketball by telling my team how they should have an Etch-a-Sketch mindset with how they treat people, too. Shake off any past mistakes or hurts they've caused, I told them, and love people brand-new each day. First place doesn't matter if you haven't placed love first, for you can never hold the ultimate trophy of life if you're holding a grudge against someone.

"Etch-a-Sketch any pain they have caused you and forgive them fully if you want to be a fulfilled person," I told them. Then I added, "Think of the worst thing that's ever been done to you. The best thing you can do about it is to love the person who did it by forgiving him or her."

As those words rolled off my tongue, I saw my reflection in the Etch-a-Sketch I was holding. Instantly, I thought of my co-worker and came to the hard realization that I wasn't following my own advice.

When I got home, I did something I had never done before: I thought about my "adversary" at work and only thought positive thoughts about him. I prayed for prosperity for him and asked for forgiveness for myself for my part in doubting his intentions. By seeking forgiveness for my actions first, feeling forgiveness for him became easier.

About a week after this revelation, it was announced that the very same co-worker I had just prayed for had received his doctorate degree in education. I didn't even know he had been in school. Love told me it was time I stood up for the person I once couldn't stand. I sent him a handwritten letter congratulating him on his achievement.

A few months went by, and I had to go to his office for something. It had been months since I had been in there, and to my surprise the letter I had sent months earlier was hanging on his wall. I was stunned! He told me how much he appreciated it and how I was the only one in the school to send him something like that.

During the winter of the next school year, I was rushed to the emergency room with some intestinal problems and was admitted to the hospital for three days. Guess who texted me every single day I was in the hospital!

That is the power of grace, of forgiveness in action. Two people who didn't click were able to connect when they got their egos out of the way and let love lead the way. When we learn to Etch-a-Sketch each day and give everyone a clean slate, adversaries can become allies.

— Steve Schultz —

Thrown into Positive Thinking

A bridge can still be built while the bitter waters
are flowing beneath.
~Anthony Liccione

I hadn't spoken to my mother in almost three years, and with good justification. There was a lot to forgive her for over the course of my fifty-two years. She was emotionally and sometimes physically abusive throughout my childhood. She cut me off financially during my senior year in college when I'd done something she didn't like, forcing me to drop out of school and get a full-time job. Shortly after that, she systematically and deliberately destroyed my relationship with the man I thought I was going to marry. And, the worst by far, she caused me to miss the moment my dying brother took his last breath. I had cared for him, with almost no help from her or my father. I missed his last breath because she couldn't make one phone call, nor was she at my brother's side.

For reasons that are a mystery to even me, I always have difficulty with the tenth anniversary of any major loss. On the tenth anniversary of my brother's death, in order to cope, I decided to use a technique I'd learned in psychotherapy. I wrote a letter to my brother, allowing myself to say anything and everything I needed to tell him. I had used letter writing before, whether someone had left my life because of death, divorce, moving away, or simply because our paths had divided. This

Resetting Expectations |

method of coping had helped me heal some deep wounds. I hoped it would this time, too.

So, late one night, I sat at one of my favorite restaurants, being served by my favorite waitress (I eat out *a lot*), got out my favorite pens (with purple ink) and my journal (with a bright red cover — I loved that the ink and the journal cover clashed), and began to write. What came out surprised me. It was not a missive from me to him, but one from him to me:

Dearest Robyn,

How could you possibly think you failed me in any way? You have every right to be angry with Mom. She wasn't there for you in the way you needed her to be. But even if she had been, my Beautiful Sister, it wouldn't have changed the outcome. I would still have left in the very same moment I did. Yes, it would have changed how you felt about it all — I get that. But I wonder if it's really me you're angry with — because I didn't hang on for a few more minutes until you could get back to me. I chose the moment I left for two reasons: 1) because Dad was finally ready to let go and 2) so you wouldn't have to endure more pain and watch me leave.

Everything happens for a reason. You know this to be true, even if we don't know what the reasons are. There was a reason I left when I did; there was a reason Mom couldn't do what you needed her to; and there was a reason you were not in the room when I slipped away. The reasons have everything and nothing to do with the obvious ones.

It all happened the way it was supposed to. I'm not asking you to necessarily like it, but you might consider accepting it. And by accepting that, maybe you can find it within yourself to forgive Mom. Or at least understand there were other forces at work besides her narcissism. [In my mind, I could see him grin at me.] I love you, and I love that after ten years you can still feel so outraged and hurt on my behalf. Perhaps it's time, however, to consider letting it all go. I'm happy and healthy here, and I want you to be happy and healthy, too. Give it some thought. Let me know what you decide.

With love always,
Scott

Astonished, I read what I had written. I had no idea where those thoughts had come from. Both my brother and I were writers, but the words that had flowed from my pen were much more his style of writing than they were mine. He had been a journalist by trade. I am a fiction writer. I read the letter again, and tears streamed down my cheeks. I ducked my head low so none of the other diners would see. Could I forgive my mother? After everything she had done and not done? Was it in my heart to accomplish what seemed like a monumental task? I didn't know. I closed my journal, with the letter in it.

Several weeks after I wrote the letter, I received a text message: "This is your mother. I thought we might try communicating again. I know we'll never be shopping buddies, but I thought we could talk once in awhile." I'm not proud to admit my first couple of responses were not as warm or loving as a daughter's should have been. Then I thought about the letter in my journal and heard Scott's voice reciting it again. After a few messages back and forth between Mom and me, I decided to give it my best effort.

Over the next few weeks, Mom and I texted, she came to a family Easter dinner for the first time in three years, and we met friends for brunch. Slowly, we built something resembling a relationship. This provided the foundation for the shock our family received later that summer when my eighty-two-year-old aunt, who we thought was in perfect health, was diagnosed with cancer in four major organs. The recommendation for treatment: none. It was so far advanced that the oncologist encouraged Aunt Marie to go for quality of life over quantity, to which she agreed.

When my aunt died, Mom was devastated. They had been inseparable since my father had died thirteen years before. Aunt Marie (married to Mom's oldest brother) had been a widow for almost twenty-five years.

Have I forgiven and forgotten everything that Mom has done to me? Not exactly. I have tried, though, to leave the past in the past and create a different relationship with her in the present. She's correct in that we're never going to go shopping, and I'm never going to send her a Hallmark card of any kind talking about what a wonderful mother she's been. But we're trying, and that's what possibilities are all about.

— Robyn R. Ireland —

It Begins with You

*Tolerance is accepting differences in other people. It is
thinking, "It is okay that you are different from me."*
~Cynthia Amoroso

In our Italian household, the kitchen was Command Central. It smelled of garlic, onions and fresh herbs, and felt like a warm embrace. It was where we had family meetings, played board games, and gathered after school to do homework while my mom chopped and sautéed. Often, we had one-sided conversations during which my mom would listen and nod her head, with an occasional obligatory "I see" or "Oh wow," as I talked a mile a minute about the injustices of my day. It was a special time when I was allowed to decompress and purge whatever was on my mind. Invariably, I would begin complaining about classmates treating me unfairly or being cruel. "She didn't even save me a seat!" or "He broke my pencil!"

One afternoon during my emotional-release session, my mom stopped stirring the sauce, put down the spoon, and in the calmest and kindest way possible said, "If everyone around you is being a jerk, then it is you who is behaving like the biggest jerk of all."

I was aghast. I thought, *What? No way. It was all on them, the other kids, not taking turns or not sharing, not me! What a frustrating notion. My own mother, too!* I didn't think I could ever forgive her.

But a few weeks later, after a particularly rough day, I had my light-bulb moment. Could it be possible that my mother was right? Was *I* the biggest jerk of all? After a good night's sleep, I decided to see if Mom's off-handed remark had any credence in action. It was an experiment with my own behavior.

That Monday, when I went back to school, I no longer expected everyone there to change their behavior to fit me. Instead, I changed myself to fit the situation. If someone was upset, I no longer reacted. If someone was hurt, I took the time to show that I cared. If I forgot an assignment, I didn't blame the teacher. I guess I just let things roll off my back and took control of the only person I could control: myself. I blew off not being invited to a party and took my younger brother to a movie instead.

Taking control of my emotions and reactions to things around me changed everything. I no longer felt like I was a victim, but a victor. I felt empowered. I forgave my own shortcomings and those of my classmates. It was transformative.

Now that I am an adult, I continue to work on this lesson. For example, my father has always done his "own thing." When I was growing up, he had his hobbies (which became our family's hobbies), his schedule (which became our schedule), and his agenda (which became our agenda). It was how he was wired from birth.

Since he never inquires about my children or me, I have learned to volunteer information. When I do, he readily delights in hearing the news. I have accepted this trait in him, and instead of asking him to change, I have altered myself to a point of understanding and forgiveness. It is easier and less harmful to our relationship when I don't expect to move his mountain to fit me. Along with his selfish traits, I also recognize that he is intelligent and hardworking. And while most of the hobbies he forced us into growing up, such as archery or fishing, have no place in my adult life, I am glad I have the foundation of that knowledge.

If we can recognize the shortcomings within ourselves, it becomes easier to forgive and see past the shortcomings of those around us. I look at my three children, for example. Their personalities at birth, childhood and young adulthood have stayed true from the get-go. The laidback one who never cried is still laidback and unruffled. The colicky one is still colicky, and the busy one still runs circles around me. I guess we are all hard-wired.

Tolerance in our own imperfections helps us to recognize and accept the imperfections in others. Like my mother taught me, "If everyone is a jerk around you, chances are you are the biggest jerk of all." But now I put my own spin on it: "If everyone is kind around you, chances are you are the kindest of all."

— Kim Kelly Johnson —

Table #10

A mother's love for her child is like
nothing else in the world.
~Agatha Christie

I close my eyes as the heat of the mid-summer sun hits my face through the passenger-side window of the van. For that moment, I could be anywhere. I bring to mind a picture of a beach where I spent countless days as a child. I imagine sitting on the warm golden sand, feeling the warmth radiate through my body as I sit grounded to that space on the beach. The sun is shining its healing rays down on me, and the sounds of the waves bring a powerful energy along with them as they rush into the shore. I can hear the sound of my own breathing match the sound of the waves as they sweep across the shoreline. I smile. Then I feel the familiar sensation of my heart pounding in my chest, beating so loudly that I can hear its rhythm in my ears. I take a deep breath to settle my racing thoughts.

Only a few moments pass before I open my eyes and see that foreboding landscape. Ironic how a person can have such a deep and longing desire and a feeling of dread simultaneously. Deep breath. I've done this before. Many, many times. I can't say that it is any easier today than it has been any one of the hundreds of other times. I wonder, just for a fleeting moment, if it will ever get easier. Deep breath. I know that in a very short time I will be sitting across from my beautiful boy, whom I love with my whole heart. I will be looking into his eyes as he tells me tales of his days. I will see that spark in his eyes of curiosity and passion, a spark he has had since he was just a little boy. Then he will smile, and my heart will melt.

Today, we will celebrate my son's twenty-first birthday — the sixth time we will celebrate this way. Be still my beating heart. Deep breath. Don't cry. Today is a happy day — the celebration of the glorious day that my firstborn child came to this earth. Every day since that brisk March evening has been a wild adventure.

My husband pulls the van into the parking lot as I take a deep breath and sigh. He looks over at me and says, "It's okay. You've got this." I know he is right, but his words reassure me anyway.

I get out of the van, and as I cross the parking lot and enter the bleak, institutional dwelling, I can feel that pounding in my chest again. Deep breath. I've got this. The large, heavy metal doors are buzzed, and I walk inside the main entrance. I start my usual mantra, the same mantra I have repeated every week when I visit.

I forgive you… I forgive you.

I sign my name and go through the same procedure as always: ion scanner, metal detector, drug dog search. My heart pounds. "I forgive you," I repeat in my mind and under my breath.

I forgive you for making choices I don't understand or agree with.

I forgive you for bringing fear and deep sadness into my life by the choices you have made.

I forgive you for stealing my attention from your brother and sister and, in some ways, stealing their childhood joy.

I forgive you for living by a different set of rules than I do — a way of living I will never understand.

I forgive you for the sleepless nights and unending sobbing.

I forgive you for your absence around the dinner table at Christmas and the presents that remained unopened and sadly tucked away for another day.

I forgive you.

Once the usual formalities are over, I can breathe a sigh of relief. I walk through the second set of heavy metal doors and the corrections officer tells me to take a seat at table #10. I make my way across the visiting room and find our table. It's nothing like the table we sat around on his birthdays growing up. There are no presents, birthday cake or candles to blow out. There are no family or friends waiting to sing "Happy Birthday." There is a small table with four chairs secured to the floor, one marked with red where he will be seated.

Then I look over and see him. There is a smile on his face. Nothing else matters now. There is nowhere in the world I would rather be than right here at this moment. My heart is no longer pounding with anxiety; my heart is suddenly full and even overflowing with love. There is nothing else, only joy as I feel his arms around me and hear the whisper in my ear: "I love you, Mom."

— Trish L. —

88

Chicken Soup for the Soul

Finding the Freedom in Forgiving

Anyone can be a father, but it takes someone
special to be a dad.
~Wade Boggs

When I was six years old, I found out that I had a biological father—and he wasn't the dad who was raising me. My parents opened communications up for me to meet my biological father's side of the family and my half-sister. They welcomed me with open arms. My biological father did not want to meet me, though. That was hard for me to grasp at six years old, but I had a mom and a dad, so I didn't really feel like I was missing out by not meeting him.

Through the years and many visits, I established a relationship with my grandparents, aunts, uncles, cousins, and half-sister, but I always felt like something was missing. I really wanted to meet my biological father. I didn't need him to be my dad; I just needed to know why he made the choice he made. Why didn't he want me or want to know me? At the same time, I also wanted to know him as a person. After all, he made up half of my DNA, and I had so many questions for him.

I waited until I was sixteen years old to make contact with him. Over the years, I had gotten his cell-phone number and saved it for one day. After working up the courage for a long, long time, I called him.

"Hi, is this Jim?" I asked quickly after his hello.

"Uh, yeah," he answered.

"Sorry, I called the wrong number," I blurted in a panic before hanging up quickly.

I took a deep breath and then about five more before I decided to send a text message to him instead since I had always been better with the written word. I told him that I was his daughter and I would really love to talk to him. I told him I didn't want anything from him, but I just wanted to get to know him and thought maybe he would like to get to know me. I gave him my cell-phone number so he could call me back.

I waited a few minutes, then a few hours, and then a few days. He never sent a reply or called back, but I got the message. He didn't share my feelings, and he still did not want to know me. I was crushed, angry, and hurt.

For years, I was so angry. The feelings of rejection and unworthiness that came from the person who was half responsible for my existence on this planet messed with my head and self-worth. I carried these feelings around for a long time, and my anger weighed heavily on me. I told my dad (the one who raised me) how this rejection was still bugging me. He told me, "Megan, have you thought about being the bigger person and just forgiving him? What good is it doing anyone for you to be so angry?" My dad is a good man. He's always trying to teach me to be the bigger person and leading by his own example.

I didn't listen, though; my biological father hadn't asked for forgiveness. Besides, I was content to live with my anger. I had it all worked up in my head what I would say to him if I ever ran into him, which wasn't likely as we lived about two hours apart. I made it my mission to succeed in spite of him, to prove that he was the one who had missed out.

Years later, I became a parent myself. I remember so clearly the moment I decided to forgive my biological father. I was staring at my brand-new, beautiful little boy and realized that my biological father was missing out on this. He would never know this tiny baby who was asleep on my chest as I sat in the rocking chair at the hospital. In just his first few days of life, that baby, my husband and I had been surrounded by family and so much love. We weren't missing out on anything.

I have the most amazing dad who would literally jump through fire for me. He has been by my side since I was one year old, cheering me on, supporting me, and loving me. My son has the kindest grandpa who plays sports with him and spoils him. The anger and hurt I was carrying around just weren't worth it anymore. I didn't need to confront my biological father to relieve myself of that. I just had to forgive him, even if he didn't ask for it and doesn't know. Sitting in the dark hospital room with my baby boy on my chest, I forgave him.

Perhaps the choices my biological father made were the best he could make for himself, and I have realized they were the best for me, as well. I forgive him for not stepping up to be a dad because his absence allowed the best dad a girl could ask for to step up and fill that role. I wouldn't be the woman I am today without him.

— Megan Vollmer —

89

Square Peg, Round Hole

To thine own self be true.
~Shakespeare

I was twenty-four, and my college boyfriend of five and a half years had just broken up with me. Devastated and depressed, I had been crying to my parents for days. What had changed his feelings? Was there someone else? Had the long distance finally gotten to him? Whatever it was, I was determined to fix it. The problem was that my dad was completely against me calling him.

"You're trying to fit a square peg into a round hole, Krista," my dad said. "You can't force things that aren't meant to fit. Let it go. This is the second time he's done this to you. You tried to work it out once before, but you can't make someone love you. Remember — square peg, round hole."

Though my dad's guidance had never steered me wrong in the past, his wisdom did not sink in right away. I was horrified at the possibility of my college boyfriend finding and falling in love with a "better" version of me. My self-worth plummeted. My anxiety kicked in. I doubted, questioned and analyzed what I once saw as my strengths — my creativity, compassion, and sense of humor — and viewed them as toxins to be expunged immediately.

I could turn into the person he wanted me to be, I told myself desperately. I could adopt his ideals and change my ways to make him happy.

"Just because he broke up with you doesn't mean you're not good enough," my dad explained to me during another one of my sobbing fits. "It just means you're not what he's looking for, which isn't necessarily a bad thing. It's his loss and someone else's gain."

But if it was his loss, why did it feel like mine?

I no longer enjoyed my usual pastimes — watching a movie, reading a book, socializing with friends. Instead, I paced anxiously around the house, my body present but my mind very far away. I was stuck in a rut, and I despised the empty shell of a person I was becoming.

Eventually, one of my girlfriends suggested therapy, so I called and made an appointment at a local counseling service. Under the tutelage of my counselor, accepting life without my college boyfriend took me close to a year — a year of self-analysis and self-discovery. It was a year of digging and sifting through who I was and who I wanted to be. I read more books, went out on some dates, and focused on my writing. It was a year of prioritizing what was important in my life and what I needed to let go.

Therapy helped me realize what my dad had been trying to tell me all along. My ex-boyfriend had ended our relationship because it wasn't working for *him* anymore. Something wasn't fitting. To him, breaking up was the right thing to do, even though it broke my heart. I didn't have control over his decision, but I did have the power to adjust my perspective. I had the power to forgive. I had the power to move on.

Square peg, round hole.

Countless times this simple phrase has saved me from myself. There have been unforeseen career roadblocks, promising writing ventures ending in rejection, exciting prospects that have crashed and burned. And when that hamster wheel is turning one hundred miles per hour, and my brain is spitting out questions or replaying encounters or inventing scenarios that might never even happen, it's sometimes taken all I've had to conjure up that square wooden peg and that defective round hole that will never, ever accommodate it.

Sometimes, things are just not meant to be. Sometimes — even though I approach every possible angle and redouble my efforts to the point of near insanity — things just do not work out the way I want.

Why? Because I am trying to fit a square peg into a round hole.

Once I made peace with that, once I inhaled my faith and exhaled my control, everything eventually fell into place. My dad proved to be right again. I never did call my college boyfriend. It was not an easy choice, but it was the *right* choice. And a few years later, I finally found the right wooden peg.

—Krista Harner—

As Good as Gold

*Forgiveness is the only way to dissolve
that link and get free.*
~Catherine Ponder

The e-mail's subject line read, "Gold Party." The message said: "At this private event, you can bring your old, broken, unwanted, unused and unfashionable gold/silver/platinum items and get paid for them. If you are content with your appraisal, you will be paid cash on the spot!"

A search through my old jewelry box yielded nothing until I spotted the gold wedding ring lying at the bottom. In my youth, the beautiful rose- and white-gold ring had held much promise and signified undying loyalty — until the promises were broken, and the loyalty died a painful death. The ring had long been forgotten in the bottom of the jewelry box, where I'd left it for more than twenty years.

At one time, I'd thought about melting down the ring and reforming it into a phoenix, something that would help me rise up from the ashes of my marriage and heal myself magically. But life wasn't that simple, and the healing didn't come quickly. Unable to decide what to reform the ring into, I left it in the jewelry box and set about reforming myself.

I'd had a hard time forgiving the broken promises of my failed marriage. I felt old, broken, unwanted, unused and unfashionable. I couldn't let go of the hurt for a very long time. As the first person in my family to get a divorce, I didn't know how to do it. But there didn't seem to be any other way to move forward. Even though I felt wounded and betrayed, and I wasn't able to magically forgive and move on, I decided to get on with living my best life.

A stock option at work paid out, allowing me to become sole owner of my house (formerly "our" house). I was relieved that I didn't have to move. Still young, in my thirties, I learned how to care for the house and live life on my own as an independent adult. The years went by, and life went on.

Now, twenty years later, the ring was doing me no good at the bottom of the jewelry box, so I considered taking it to the Gold Party. Amazingly, I felt no hard feelings. No knot in my stomach. No sinking feeling in my gut. No outrage or even suppressed anger. The ring no longer held the significance it once had. I had let go of the old disappointment and resentment, and my heart didn't hurt. Time had healed me, and I felt free.

I didn't feel like blaming anymore. I had a new perspective and saw both of our parts in the failed marriage. It had taken a long time, but I had truly moved on. I was grateful that I hadn't wasted the past twenty years with someone who hadn't treated me well, because I knew I deserved better. In spite of my initial fears of the unknown, the past twenty years had gone pretty well for me. I was glad to be free of him, and I hoped his separate life had gone well, too.

I realized that forgiveness can't be forced. But with time and the determination to get on with life, forgiveness can grow from the tiniest seed of hope. My seed was that stock option that allowed me to stay in my home — at least that one part of my life had not been uprooted.

I sold the ring without hesitation or regrets. Since I've learned over the years that dogs bring me joy, I put the cash toward adopting a rescued Corgi mix who'd been abandoned in a Texas grocery-store parking lot. We both know what it feels like to be left behind and start over. I call him Herbie the Love Bug, and he's as good as gold. In fact, he's even better.

— Jenny Pavlovic —

Emotional Shackles

To give vent now and then to his feelings, whether of
pleasure or discontent, is a great ease to a man's heart.
~Francesco Guicciardini

"Just don't let it bother you," my father advised after I broke into tears while reporting that my third attempt at infertility treatment had failed.

"But, Dad, this was our last chance," I sobbed. "We will never have children. I will never be a mother!"

"Well, there is nothing you can do about it. You just have to get over it and move forward," he responded mechanically before changing the subject abruptly.

My mouth dropped. For months, I had tended to my father's grief over my stepmother's death. As a dutiful daughter, I called him daily and visited him twice a week. How could he so carelessly dismiss the important benefits of having a child?

Weeks later, when we sat down to a special dinner I had prepared for his birthday, the subject of my not having children came up. Once more, I started to cry.

"What's your problem?" my father asked coldly as he heaped a second serving of beef stroganoff and wild rice onto his plate. "I wouldn't have cared if I never had children."

Again, my mouth dropped as his words seared through my mind and stabbed through my heart. Shocked at hearing such a pronouncement, I said little for the remainder of our dinner. After he left, I ran to my bedroom and wept uncontrollably for over a half-hour. Not only did my father fail to offer any comfort for my devastating loss, but he completely invalidated me as his daughter—his only child. *Certainly, he could not have meant his hurtful words,* I thought hopefully. *Maybe he will apologize after he reflects on his words more carefully.*

But that apology never came. In fact, my father's demeanor grew colder toward me during our visits and phone calls. Consequently, my contacts with him decreased as my resentment increased. For months, I harbored anger much of the time, even about issues that had nothing to do with having children or my father. Then my body reacted to my anger with migraine headaches and digestive troubles. In my unwillingness to forgive, my regular practices of prayer and meditation went by the wayside as I struggled with my faith in God.

Then a miracle happened. In the middle of a deep sleep, I had a profound dream about my mother who had died twenty years before. In this dream, she said, "Well, your father didn't listen to me for twenty-seven years. What makes you think he would listen to you?" I woke up laughing. Suddenly, I realized how silly my expectations of my father were. He's a great "fixer," but not a good "consoler." All this time, I had been trying to get a rich outpouring of blood from a dry, empty turnip.

For weeks, I laughed heartily every time I thought of my mother's words in my dream. At times, I could even imagine her laughing with me. Gradually, I released my anger and unrealistic expectations as I found gratitude for the things my father could give (like fixing my thermostat, driving me to a repair shop when my car broke down, and keeping me informed of the latest news and technological developments). In short, I forgave him.

As time passed, my father still made comments that struck me as insensitive. However, I reminded myself of his good qualities and my decision to lower my expectations of his emotional capabilities. Instead, I turned to compassionate friends and a professional counselor to support me in my grief over never having children. Although my grief lingered a long time, my father and I got along better. I stopped being so angry, my headaches and stomachaches subsided, and I started practicing my faith again.

About two years later, another miracle happened. Amazingly, my father started to express his emotions much more deeply. For example, he tearfully related painful stories from his early childhood in which his siblings teased him for being a sissy when he cried. He also described how he learned to follow his parents' unhealthy teaching that it is best to ignore your feelings. Later, he would tell sad stories about his golf friends with a good deal of empathy. Finally, he even told me the reason why he was so insensitive about my inability to have children. "I felt that my world was falling apart after your stepmother died, and I couldn't handle hearing about your loss, too."

After my father died, I reflected on his lifelong struggle with expressing his feelings and his later success in freeing himself from the emotional shackles of his childhood. When I valued him for who he was and where he was on his life journey, he was able to find his inner resources to heal. Now, when I struggle with forgiveness, I remember how I forgave my father. As a result, it becomes a little easier each time I need to forgive.

—Jessica Loftus—

I'm Not Going to Hate You

*Darkness cannot drive out darkness; only light can do
that. Hate cannot drive out hate; only love can do that.*
~Martin Luther King, Jr.

My wife sat on the edge of the couch, her head down and hands fidgeting in her lap. She played with her wedding ring, slowly spinning it around her finger.

"You're going to hate me," she said quietly. Her lips quivered, and her blue-grey eyes began to flood with tears. "You're going to hate me."

I was confused as to what this was about and why my wife was so shaken up.

"I'm not going to hate you," I said. "I could never hate you." She'd only come home moments before, sitting down quietly on the couch, so naturally my thought was that she wrecked the car. I asked if that's what it was, and she replied that it wasn't. This left me with a brief sense of relief.

"I can't do this anymore," she said. A lump caught in my throat. I swallowed, trying to release it.

"What can't you do? Can't sell the house? Can't move into a new home? We can back out of the sale. We can stay here, save money until we are more comfortable and ready."

"No, I can't do *this* anymore," she said with a sense of frustration at my not understanding. She looked up from her lap while throwing her hands into the air, indicating our life together.

I went into a sort of panic mode, asking if she'd cheated on me. "No," she reassured me while looking directly into my eyes for the first time. "I didn't cheat on you."

"Then what is it? Why can't you do this?"

She went back to fidgeting and then started to sob uncontrollably with her face in her hands. I watched her shake as she cried there alone on the couch, helpless and scared. I wanted to wrap my arms around her and pull her in close to reassure her nothing was wrong. But I wasn't even sure myself if that was the case, and I was strangely frozen where I stood from the shock. The sound of her struggling to breathe in between the tears was heartbreaking. I just wanted the moment to pass and not be real. I wanted everything to be okay.

"I think I like women," she said.

At that moment, my whole world fell to pieces and slipped away completely. I couldn't fix this. All I could do was let it happen while I sat and watched. My wife no longer loved me the way a wife should love her husband.

I went from having my whole life planned to not knowing where I was going to be in the next five minutes. I went from building a dream home to living in a hotel alone. I lost my best friend. But the worst part was the hate and anger that bubbled up inside me. It was an anger I never knew I was capable of feeling, especially toward someone I'd loved with all of my being.

I let it consume me as I became more bitter with each passing day. I felt sorry for myself for what I had just been put through, blaming it all on my wife's selfishness to have only what she wanted. I spent the first night on the floor of my empty apartment with my dog curled up next to me on the cold carpet. I stared at the ceiling through flooded eyes with a fire still raging inside me. I was there because of her, and I hated her for it.

Then one day while walking along a trail, I cleared my head of hate long enough to put myself in her shoes. I tried to imagine the struggle she had dealt with alone — the secret she had held onto for a year before telling me. I imagined how alone and confused she must have been, knowing this life with me wasn't what she wanted or needed. I thought about the fear she must have felt, not really wanting to leave me, but knowing that if she stayed and tried to make it work, she might never find and feel the deep unwavering love like I had for her.

I knew then that I couldn't rob her of that. She had taught me what true love was and the passion that came with it. I couldn't continue hating her for wanting to find what I felt for her. To me, there is nothing better in the world than to experience true love. And I wanted more than anything for her to have that—even if it meant giving it all up myself.

After getting home from the trail, I sat down and typed these words to her:

Words cannot express how deeply sorry I am for how I treated you at times the last few months. I was mean, hurtful, rude. I wish I could take it back and do it differently. It was hard to control my anger because of you ripping my life away from me. I hated you for it, and it felt like everything you were doing was to spite me and make me even madder. I am truly sorry for all of it. I've never wanted to hurt you, but I did, and I am sorry.

Most importantly, I just want you happy. I don't want you struggling and having bad days. You've been through a lot, and you deserve nothing less than to be happy. I have loved you more than anyone could ever love another person. I probably always will, but it wasn't what you wanted or what you needed. I am so sorry for that. I am sorry you didn't know sooner. I know you couldn't control any of this, and I want you to know that I honestly and completely forgive you for it. For all of it. That's a huge burden you carried that I will never understand, and I will never understand the things you did to me. I can't do anything but forgive you. You were in a lot of pain and carried a lot of mental stress. I can't imagine what you went through, or what you are going through still. Just know I am always here for you. You don't need to do it alone anymore.

Thanks to those few words of true forgiveness, the hatred lifted completely off my heart. We were both able to begin letting go of the last bit of guilt and start healing in order to live and love again.

— Dustin Urbach —

When You're the Victim

A Chance Meeting

There is nobility in compassion, a beauty in empathy,
a grace in forgiveness.
~John Connolly

I was in my second year as a food-service employee at the local elementary school, work I enjoyed very much. My days always began on a positive note due to my scenic commute: a narrow, winding country road.

The morning of March 6, 2017 was drizzly and cold. I listened to the radio on my drive, braking to navigate a curve at the bottom of a hill. Suddenly, something caught my eye out the driver's side window. I turned to look and saw the chrome grill of an SUV right in my face.

I don't know how long I was knocked out. When I opened my eyes, all I saw was my shattered windshield. It didn't take me long to realize I couldn't move either arm. I couldn't undo my seat belt or touch my face, which was bleeding heavily.

A witness called the paramedics. Air Care couldn't land because of the wooded valley I was in. I was taken via ambulance to the nearest trauma center, about thirty minutes away. By the end of the day, I learned I had eight fractures and would need two surgeries. My neck had broken in four places, the seat belt had snapped my collarbone in two, and I had also broken my right elbow, a rib, and a kneecap.

Over the next few days in the hospital, I began to get a clearer picture of what had happened. A local high school student, rushing to class, had crossed the center line and hit me head-on. I heard through friends of mine who knew his family that he was very, very upset by what had happened. I felt bad that he had such a burden to bear at such a young age.

My recovery was steady but slow. I needed assistance in everything — getting up, sitting down, and walking. I couldn't shower or wash my hair for more than two weeks, thanks to the neck brace I was not allowed to remove. I had no use of my right arm or hand (and I'm right-handed). The medications I was on affected my ability to read books (one of my favorite pastimes). I couldn't focus on small print. I spent a lot of time just thinking. One of the things I thought about was the teenage boy. I wondered how he was doing, both physically and emotionally.

By mid-July, I had finished physical therapy and was doing very well. I was looking forward to the next school year. I felt ready to go back to work — but maybe I'd find a different route to drive.

Fourteen months after the accident, I was grocery shopping when a woman I didn't know approached me and asked if I was Suzanne. She introduced herself, and I realized it was the young man's mother. I thought she was very courageous and kind for reaching out to me. I appreciated learning how he was doing. He had also been injured, breaking his wrist, and had needed counseling to help with the emotional trauma of causing the accident. He was now in college and had anxiety driving to class. I could certainly empathize with the difficulty of getting back behind the wheel of a car.

Secretly, I wished I could talk to him myself. I was hoping he had moved on with his life and wasn't distraught any longer. I wondered if I would ever get to meet him. Would I even recognize him? I had seen his photo early on, but I would not know him if he walked by me on the street.

Seven months later, it was time for our daughter's Christmas band concert at the high school. The first adult I recognized upon entering the auditorium was the mother who approached me in the grocery store. I wondered why she was there. I didn't realize the choir was performing as well, and the boy's brother was in the choir. It was easy to pick him out, as he resembled their mother.

At the end of the concert, the choir director invited alumni of the high school choir who were in attendance to come up on stage and sing one last song with the current members. A bunch of people hustled up on stage, excited to sing. One young man in a white hoodie and ball cap ran up and stood by the brother. Suddenly, I realized that it was him, the driver.

The concert ended. I weaved my way through the crowd and up the stage stairs until I was next to him. He was smiling, happy, and joking around with his friends and brother. Finally, he looked at me, all smiles.

"Hi, I'm Suzanne," I said.

His expression turned to utter shock. He knew who I was.

I had not really rehearsed what I was going to say, even with all the thought I had put into wanting to meet him someday. I reiterated what I had told his mom in the grocery store several months earlier.

"I just wanted to say that I'm okay. I'm really okay, and I was never mad at you," I told him.

Suddenly, he threw his arms around me, as if he didn't care about all the people around us — his brother, friends, and an auditorium still full of people. Neither did I. In that moment, no one else was there. I kept talking.

"I know this was hard on you, and I'm sorry. I'm a better person for what happened that day. I really am. And I think about you all the time."

"You do?" came a slightly muffled answer.

"Yes, I do." I was running out of words and beginning to lose my composure, tearing up and getting shaky. We let go of each other, and I looked him right in the eye.

"I'm really okay," I added. I patted his shoulder, turned, and ran down the stairs.

They say that forgiveness is for yourself, not the other person, but I never felt like I had anything to forgive. It was an accident, and I was never angry or depressed about it. I felt like he needed to forgive himself, and the only way that would really happen was if he could see me and hear from me that all was well. I was the only person who could give him that gift. When he hugged me in that moment, I felt that any feelings of guilt, shame, or sadness he might still have had were swept away. In truth, though, it was healing for us both.

—Suzanne Caithamer—

94

You're Forgiven

*Forgiveness is the key that unlocks the door of
resentment and the handcuffs of hatred. It is a
power that breaks the chains of bitterness.*
~Corrie ten Boom, Clippings from My Notebook

The ringing of the phone woke me from a deep sleep at 4:30 in the morning. I jumped out of bed and picked up the receiver.

"Hello, is this Mr. Pollock?"

I answered, "Yes, this is Mr. Pollock. What can I do for you?"

"This is the dispatcher for the Treasure County Sheriff's Department. There has been a series of burglaries in Hysham. It is possible that Hysham Hardware was one of the businesses burglarized. The sheriff would like you to come to your store. He would like you to park by your door and wait until the sheriff contacts you."

"Okay," I said. I sat down in a chair. My emotions went from surprise to anger like a racecar on a drag strip, zero to sixty in less than two seconds. I put on my clothes, told my wife what had happened, and headed out the door. It had snowed through the night, but I was so hot that the snow should have been melting wherever I stepped.

As I drove to town, I remembered that just a few days earlier I had felt like someone was watching as I closed for the night.

When I got to the store, I parked and sat there wondering where the sheriff was. The back door was wide open, and I was sure the furnace was running full blast. I felt violated.

I sat there stewing. The sheriff knocked on the window and brought me back to reality. He confirmed we had suffered a burglary. Together, we entered the store and looked to see if anything was gone. They had pried open the front door. On the floor was a pile of tools the thief or thieves had used to try and open the safe. They used a half-inch drill with a hole saw, a reciprocating saw, a sledgehammer, and some chisels, which they had taken off the shelves of my store.

Papers from my desk covered the office floor like a tornado had hit the place, but as far as I could tell all the expensive merchandise was still there. The sheriff then asked me to return to my pickup and wait for them to check for fingerprints.

While I sat in my pickup, anger raged through my mind. I probably could have chewed on nails and spit out bullets. Soon, the sheriff and deputies left, and I began the process of cleaning up the mess and fixing the broken lock and door. My wife arrived, and together we worked. When she saw all the chaos, she also felt violated and filled with anger.

Later that day, we learned that law enforcement had caught the thieves. One of them had stolen a car, but the law had him in custody before he could get out of town. The other one had hitchhiked on a truck to Billings. When the truck driver dropped him off to call a cab, he flashed a wad of bills. The truck driver was suspicious, so he called the police. When this thief reached his home, the law was waiting for him.

When the trial came, I wanted these crooks prosecuted to the full extent of the law. They must pay, and pay they did. The jury found both guilty. With them both in prison, the fire in my heart began to cool, but I didn't realize just how much it had cooled until sometime later.

One morning about three years later, I was in the store by myself when a man I didn't know walked through the door. This was an odd circumstance as I knew everyone who lived in Treasure County.

He walked up to the counter and turned to me. "Are you the owner of this store?"

I smiled and replied, "Yes, I am."

"Have you owned it for a while?"

My eyes met his. "Yes, a little over twenty years."

He looked away. "Then you owned it three years ago."

I started to say, "Well, duh," but for some reason, I didn't. Instead, I replied, "Yes."

Then he made a statement I will never forget. "I need to ask for your forgiveness."

I had no idea what he was referring to. "My forgiveness for what?"

Once more, he lowered his eyes. "I'm the one who broke into your store and made all the mess."

Without thinking, I said, "You're forgiven, brother." Somehow, all the pain, hurt and emotions were gone. This man had admitted his guilt and asked for forgiveness; I knew I must forgive him. I felt a weight lift from my heart.

He turned and walked out the door, and I never heard from him again.

I had always been one to hold onto a grudge, but I was able to forgive. Forgiving this man gave me a newfound freedom. My chains of anger dropped right to the floor.

—Lee E. Pollock—

95

Thrown Away

We think that forgiveness is weakness, but it's
absolutely not; it takes a very strong person to forgive.
~T. D. Jakes

"If I was in a room with that man for just two minutes, and I had a gun," I told Charlie, "he would be dead."

Charlie was my husband of twenty-six years. He just shook his head. "You're not like that," he said.

After all that time, he thought he knew me. I guess he was wrong. I knew my heart, and I knew what I would do to the man who, just two months before, had murdered my child.

Chad had been twenty and our only son. We had three daughters, but there is a different relationship between a son and his mother. That broken bond left me despondent and depressed. It drove me to the cemetery to curl up and weep beside the little brass marker that indicated Chad's grave until a headstone could be erected. It filled me with a feeling I had never harbored before: cold hate.

The young deputy sheriff who had come to our door at 2:00 that morning didn't know how to soften the blow. "It's Chad," he stammered. "He's dead." Murders don't happen in tiny rural communities, though, and we thought it must have been an accident. We could have lived with that, but not a shotgun blast to the face. I shook my head to dislodge the image left by the deputy's words. It didn't work.

The next weeks and months swam by; I don't remember much of what happened. I threw up at the funeral. I blew up in the courtroom.

I dropped thirty pounds the first month because I stopped eating. I wanted to die, too. Then things began to get better. I started to function again, but the hate refused to leave.

I saw a news report about a little girl who had been maimed by a hit-and-run driver. She forgave him from the witness stand. I saw a story about a man who had survived a concentration camp and forgiven his captors. Every day I heard about someone else who had overcome his or her anger and had forgiven. Every church sermon seemed to contain the need to forgive and let God deliver justice. I knew it was true, but I also knew my son would never give me little red-haired, brown-eyed grandchildren. I knew he would be absent from family holidays and celebrations. I couldn't let go.

People told me they were glad this had happened to a strong Christian; a weaker person would have been destroyed by it. I smiled weakly and answered them in my head: "You are an idiot." The young man who killed Chad was in jail, awaiting trial. I imagined killing him in so many ways. Then he was in prison, and I still fantasized about his death. I prayed for it.

Our thirteen-year-old daughter became a virtual orphan, cared for by her older sisters. I saw it happening, but I was powerless to change. I was sickened by the person I had become. Charlie found a flyer blowing across a parking lot that advertised a church service in a neighboring town and thought maybe God could touch me there. I don't remember the message delivered. I don't remember the songs that were sung. I only remember that well-meaning people followed the haunted woman I had become out to the parking lot to pray for her. I hammered at the car door, screaming at Charlie to unlock it.

Then, one Sunday, a special speaker came to our church. He spoke about forgiveness. I shut him out until I heard him say, "I don't think most people understand what forgiveness is."

He seemed to look directly at me and continued. "Forgiveness doesn't mean throwing your arms around the person who hurt you and telling them what they did is all right."

My breath caught in my throat.

"People should be held accountable for the terrible things they do," he continued, "but the justice system doesn't always work the way it should. People don't always get found out. Sometimes, it looks like evil wins."

Now he had my full attention.

"There is a final judgment, and God's sentence is harder than anything courts could impose. Perpetrators usually don't care whether they are forgiven, but unforgiveness will certainly take a toll on you."

He went on to explain that forgiveness was about the victim. He suggested writing the name of the person who held our thoughts hostage on a piece of paper and then wadding up the paper and throwing it into the trash. He suggested doing it every time our thoughts went to that cold hate. Every time. He said some days we would have to do it twenty times and some days only ten. Later, it might be only twice, or maybe there would be a day when we didn't do it at all and were no longer held captive by our hate.

I could manage that, I thought, and I did. Piece after piece of paper with only that detestable name was crumbled and tossed away. Then, one day, I realized I hadn't thought about him at all. Oh, I had thought about Chad, but those thoughts were not buried in garbage; they were warm and even joyous. I felt cleaner than I had in the time since Chad was killed. Freer.

The image of my boy lying in a pool of his own blood no longer haunted me. Instead, the picture of Chad that came to me again and again was of my son, clad in jeans and a "muscle shirt," running across a grassy field. Someone had once told him to "go fly a kite," and there it was… dancing in a warm, spring breeze.

— Caryl Harvey —

96

Losing Sophie

*Forgive, forget. Bear with the faults of others as you
would have them bear with yours.*
~Phillips Brooks

My friend Sandy and I sat across from each other at our favorite Mexican restaurant, munching on chips and salsa while we talked and laughed. My cell phone rang. I didn't recognize the number, so I didn't answer. Less than a minute later, it rang again. Same number. Then a third time.

"Hello," I said.

"This is your neighbor, Dexter," the voice on the other end said. "I got your number off Sophie's collar."

Sophie was my eight-year-old, mixed-breed dog, part Boxer and part who-knows-what. Adults and children alike seemed to adore her. She didn't chase cats. She didn't turn over garbage cans. She didn't put her muddy paws on clean clothes.

Sophie had only one bad habit. She'd escaped my fenced-in yard so many times. She loved to chase the UPS truck. I couldn't quite figure out why. She didn't chase cars or motorcycles or bicycles. She was completely uninterested in the postal truck and the FedEx van. But something about that big brown UPS delivery truck lit a fire under her. The moment she heard its engine turn onto our street, she was after the truck like a shot. The surprising thing was that she loved Mike, the driver. As soon as he parked and descended the steps, Sophie wagged all over.

Dexter was calling to tell me he'd been in his front yard when the UPS truck came tearing around the corner. "Sophie was in hot pursuit," Dexter said. "The driver took the turn too sharp and clipped her with his rear wheel."

Tears filled my eyes, and my hands starting shaking. "Is she…" I didn't dare say the word. "Is she hurt?" I stammered.

"It's hard to tell," Dexter said. "Her back legs are scraped and bloody, and she's breathing real shallow. But her eyes are open, and she thumps her tail when I talk to her."

I pulled a wad of cash from my wallet and tossed it on the table. "I'll be there in five minutes."

Sophie was just as Dexter had described. She raised her head when she heard my voice and licked my hand as I sank down beside her and cradled her head in my lap. I dialed my veterinarian's work number, hoping against hope that he might still be at the office on a Friday evening. No answer. Same with his home number.

There was nothing to do but call the emergency veterinary clinic in a nearby county. The on-call doctor promised to meet me there. Gently, Dexter placed Sophie into the back of Sandy's van, and we sped to the clinic. Sophie whimpered softly for the entire half-hour journey. Dr. Cunningham slid her carefully onto a stretcher and rolled her into the examining room. Sophie's big, brown eyes stared into mine.

I stroked her silky ears and put my face close to hers. "It's gonna be okay, sweet girl," I whispered.

"We'll need X-rays to assess internal damage," Dr. Cunningham said. "But I think the best thing to do now is get a catheter in and start an IV. That'll keep her comfortable overnight so we can take pictures in the morning. You go home and get some rest, and I'll call as soon as I know something."

Sandy and I drove away feeling good about Sophie's diagnosis. I even joked that I hoped this would teach her to never, ever chase the UPS truck again. My phone rang when we were about halfway home. I could hear the pain in Dr. Cunningham's voice. "Sophie coded while I was working on her," she said. "She passed away. I'm so, so sorry."

I sobbed. So did Sandy. I went down a long list of what-ifs. And then I let my grief turn quickly to anger. And hate. This was Mike's fault, no doubt about it. Everyone in the neighborhood knew he drove too fast. We worried he might hit a child on a bike, a young mother pushing a baby stroller, or an animal. Now he had. He'd hit and killed my beloved Sophie. And I was never going to forgive him for it.

I didn't call UPS management to report Mike, although I considered it. Instead, I seethed. I ignored his wave when I passed him on the street. I taped a PLEASE LEAVE PACKAGES ON PORCH note to my front door so I wouldn't have to answer his knock. For almost a year, I let my ill feelings toward Mike fester. Then one day, while walking out of the library, I came face-to-face with him. He set down the packages he was carrying and touched my arm.

"I've been wanting to talk to you," he said softly. "How's Sophie?"

Before I could choose my words, they came spilling out. "She's dead is how she is," I said. "And it's all your fault."

I wasn't prepared for Mike's reaction. Instead of defending himself, he burst into tears. "I'm sorry to hear that," he said. "So, so sorry. I knew I'd clipped her with my tire, but she got up and walked off, so I didn't stop. I figured you'd been keeping her fenced up since it happened."

I shook my head. "Her injuries were way worse than they looked."

Mike's hand was still on my arm. "I'm used to dogs chasing me," he said. "There's something about the whine of our truck engine that sets them off. But I want you to know I looked forward to being in your neighborhood because Sophie was always so glad to see me." My mind flashed back to Sophie's joy when Mike stepped down from the truck. I remembered how she walked with him to his customer's door and how he always bent down to scratch her ears after he'd handed over his packages.

Mike swiped at his eyes with the back of his hand. "I know I drive too fast sometimes," he said. "But you wouldn't believe how many packages I have to deliver every day. I hope you'll forgive me."

Right then and there, I did. I let go of the anger. I let go of the hate. I forgave Mike. And I told him so. Forgiving hasn't made me miss Sophie any less. The memory of her lying on the stretcher in the animal hospital will never go away. But, day by day, it's being replaced by happy memories. I wave at Mike now when I pass him on the street. I answer his knock when he brings packages to my door. I've even given him a print of my favorite picture of Sophie. Someone once said, "To forgive is to set a prisoner free and discover that the prisoner was you."

I'm no longer a prisoner. And for that I'm grateful.

—Jennie Ivey—

97

Mindful Mercy

To understand somebody else as a human being,
I think, is about as close to real forgiveness
as one can get.
~David Small

An unearthly, primal scream assaulted my ears and chilled me to the bone. I wondered what could possibly create such a noise. Then I realized that awful sound was coming from me. I had just been given the news that my mother, who was my best friend, had been killed the evening before by a drunk driver.

The days following the horrific news became a blur of trying to be strong for others, putting on a brave face, and making funeral arrangements. Staying busy postponed having to deal with the real emotions bubbling beneath the surface.

Then the funeral was over, the related activity died down, and the well-wishers began to fade away. In the silent aftermath of those days, the storm of emotions hit like a category 5 hurricane.

Unadulterated rage filled my mind with thoughts of painful "justice" dished out by the court. The drunk driver, whom I will refer to as "Mary," surely deserved "an eye for an eye" treatment.

Mary had stripped my best friend from my life. She had deprived my mother of her golden years. For months, I caught myself picking up the phone in order to cry to my best friend about the pain I was feeling, only to realize it was my now-deceased mother I was calling.

My mother and I had not always had such a great relationship.

In fact, there was a twelve-year period of time in which there was no communication between us.

But then a family party brought us into the same room, and things changed. With both of us being adults, we were on equal footing and had learned enough through our time apart to find a way to be together again.

And together we were for five years. We traveled together, shopped together, did charity for others together, and crafted together. We had started working on a dollhouse and quilts for others.

We had plans for the future, and she'd even asked me to care for her when she could no longer care for herself. That is how close we had become.

And then, in one reckless, thoughtless moment, Mary had taken all of that away from us. She killed my mother and all our plans for the future.

Once the anger subsided, I was lost, desolate. Where could I possibly find comfort, and what could possibly make what had happened right?

After much thought and prayer, I realized there was nothing that could make it right. Mary could not make restitution because she could not give me back my mother.

At the same time, there had recently been a spate of articles in the newspaper about repeat-offender drunk drivers. Some had been arrested as many as five times and still continued to put lives at risk.

That gave me a starting place. Maybe there was a way to help Mary not become a repeat offender. Maybe other families could be spared loss at her hands.

The research I did showed that throwing drunk drivers in jail did not prevent recidivism. Across the nation, other measures had been taken that showed positive results.

In the midst of this process, I thought about some *Oprah* shows I had seen. Victims of horrific crimes had forgiven those who had killed their loved ones. At the time, everything inside me said they were crazy and there was no way I'd ever forgive someone who did such a thing to me. But now that I had experienced such loss myself, I suddenly understood why the victims chose to forgive.

Forgiveness, I learned, is not about saying that what was done is okay. It isn't. But it is about giving yourself the freedom to live again. It is about refusing to add to the damage done by the guilty by condemning yourself to the soul-rotting, festering darkness that can fill you when you hold onto the rage and pain.

When the time came to write a victim-impact statement that the judge would read, I included the research I had done and explained why it was important not to jail her, but to help her avoid driving drunk again.

I added in my letter that I had done more than my share of bonehead things in my life, but none had resulted in the taking of a life. I could not imagine what that would be like to live with.

I told the judge that, in the end, justice was not truly just without mercy. I had come to a place of forgiveness.

The hearing fell on the day after Mother's Day, and I spoke, saying much of the same things I had stated in my letter to the judge.

When the judge ruled, he did all I asked and more. He (or his clerks) had done more research and added additional measures to help Mary not drink and drive again. As he gave his ruling, he pointed out what I had said about justice and mercy, noting that he agreed and was influenced by that.

As I left the courtroom, I knew I had one more thing to do: talk to Mary. But cameras and reporters prevented that.

Hesitantly, I wrote a letter to Mary, telling her that I forgave her and wishing her a better future. I didn't want to intrude in her life, but I felt it needed to be said.

Weeks later, I got a response. With trembling hands, I opened it and read. She didn't want to intrude in my life, either, but also felt she had something important to say.

She told me how much my letter and forgiveness meant to her. She added that I was the only person in her life who had treated her like a human being.

Years have passed and, to my knowledge, Mary has not become a repeat offender. From all appearances, she is reformed and living a better life.

Forgiveness didn't bring back my mother, but it did potentially spare others from the same fate. And I have peace in knowing that somehow things were made right, both for Mary and for me. It all came about because of forgiveness and mercy.

— Kara Pendleton —

98

An Unexpected Ending

When a deep injury is done to us,
we never heal until we forgive.
~Nelson Mandela

I'd never before kept company with such dark emotions or the kind of hatred that filled my heart. It shamed me, but more than that, it horrified me to think that if the man who had molested my daughter had been standing before me, I'd probably reach out and strangle him.

My ex-husband had known this man and his wife well. An older couple, my ex had stayed with them when he had to work out-of-town. He considered them close friends, and many times we'd taken the kids and stayed overnight at their house. I hadn't seen them since the divorce, however. But then one day, the husband passed through our town on the way home from a fishing trip. He stopped to visit us. In the comfort of my home, with me nearby, he changed our lives forever.

After that night, I barely recognized my daughter. I watched her turn from a vibrant, straight-A student into a terrified little girl who woke up crying from nightmares. She started wetting her bed, which she'd never done, and brought home Ds and Fs on her school papers.

Many times, I'd sat with my children and discussed this exact scenario. I felt confident that if they ever faced a sexual predator — even if they trusted the person and knew them well — they'd know what to do and would come to me right away. Despite my efforts, the worst had happened while I stood in the kitchen brewing the pervert's coffee.

Our lives became a whirlwind of visits to police headquarters where we answered non-stop questions. We had tons of counseling appointments, trying to get our world back on track.

Finally, they brought this perpetrator in from out-of-state. The man's wife had come with him, and I wondered why she stayed with him, knowing what he'd done.

At first, my daughter's abuser denied the allegations brought against him. That meant a trial and putting my daughter on the stand, forced to look at this man. Thankfully, it never came to that. After failing his lie-detector test, he admitted his guilt and signed a full confession, claiming he was sorry for what he had done.

Once her culprit pleaded guilty, the prosecution called my daughter and me in for a conference to update us on our case and take the next step.

"I've got one question for your daughter," the detective said. He looked deep into her eyes. "I want you to know that we have enough evidence to prosecute this man and put him behind bars for a long time. As you know, it's not the first time he's done this to a little girl. It's your decision. Do you want him to go to jail for what he did to you?"

My daughter thought for a moment, but didn't take long to answer. "I don't want him to hurt anyone else, but I think everyone has suffered enough. He needs help… but, no, I don't want him to go to jail."

Tears filled my eyes. Not in my wildest dreams had I expected this ending. I'd wanted this man punished for turning her life upside down. Even though she was still struggling to pick up the pieces of her shattered world, my daughter had already forgiven him and let it go.

Watching someone so young lead the way to forgiveness opened a portal in my heart. The overwhelming darkness and hatred I'd hidden and held on to for so long flowed away with my tears. If my child could move on with her life and try to leave behind the anger, betrayal, and hurt that this man had caused her, I could, too. I'd never forget what he'd done, and neither would my daughter. But through mercy and forgiveness, we could finally start healing and move on with our lives.

—Jill Burns—

99

For the Love of a Child

We are all mistaken sometimes; sometimes we do
wrong things, things that have bad consequences.
But it does not mean we are evil,
or that we cannot be trusted ever afterward.
~Alison Croggon

O n May 1, 1998, I got the call no parent ever wants to hear; my middle child, Robert, was with some friends on their way to see a movie. My son had fought for sobriety for many years and was the only one in the car sober. His friends were all drinking. I don't know what possessed Bobby to get into a car with a driver under the influence, and I'll never know that answer.

When I finally got to the hospital, the doctors pronounced my son brain-dead. We waited for his siblings to arrive before we made any decisions—they were coming by bus.

It was a grueling and exhausting wait, but finally almost all my children were there; each, except for my eldest, said their good-byes. My eldest was living in North Carolina at the time, but we were able to conference call with her so she also had a choice as to what to do.

When it was finally time to pull the plug, no one else wanted to be in there except me. My son had just taken his final breath, but I felt like something else needed to be done.

There was one other person I needed to visit—the young man who was driving while intoxicated. In my opinion, that young man had just made a bad choice; he got behind the wheel of a car and chose to drive drunk. I didn't feel like he had planned to do it, or had planned to cause the death of his passenger. I told my husband to drive me to the other hospital so I could see Jason.

When we got there, he was in intensive care. He had suffered some pretty serious injuries. I spoke to the nurse and asked permission to visit with Jason. She was more than apprehensive until I told her why. There he was, lying in a hospital bed, looking pretty beaten up. My heart knew what had to be done. I pulled up a chair so I could sit close and reached for his hand.

"Jason, I'm Bobby's mom," I said. I held his hand and stroked his arm. "I want you to know that I forgive you. I know that the pain we are feeling will never go away, but I need to let you know that I hold no ill feelings or anger. I only hope that Bobby didn't die for nothing, so promise me that you will live your life and make every moment count."

Jason looked down at my face as tears fell down his cheeks. I reached over and gave him a hug. I felt as if I was holding my own child! As I looked over at the watchful nurse, I noticed her sniffling, and then I heard a little gasp and a soft sob from the young man.

After a few months, Jason's hearing was set, and I made another journey to Colorado to attend. Jason was in the hallway as I walked toward the door of the courtroom. We took one look at each other and then embraced. I made my victim's statement and begged the judge not to sentence him to prison. I asked that he be allowed, through community service, to teach others about what it feels like to wake up and realize your friend is gone because of a bad error in judgment. It didn't work; the judge sentenced him to prison.

It's sad to see not only one life and one family changed forever, but now another young man's life and his family also pay the price.

Some people have said they could never do what I have done, that forgiving someone who was responsible for the loss of a loved one did not deserve forgiveness. I say this young man did not decide to drive drunk in order to murder my son. They were just a group of friends having fun. Jason didn't do this with a weapon; it was not premeditated murder. It was a stupid mistake. I have been guilty in the past of drinking and driving, of putting others and myself in danger, not ever realizing the cost. This tragedy has taught me the importance of not drinking and driving, too.

I did not stay in touch with Jason because the grief of losing my child is great. I only hope that he learned this incredible lesson and also teaches others.

— Catherine Inscore —

My Journey to Forgiveness

When you hold resentment toward another,
you are bound to that person or condition
by an emotional link that is stronger than steel.
~Catherine Ponder

When I was twelve years old, my father hit me in the face and broke my nose. It wasn't the first time I had felt the sting of my father's hand, but it was usually delivered through the swing of a belt or the whip of a switch. (For non-Southerners, that's a branch cut from a tree and used to exact swift punishment to children for the error of their ways.)

Growing up in the South, harsh discipline was a way of life — spare the rod, spoil the child. And my father seemingly took that adage to heart. But this was the first and only time that my father struck me in the face.

While that physical blow had a profound impact on my life, it would not be the only lasting gift my father would leave me. Aside from the physical trauma experienced at the hands of my father, there was also verbal abuse. In addition to being a tough disciplinarian, my father was very critical. He rarely doled out praise or compliments. When I did something good, the question usually was why I didn't do it better. Some might say that was just his way of pushing me to reach my potential. That might have been what he intended, in his own misguided way.

As a result, though, not only did I grow up unsure of myself because of my appearance, but I also lacked overall self-confidence. I didn't believe in myself or think I was good enough. Though I'd been mostly a straight-A student in adolescence and represented my school three years running in the county spelling bee, I later dropped out of high school and took a factory job.

As I grew older, I began to build some self-esteem. I dabbled in photography, passed the GED and took a few college classes. Ultimately, I decided to leave my factory job and attend college full-time. My father literally laughed at my plans.

My parents were much older when I was born. I was a very unexpected third child, coming twenty years after their second. My father was just nineteen at the end of the Great Depression, and I'm sure he had a hardscrabble life with little time for education and lots of need to work.

I guess my father viewed college as unattainable, too far out of reach — even for his bright young daughter. He died a month before I began my college classes, so he didn't see me graduate with my associate or bachelor's degrees. He didn't see my successful career at the local newspaper.

As an adult, I was able to repair the outward trauma to my nose through surgery, but the inward trauma has proven to be much more challenging. At one point, I thought I'd beaten it, but during a recent time of turbulence and self-doubt, I sought the services of a professional counselor and realized that the trauma and resentment were still lurking inside me, not yet resolved.

I thought I could say all was forgiven but still hold on to my resentment. After all, the ghosts of my childhood still haunted me. I deserved to cling to my resentment like some sort of prize. It was mine. I earned it, right? But as I learned from author and minister Catherine Ponder, forgiveness and resentment go hand in hand. You cannot consciously proffer one while clinging to the other.

In a recent session, the counselor posed a series of questions: What is forgiveness? What would it take to achieve and what would it look like? I answered the questions, but was left wondering *how*. Having come to the realization that holding on to my resentment only served to keep me in the prison of victimhood, my answers were focused on taking back my power, and on being confident and positive about myself, my abilities, and my future.

And therein I discovered the *how*. The only way to let go is to focus on what's ahead and keep moving in that direction. It doesn't mean that my father's bad behavior was okay; it means that I am allowing myself to be free. Rather than remain a victim, I must reclaim my power on a daily basis—my power to believe in myself and know that I can succeed. The only way to find peace for myself and forgiveness for my father is to address what happened and put my resentment to rest.

As I write this, I notice it is my father's birthday. This realization feels like a wink of sorts from him that it's okay to write this story and put it out in the world. So, I guess this essay is my gift to both of us.

As an adult, I sometimes think of the little girl I used to be; I want to hug her and encourage her. Sometimes, this leads me to think of my father as a little boy and a young man who had scant opportunity, who would only survive through hard work. I want to hug that little boy and encourage him, too.

I told the counselor what forgiveness looks like to me, but how can I be sure it's actually happened? Forgiveness is a journey for me, something that will take place over time. For some of us, it takes a very long time, but it begins with wanting to let go and be free. And, one day, while you're busy living—focused on being your best real self—you suddenly realize it's happened. You realize that you've let go. I haven't reached my destination quite yet, but I am definitely on my way.

—Diane Hughes—

Unexpected Blessing

True repentance means making amends
with the person when at all possible.
~Lawana Blackwell

I t was a cool evening in spring. I was just finishing the dinner
dishes when the phone rang. It was unusual because our landline
seldom rang. Most everyone we knew contacted us on our cell
phones.

"Is this Linda Newton?" questioned a familiar voice that I struggled
to place.

"That's me," I replied, still trying to figure out who was on the
other line.

"This is Janet Rhodes."

That name seemed familiar, too, and I scrambled to place it. I
knew a lot of people, having lived on two coasts and in most major
cities in California while pastoring a busy church with my husband
for the past thirty years.

Janet shared some small talk about how she lived in Hawaii, and
it had been no small feat to get my number and find an opportunity
to call me with the three-hour time difference between us.

"I am calling because I need to apologize to you," she stated.

That's when I suddenly realized who she was.

"That day when I came into your classroom and chewed you out
for disciplining my daughter, I was way out of line. I know now that
you were doing what was best for her. You were right. I was wrong.

I am in recovery now, and part of my healing is to make amends to people I have harmed. I would very much like to make amends to you for my behavior."

Wow! I had not thought about this situation for a while, but twenty years earlier it was all I could think about. I was young, and it was only my second year of teaching. Janet's daughter, Stephanie, had acted out toward some of the other girls in the classroom, and I had made her stay in from recess. I was kind and fair when I meted out her punishment. The truth is I really liked Stephanie, but she clearly didn't like being disciplined. She told her mother, and Janet felt the need to defend her disruptive child.

After school, she flew into my classroom and accused me of everything from being unfair to playing favorites to not caring about my students. She was yelling so loudly that every teacher in the building heard her accusations, including my principal.

Her words devastated me because none of the things she blamed me for were true. I managed to keep from crying while she stood in front of me, but as soon as she left the room, I broke down. I cried all evening and on and off through that sleepless night. The school was small, so her attitude ruffled feathers among some of the other parents. I had once felt such joy teaching my kids, but now I felt like I was under a microscope in my classroom. For the next few weeks, her incriminating words caused me to second-guess everything I did with my students. I doubted my ability and even my own heart. I was miserable.

I made an appointment with the principal to discuss the situation. She didn't make me feel any better, but she didn't make me feel any worse either. Her attitude was wise: "Let's wait and see if there is any more fallout from this angry mother's behavior for the rest of the school year."

The school year was nearing an end, and I was grateful. Despite how her mother had treated me, I knew I would discipline Stephanie again if she acted out. It was the right thing to do.

And now, two decades later, the irate mother was apologizing to me. Two thoughts came to me as I quickly processed our conversation.

One was that this hurtful episode, resulting in intense self-doubt, had become ancient history to me. At the time, I let her words affect me way too deeply for much too long. I've now learned to process criticism much more quickly, accepting what's true, dismissing what's not, and moving on with my mission in life. The truth at the time was that I didn't play favorites and I did care deeply about my students, despite one woman's opinion. So, in essence, her apology wasn't necessary for my wellbeing because I had done the work of restoration on my own. I was grateful for that.

The second thought was how much courage this lady had to muster to make this call. It moved me.

"Can you find it in your heart to forgive me?" Janet asked finally.

"Certainly," I responded. "And I have to say that you're a hero to me. After all these years, you could have just forgotten about this. But you went to such effort to make things right. I am both blessed and impressed."

"Thank you for being so gracious," she added.

"Thank you for caring enough to call me," I told her.

We spent the rest of our short conversation asking about each other's children before we hung up. As I reflect on that evening, I am still in awe at Janet's growth, courage, and tenacity to make amends for the hurt she caused so many years ago. Her apology truly was an unexpected blessing.

— Linda Newton —

Meet Our Contributors
Meet Amy Newmark
Thank You
About Chicken Soup for the Soul

Meet Our Contributors

Penny Radtke Adams graduated with a B.S. in Education in 1969. She taught for twenty-five years in South Dakota and Wyoming. Penny and her husband retired in Texas, where four of their five children live. She loves visiting her fourteen grandchildren and is currently working on her memoir. E-mail her at penradtke@yahoo.com.

Lucy Alexander is a former European fashion marketing director. Now a full-time mom, she owns a branding and consulting business in her hometown outside of Philadelphia.

Monica A. Andermann lives and writes on Long Island where she shares a home with her husband Bill and their little tabby Samson. Her writing has been included in such publications as *Woman's World*, *Guideposts*, *Ocean* as well as the *Chicken Soup for the Soul* series.

Sue Armstrong is a novelist and poet with three books in publication. Retired from teaching preschoolers, their parents, and Early Childhood Education students and staff, she still dreams of setting up a classroom every August. She loves spending time with her five grandchildren, who all live close by.

Gretchen Bassier writes short stories and really long novels. She is crazy about animals, addicted to superheroes, and forever grateful to her awesome writing partner, Anna, who will one day be a famous romance novelist. For writing resources, tips, reviews, and more, visit Gretchen's blog at www.astheheroflies.wordpress.com.

Nancy Beach received her Bachelor of Science in Bible, with honors, and is working on a Master of Arts in counseling. She has been married for twenty-six years and has two grown children. Nancy enjoys reading, sunsets, and sand between her toes. She writes devotionals and inspirational fiction. Learn more at www.filledtoempty.com.

Abigail A. Beal is a freelance writer and a published author. She has a B.A. degree in English and an M.S. degree in Communication Studies from The College of New Rochelle. She is writing a children's book. E-mail her at abigailwrites@gmail.com.

Glynis M. Belec is an award-winning children's author, an inspirational speaker and a busy freelance writer. If she isn't engaging in interesting conversation with children, she is likely somewhere being thankful for every breath and preparing for her next exciting adventure.

Michele Boom has taught elementary school both in the traditional setting as well as online. She also works as a freelance writer and is a frequent contributor to the *Chicken Soup for the Soul* series. She lives in Bend, OR with her family, two cats, a bunny and two aquatic frogs.

Jill Burns lives in the mountains of West Virginia with her wonderful family. She's a retired piano teacher and performer. She enjoys writing, music, gardening, nature, and spending time with her grandchildren.

Suzanne Caithamer received her B.A. in English and Journalism from Indiana University and a B.S. in Food and Nutrition from Purdue. She is currently working on projects in nutrition and food writing. She lives with her family in Kentucky and enjoys reading, cooking, and selling on eBay. E-mail her at caithamers@fuse.net.

Anthony Clark is a college professor and writer living in St. Louis, MO.

Christina Ryan Claypool is a national Amy and Ohio APME award-winning freelance journalist and speaker who has been featured on Joyce Meyer Ministries TV show and on CBN's *The 700 Club*. Her inspirational novel, *Secrets of the Pastor's Wife*, was released in fall 2018. Learn more at www.christinaryanclaypool.com.

Laura Connell has published personal essays in *The Globe and Mail*, *Toronto Star*, *Calgary Herald*, *Homemaker's* and *Holl and Lane* magazine. She lives in Toronto with her two teenage daughters and enjoys travel, the outdoors, and reading library books. She is writing a memoir about recovery from alcohol addiction.

Eilley Cooke is a Vermont-based author who enjoys writing flash fiction, horror, and short stories. Eilley enjoys spending time with her two children, and their turtle, Shelley. She tries to see as many movies as possible, preferably while they're still in the theater. Music is always present in her life, and she believes one cannot live without it.

Shannon Cribbs received her Master's in Education in 2010 from Walden University. She has three boys and one girl. She was a public school teacher in Georgia before resigning to become a stay-at-home mom. She enjoys traveling with her family.

William Dameron is an award-winning blogger, essayist and the author of *The Lie: A Memoir of Two Marriages, Catfishing & Coming Out*. His work has appeared in *The New York Times*, *The Boston Globe*, *Salon*, the *Huffington Post*, and in the book, *Fashionably Late: Gay, Bi and Trans Men Who Came Out Later in Life*.

Marianne L. Davis received her B.A. in English from the University of Idaho and has twenty years experience writing professionally in the tech industry. She's currently working full-time on her first book, a suspense-thriller trilogy. Marianne married her college sweetheart, Steve, in 1991 and they have three children.

Kathy Dickie lives in South Surrey, BC. She retired from the corporate world a couple of years ago. Since then, Kathy and her husband have been enjoying extensive worldwide travel. When she isn't traveling, Kathy enjoys family visits, writing, quilting, and documenting ancestry research.

Christine Dubois is a widely published writer/editor and popular writing instructor. She lives with her husband near Seattle and is the mother of two fabulous millennial sons. In her spare time, she likes to go birding. This is her first contribution to the *Chicken Soup for the Soul* series. Learn more at www.christinedubois.com.

L.N. Felder lives in Southern California with her partner and son. She has been writing since she was a child and has loved telling stories from as far back as she can remember. In addition to writing, she loves reading, art, knitting, and playing games with her son. She plans to further pursue a creative writing career.

Shari Getz is a writer and entrepreneur with an irrepressible penchant for creating things, telling stories, and advocating for arts education. She infuses humor, from the subtle to the absurdly whimsical, into stage and screenplays, picture books, gift books, and even her own line of greeting cards at RandomGreetingCards.com.

C. Goodheart uses writing as a means of processing her own traumatic past. She is most at peace when out in nature. She loves to run, hike, garden, and photograph the fine, minute details of flowers.

Dale Mary Grenfell is a retired educator, prolific freelance writer, storyteller and workshop facilitator. Loving life in the foothills of the Rocky Mountains, she also volunteers with the CSU International

Friends program and with the Office of Restorative Justice. E-mail her at grenfell@q.com.

Judith Hackbarth is a retired educator/children's theater director. She has published a book on children's theater plus numerous educational materials for the classroom and stage. She and her husband reside in Wisconsin where she enjoys spending time with family and friends.

Shannon Hanf is a social worker, mother, and avid dog lover. She lives in Troy, OH, with her teenage son and three rescue dogs. Judah, the subject of her story, is one of those three dogs. Shannon and Judah are proud to raise awareness of Pit Bulls and their sweet dispositions.

Krista Harner received her B.S. in Secondary English Education from Millersville University and her M.A. and MFA in Creative Writing from Wilkes University. She has been an English teacher for the past fifteen years and enjoys reading, writing, and ice cream. Krista lives in rural Pennsylvania with her husband and two sons.

Caryl Harvey is a writer and former foster parent. After the death of their son, she and her husband Charles fostered sixty-eight children, adopting three of them. Caryl is also an avid amateur historian who has performed Margaret (Molly) Brown, a Victorian Irish maid, a pioneer woman who walked the Oregon Trail, and Helen Keller.

Christy Heitger-Ewing is an award-winning writer who has written more than 1,000 human-interest stories for national, regional, and local magazines. She's also contributed to twenty-three anthologies and is the author of *Cabin Glory: Amusing Tales of Time Spent at the Family Retreat*. Learn more at christyheitger-ewing.com.

Rose Hojnik was born in the rough and tumble streets of Chicago, a city that taught her a great many lessons.

Lillie Houchin began her writing career shortly after retirement hoping to fulfill her teenage dream of becoming a published author. Her manuscripts have been published in a host of anthologies and magazines.

Cindy Hudson is the author of *Book by Book: The Complete Guide to Creating Mother-Daughter Book Clubs.* She lives in Portland, OR with her husband and two daughters and enjoys writing about things that inspire her: family life, her community, reading, and family literacy. Learn more at CindyHudson.com.

Diane Hughes is a former newspaper writer/editor who lives in Nashville, TN, and currently works in education advocacy. She and her husband, Michael, enjoy camping, hiking, kayaking, photography, and travel in their free time. She also enjoys dabbling with watercolor. Diane occasionally blogs at www.dianewordsmith.com.

Sharilynn Hunt is a retired medical social worker and founder of New Creation Realities Ministry, a teaching and prayer ministry. Her writings include a 31-day devotional, *Grace Overcomes Today,* and other inspirational nonfiction stories published in various compilations. Her four grandchildren fill her life with joy!

Judith Ingram is the author of *A Devotional Walk with Forgiveness* and posts weekly devotionals about forgiving on her blog. She earned her Master's degree in counseling and a certificate in biblical studies, and studied two years at Fuller Theological Seminary. Judith lives with her husband in the San Francisco East Bay area.

Catherine Inscore, mother of seven, works at Copper Mountain College, Greenleaf Library, in Joshua Tree, CA. Catherine is a certified instructor for Mental Health First Aid, and a commissioner for San Bernardino Behavioral Health 3rd District. She loves acting in local community theaters with her husband, Barry.

Gina Insinna-Rice is a full-time caregiver to her twenty-six-year-old son, Chris. Chris was born with cerebral palsy and is a complete blessing. Gina is the author of *Finding Christ through Chaos*, which made the bestseller list in 2017. Gina enjoys sharing her stories to inspire other parents of children with special needs.

Dea Irby has been the wife to Tom since 1974, mom of eight, grandmom to seventeen-plus, and a Realtor. She enjoys Toastmasters, networking, "Chicken Coup" writers group, PEO, The Alliance, and traveling the world to visit her children. E-mail her at deairby@gmail.com or visit deairby. com to learn more.

Robyn R. Ireland has made her home in the thirteenth largest city in Iowa, and works for a local newspaper as a full-time reporter/ photographer. She's comfortable with the first title. Not so much with the second, though she's been told her photos are improving. In her spare time, she enjoys reading, writing fiction, and being outside.

Jeffree Wyn Itrich recently relocated to a small farming town in Central Texas where she sees everyday wonders with a new point of view. She enjoys quilting, gardening, baking, and giving new life to old furniture.

Jennie Ivey lives and writes in Tennessee. She is the author of numerous works of fiction and nonfiction, including dozens of stories in the *Chicken Soup for the Soul* series. Learn more at jennieivey.com.

Cat Jerome is a Canadian author and artist who writes psychological horror fiction and inspirational nonfiction. She studied creative nonfiction at Oxford University. Cat's work has been featured in several horror anthologies and she's currently writing an anthology with brain injury survivors.

Kim Kelly Johnson is a southern girl who has always loved to write. From doodling on the back of napkins to the bottom of receipts, her creative juices are always flowing. She derives the inspiration for her stories from life's little ironies and the antics of her family — especially her newly arrived first grandchild.

Jill Keller is a novelist who lives in a small town against the Appalachian Trail in Pennsylvania with her husband and two children. When not writing, she enjoys pursuing her passions for cooking, volunteering at the library, taking walks on the trails, and reading to her children. Learn more at kellerjf.wixsite.com.

Former history teacher and newspaper columnist **Pam Kennedy** is a freelance writer from Illinois. She is the wife of one, mom of two, grandma of three, and servant of three (cats). Her hobbies include gardening, dining out, and finding ways to avoid housework.

S. Kling enjoys reading, writing and inspiring others.

Terri L. Knight has a degree in psychology, substitute teaches elementary school, and writes in her spare time. She has several pieces published in literary magazines, books, and newspapers and she has won several writing contests. When she is not writing or working, she takes care of her family and three rescue animals.

Trish L. is the mother of three children. Through a difficult journey with her oldest son, her family has maintained hope for a beautiful, bright future. Trish is a yoga teacher and works with at-risk youth. She brings hope into the lives of others through her life experience and a genuine belief that life is a beautiful adventure.

Mary Elizabeth Laufer has a degree in English from SUNY Albany. As a Navy wife, she moved thirteen times in twenty years, working as a substitute teacher, library assistant, and private tutor. Now that her children are grown, she devotes most of her free time to writing.

Allison Wilson Lee has served with interdenominational ministry Cru on three continents and now home schools her sons in Orlando, FL.

She has been published in magazines such as *Threads*, *Today's Christian Living*, *PRAY*, and *Purpose*, as well as *Chicken Soup for the Soul: Random Acts of Kindness*.

L. Y. Levand is a fantasy author who occasionally writes nonfiction. She lives with her husband and their two cats — Frodo and Rosie — who remain convinced that they are, in fact, supreme rulers of the world.

Monica Anne Levin has connections with three continents: born in Africa, grew up in North America and currently living in Asia. After a lengthy teaching career, she has since written five novels including *Hidden Heritage* about international adoption.

Lindsey Light spends most of her time raising two ginger babes, Deacon and Nora, her fur baby, Larkin, teaching writing at the University of Dayton, and pursuing a Ph.D. in educational leadership. In her "free time," she reads, writes, keeps up with the local sports teams, and watches the same three shows on Netflix.

Vickie J. Litten lives in South Florida with her husband, two sons, three grandchildren, her deaf dog and Savannah cat. She loves to write, and also enjoys art, photography, cooking, and gardening.

Author **Alan Livingston's** published books include the novel *Gabriel's Creek*, an historical memoir, *Intersection with History* and the historical fiction *Bogeys: Armistice*. A Texas native, Alan currently lives in Las Vegas, NV. He began writing full-time after a long hospitality career. Learn more at alanlivingston.com.

Jessica Loftus, a seasoned psychologist and career counselor, provides psychotherapy to adults in her private practice. She authored a self-help book on bad habits and hosts a blog, "Pet Ways to Ease Stress," which is featured on PsychCentral.com. Learn more at easywaystoeasestress.com.

L.M. Lush is a freelance writer, ghostwriter, and ghost editor. She's also an adjunct professor at Westchester Community College in New York where she teaches courses in Creative Writing and Music Appreciation. She enjoys playing the piano and cello and hiking with her dogs, Sadie and Oreo. Learn more at LMLush.com.

Debra Lynn is a proud mother of two amazing adult children and a teacher of many. She teaches special education at the middle school level in Minnesota. Deb enjoys reading, writing, hiking, and all things outdoors.

Paul Lyons is an inspirational comedian and writer. He works on cruise ships, in clubs, and for corporations. He has performed for AT&T, Prudential, NCAA, NFL, and hundreds of other companies. His new book is titled *Carpe Diem, Mañana*.

Amy Mac has lived all over the world, from Peru to China to Hungary, teaching and telling stories along the way. She currently lives in Montana with her husband and daughter, where she is an emerging writer.

Lauren Magliaro lives in Northern New Jersey with her husband, twelve-year-old son, and lots of fish and other saltwater creatures. She enjoys reading, Springsteen, and the New York Yankees. This is her second story in the *Chicken Soup for the Soul* series and she dreams of writing a tween book someday. E-mail her at LaurenMags19@aol.com.

Nicole Ann Rook McAlister has studied journalism and pursues an avid interest in world religion and mythology. Nicole enjoys adventures in camping, sunrises on the beach, painting, crafting and all manner of such things. Several of her pieces have been on exhibit at the Whitesbog Historic Village in Browns Mills, NJ.

Marya Morin is a freelance writer. Her stories and poems have appeared in publications such as *Woman's World* and Hallmark. Marya also penned a weekly humorous column for an online newsletter, and writes custom poetry on request. She lives in the country with her husband. E-mail her at Akushla514@hotmail.com.

Diane Morrow-Kondos loves writing about her grandparenting experiences at www.tulsakids.com/Grand-Life. Her first book, *The Long Road to Happy: A Sister's Struggles Through Her Brother's Disabilities*, will be published later this year. She also enjoys competing in triathlons and open water swims. Learn more at dianemorrowkondos.com.

Jesse Neve is a wife and mom of four from Minnetrista, MN. She is always striving to see the silver lining in every situation. E-mail her at jessedavidneve@frontiernet.net.

Linda Newton is a counselor and the author of *12 Ways to Turn Your Pain Into Praise*. She frequently speaks at retreats, conferences, and seminars in the U.S. and abroad. Learn more at www.LindaNewtonSpeaks. com, and on Facebook with her husband at www.facebook.com/ answersfrommomanddad.

Raymond C. Nolan was born and educated in upstate New York. After completing his military operations in 1973 Ray became a bi-vocational minister and is presently Pastor of Daybreak Methodist Church in Miflin, AL. As a cancer survivor he enjoys living each day to the fullest. He and his wife Methyl live in Coastal Alabama.

Linda O'Connell is a frequent contributor to the *Chicken Soup for the Soul* series and many other regional, national, and international publications. A former early childhood educator from St. Louis, Linda loves spending time with her grandchildren and helping them make discoveries. She blogs at lindaoconnell.blogspot.com.

Sister Josephine Palmeri, MPF, loves teaching Spanish at Villa Walsh Academy in Morristown, NJ. Her favorite things are teaching, singing, writing, crossword puzzles, and telling stories. She has had over twenty magazine articles and two joke books: *Tales from the Barber Shop* and *More Tales from the Barber Shop and Pittston* published.

Jenny Pavlovic, Ph.D. is the author of *8 State Hurricane Kate* and *The Not Without My Dog Resource & Record Book*, and she has published many stories. Jenny lives in Wisconsin with her cat Junipurr and dogs Chase, Cayenne, and Herbie. She loves walking dogs, gardening, swimming, kayaking, and outdoor adventures. Learn more at www.8StateKate.net.

Kara Pendleton is the author of seven books and contributing author to one. Her education includes finance, housing, consumer issues, journalism, and health/nutrition. She has an English Vocabulary Master Certification and she has been a guest on talk radio and a public speaker. This feisty, curvy, green-eyed brunette is 5' 10" in her boots.

In his heart, **Kristen Mai Pham's** father was a writer. So, Kristen is delighted to be sharing his story with *Chicken Soup for the Soul* readers. She is also an aspiring screenwriter and her next adventure will be publishing her first book. Follow her on Instagram at @kristenmaipham or e-mail her at kristenmaipham3@gmail.com.

Stephanie Pifer-Stone is an Interfaith Minister with a degree in Holistic Theology. She studied Religious Literacy at Harvard Divinity School. *Becoming Egg-straordinary*, is her first book published about releasing your inner butterfly. In addition to her husband and their furry kid, her passions include yoga, writing, and cooking.

Lee E. Pollock has had many different careers including sales, owning a hardware store for twenty-three years and pastoring churches for twelve years. He is now retired and spends his time writing and ministering in prisons. He has two adult children, six grandchildren and two great-grandchildren.

Sally Quon is a writer and photographer living in the beautiful Okanagan Valley where she writes a weekly nature blog. When not out exploring the back roads of the valley, she spends her time writing poetry and practicing the art of quiet sitting.

Rebecca Radicchi lives outside Atlanta where the summers are hot and the tea is sweet. She has ridden the messy beautiful waves of adoption, breast cancer, and being the mom of kids with medical needs. In it all, she's discovering abundance in both the uncomfortably hard and the easily beautiful. Learn more at www.rebeccaradicchi.com.

Cindy Richardson seeks to encourage, challenge, and inspire women through writing, speaking, and mentoring. Married to her college sweetheart, she enjoys the friendship of her three daughters and loves being Nana to six grandchildren. She teaches kindergarten in Missouri where the Pony Express began and Jesse James ended.

Karen Sargent is the author of *Waiting for Butterflies*, which was named the 2017 IAN Book of the Year and received the Foreword Reviews Gold for Christian fiction. After teaching high school and college English for twenty-five years, she retired to focus on writing. She is a frequent presenter at writers' workshops and conferences.

Steve Schultz is a two-time Teacher of the Year Award winner at Fountain Valley High School. He has written a monthly column on love, leadership, and elevation for the past decade for *Fountain Valley Living* magazine and has been published in six other *Chicken Soup for the Soul* books. E-mail him at personalbest22@gmail.com.

Diane Stark is a freelance writer, wife, and mother of five. She is a frequent contributor to the *Chicken Soup for the Soul* series. She loves to write about the important things in life: her family and her faith.

Gary Stein co-founded an NYSE-member investment banking firm. He was a strategy advisor to Lionsgate, Miramar and Seventh Generation and built a thirty-time Emmy-winning kids TV business. Gary is proud to be a mentor to several outstanding young women and has been a frequent contributor to the *Chicken Soup for the Soul* series. E-mail him at gm.stein@verizon.net.

Noelle Sterne (Ph.D. Columbia University) writes in many genres with over 600 pieces and two books published. *Challenges in Writing Your Dissertation* evolved from her academic editing and coaching practice. *Trust Your Life* helps readers/writers reach lifelong yearnings. Fulfilling her own, she just completed her second novel.

Lynn Sunday is an artist, writer, and animal advocate who lives near San Francisco, CA. Her stories have appeared in eleven *Chicken Soup for the Soul* books and numerous other publications. E-mail her at sunday11@aol.com.

Barbara J. Todd began her writing career by compiling "Life Lesson" analogies for her grandchildren, hoping to create a "Legacy Book" for them. Since retiring, several of her devotions and stories have been published. She loves to encourage others through her writing. Barbara lives in Texas with her husband of fifty years.

Dustin Urbach received his Bachelor's in Mechanical Engineering from Kettering University in 2012. Currently residing in Michigan, he spends all his free time with his dog Ella, backpacking, vacationing, and following his passion for writing. He enjoys writing both short and long fiction, and is currently writing a memoir.

Megan Vollmer is a wife and a mother of two. She received her Associate of Arts and Science degree in 2017. She has been published on *Her View from Home* and *BabyGaga*. She thrives on faith, sarcasm, and coffee. E-mail her at meganvollmerblog@gmail.com or find her on Instagram at meganv.writes.

Joseph Walker wrote a nationally syndicated column called "ValueSpeak" for twenty-five years. His published books include *How Can You Mend a Broken Spleen?*, *Look What Love Has Done* and *Christmas on Mill Street* for Deseret Book. He and his wife, Anita, have five children and fourteen grandchildren.

Marilynn Zipes Wallace has a B.A. and M.A. in English. She worked in publishing in New York City and then in London, having fallen in love with England after spending her junior year of college there. Her feature articles have appeared in a number of English magazines and in *Chicken Soup for the Soul: Life Lessons from the Dog*.

Diana L. Walters is past retirement age, but continues to work part-time in an assisted living facility helping residents thrive. In her spare time she develops ministry materials for people with dementia and writes. She's been published in the *Chicken Soup for the Soul* series, *Upper Room*, and *Purpose*.

Jennifer Watts is a writer living in sunny Hawke's Bay, New Zealand. She is a former journalist who has travelled and lived in several countries. She enjoys getting lost in a good book, movie or binge-worthy series. Jennifer is married and has raised two daughters. She is not a morning person.

Lea Welch was born and raised a small town, country girl. Now living in a small city, she is a wife and mother with a passion for the written word. Her goal is to, one day, publish her book.

Mary Z. Whitney is a regular contributor to the *Chicken Soup for the Soul* series, with stories in over thirty *Chicken Soup for the Soul* books. She loves sharing inspiration and faith with others. Mary lives in Leavittsburg, OH with her husband, John and their little dog, Max. She has also published *Max's Morning Watch* and *Life's a Symphony*.

Gwen Sheldon Willadsen is a retired professor from California State University, Chico. Her retirement hobbies are genealogy research, travel, spending time with her grandkids, and writing memoir and genealogy stories. Her writing has been published in *The Sun*, *Boomer Café*, and *Raven's Perch* magazines.

Mary Wilson is a secretary who has published several articles and a novel. In 2017, one of her novels was a semi-finalist for a national book award. She enjoys reading, traveling, and photography. She and her husband live in northern Ohio.

Following a career in Nuclear Medicine, **Melissa Wootan** is joyfully exploring her creative side. She enjoys writing and is a regular guest on *San Antonio Living*, an hour-long lifestyle show on San Antonio's NBC affiliate, where she shares all of her best DIY and decorating tips. Contact her at www.facebook.com/chicvintique.

Meet Amy Newmark

Amy Newmark is the bestselling author, editor-in-chief, and publisher of the *Chicken Soup for the Soul* book series. Since 2008, she has published 160 new books, most of them national bestsellers in the U.S. and Canada, more than doubling the number of Chicken Soup for the Soul titles in print today. She is also the author of *Simply Happy*, a crash course in Chicken Soup for the Soul advice and wisdom that is filled with easy-to-implement, practical tips for enjoying a better life.

Amy is credited with revitalizing the Chicken Soup for the Soul brand, which has been a publishing industry phenomenon since the first book came out in 1993. By compiling inspirational and aspirational true stories curated from ordinary people who have had extraordinary experiences, Amy has kept the twenty-six-year-old Chicken Soup for the Soul brand fresh and relevant.

Amy graduated *magna cum laude* from Harvard University where she majored in Portuguese and minored in French. She then embarked on a three-decade career as a Wall Street analyst, a hedge fund manager, and a corporate executive in the technology field. She is a Chartered Financial Analyst.

Her return to literary pursuits was inevitable, as her honors thesis in college involved traveling throughout Brazil's impoverished northeast region, collecting stories from regular people. She is delighted to have come full circle in her writing career — from collecting stories "from the people" in Brazil as a twenty-year-old to, three decades later, collecting stories "from the people" for Chicken Soup for the Soul.

When Amy and her husband Bill, the CEO of Chicken Soup for the Soul, are not working, they are visiting their four grown children and their grandchildren.

Follow Amy on Twitter @amynewmark. Listen to her free podcast — "Chicken Soup for the Soul with Amy Newmark" — on Apple Podcasts, Google Play, the Podcasts app on iPhone, or by using your favorite podcast app on other devices.

Thank You

We owe huge thanks to all of our contributors and fans. We were overwhelmed with thousands of submissions on this very important topic, and we had a team that spent months reading all of them. Laura Dean, Crescent LoMonaco, Barbara LoMonaco, Mary Fisher, and Jamie Cahill read all of them, and then D'ette Corona and Amy Newmark narrowed down the semifinalists to make the final selections.

Susan Heim did the first round of editing, D'ette chose the perfect quotations to put at the beginning of each story, and Amy edited the stories and shaped the final manuscript.

As we finished our work, Associate Publisher D'ette Corona continued to be Amy's right-hand woman in creating the final manuscript and working with all our wonderful writers. Barbara LoMonaco and Kristiana Pastir, along with Elaine Kimbler, jumped in at the end to proof, proof, proof. And yes, there will always be typos anyway, so feel free to let us know about them at webmaster@chickensoupforthesoul. com, and we will correct them in future printings.

The whole publishing team deserves a hand, including our Senior Director of Marketing Maureen Peltier, our Vice President of Production Victor Cataldo, and our graphic designer Daniel Zaccari, who turned our manuscript into this beautiful book.

Sharing Happiness, Inspiration, and Hope

Real people sharing real stories, every day, all over the world. In 2007, *USA Today* named *Chicken Soup for the Soul* one of the five most memorable books in the last quarter-century. With over 100 million books sold to date in the U.S. and Canada alone, more than 250 titles in print, and translations into nearly fifty languages, "chicken soup for the soul®" is one of the world's best-known phrases.

Today, twenty-six years after we first began sharing happiness, inspiration and hope through our books, we continue to delight our readers with new titles, but have also evolved beyond the bookshelves with super premium pet food, television shows, a podcast, video journalism from aplus.com, licensed products, and free movies and TV shows on our Popcornflix and Crackle apps. We are busy "changing the world one story at a time®." Thanks for reading!

Share with Us

We all have had Chicken Soup for the Soul moments in our lives. If you would like to share your story or poem with millions of people around the world, go to chickensoup.com and click on Submit Your Story. You may be able to help another reader and become a published author at the same time. Some of our past contributors have launched writing and speaking careers from the publication of their stories in our books!

We only accept story submissions via our website. They are no longer accepted via mail or fax. Visit our website, www.chickensoup.com, and click on Submit Your Story for our writing guidelines and a list of topics we are working on.

To contact us regarding other matters, please send us an e-mail through webmaster@chickensoupforthesoul.com, or fax or write us at:

Chicken Soup for the Soul
P.O. Box 700
Cos Cob, CT 06807-0700
Fax: 203-861-7194

One more note from your friends at Chicken Soup for the Soul: Occasionally, we receive an unsolicited book manuscript from one of our readers, and we would like to respectfully inform you that we do not accept unsolicited manuscripts, and we must discard the ones that appear.

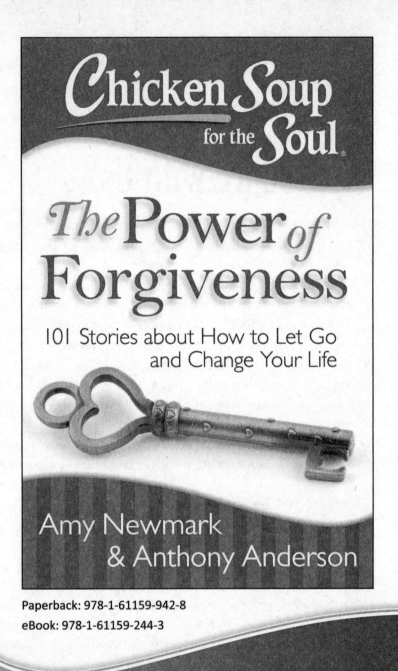

Chicken Soup for the Soul.

The Power of Forgiveness

101 Stories about How to Let Go
and Change Your Life

Amy Newmark
& Anthony Anderson

Paperback: 978-1-61159-942-8
eBook: 978-1-61159-244-3

More stories of forgiveness

Chicken Soup for the Soul

for the Soul

Think Positive, Live Happy

101 Stories about Creating Your Best Life

Amy Newmark
& Deborah Norville
Journalist and Anchor of *Inside Edition*

Paperback: 978-1-61159-992-3
eBook: 978-1-61159-293-1

and positive thinking

FROM THE EDITOR-IN-CHIEF OF THE NEW YORK TIMES BESTSELLING SERIES

Chicken Soup
for the Soul.

Simply
Happy

A Crash Course
in Chicken Soup
for the Soul
Advice and
Wisdom

Chicken Soup for the Soul
Chicken Soup for the Soul Miracles Happen
Chicken Soup for the Soul It's Christmas!
My Dog's Life
Chicken Soup for the Soul Think Positive
Chicken Soup for the Soul Food and Love

Amy Newmark

Paperback: 978-1-61159-949-7
eBook: 978-1-61159-254-2

More Chicken Soup for the Soul

Chicken Soup for the Soul

Think, Act & Be Happy

How to Use Chicken Soup for the Soul Stories to Train Your Brain to Be Your Own Therapist

Amy Newmark
& Dr. Mike Dow
New York Times Bestselling Author & Therapist

Paperback: 978-1-61159-979-4
eBook: 978-1-61159-279-5

life-changing wisdom and tips

Changing the world one story at a time®
www.chickensoup.com